A Single Roll of the Dice

A Single Roll *of the* Dice

Obama's Diplomacy with Iran

Trita Parsi

Yale

UNIVERSITY PRESS

New Haven and London

W

Yale University Press books may be purchased in quantity for educational, business, or promotional use. For information, please e-mail sales.press@yale.edu (U.S. office) or sales@yaleup.co.uk (U.K. office).

Designed by Sonia Shannon.
Set in Bulmer type by Keystone Typesetting, Inc., Orwigsburg, Pennsylvania.
Printed in the United States of America.

Library of Congress Cataloging-in-Publication Data
Parsi, Trita.
A single roll of the dice : Obama's diplomacy with Iran / Trita Parsi.
         p.   cm.
Includes bibliographical references and index.
ISBN 978-0-300-16936-2 (hardcover : alk. paper)
1. United States—Foreign relations—Iran. 2. Iran—Foreign relations—United States. 3. United States—Foreign relations—2009–.
4. Iran—Foreign relations—21st century. I. Title.
E183.8.I55P38 2012
327.73055—dc23
2011040646

A catalogue record for this book is available from the British Library.

This paper meets the requirements of ANSI/NISO Z39.48-1992 (Permanence of Paper).

10 9 8 7 6 5 4 3 2 1

To Amina, for your love;
to Darius, Jamil, and Yasmine, for your laughter;
to Monir, for your kindness

Contents

Preface

During the first two years of the administration of Barack Obama, Washington's desire for diplomacy with Iran arose as quickly as it dissipated. In the aftermath of the White House's efforts to reach out to Tehran in 2009, the narrative that emerged concludes that diplomacy was genuinely pursued and exhausted, ending in failure, and consequently Obama had to abandon engagement and opt for sanctions and, potentially, military action. In many ways, Iran has become the poster child of the Obama administration's engagement policy with America's foes. Not only does failure with Iran impact the future of U.S.-Iran relations, it may also raise the question of the benefits of diplomacy as a whole. That is why a closer study of Obama's outreach to Iran is of such importance.

In examining the diplomacy between Washington and Tehran during this period—both the respective domestic political trials as well as challenges from Iran and America's regional allies—I argue that the current stalemate has more to do with the domestic political limitations Obama and his Iranian counterparts face than it does with a genuine failure of diplomacy. Obama's political space on this issue was compromised from the outset of his presidency by pressures from Congress, Israel, and some of Washington's Arab allies. The Iranians, in turn, were limited by the fractures within their political elite, particularly after the fraudulent election of 2009. The Iranian government's internal and external conduct after the election, in turn, further limited the Obama administration's diplomatic maneuverability. Had greater time and space existed for diplomacy, and had the modalities and agenda of the negotiations been different, the outcome would likely have been more favorable. Contrary to the prevailing narrative, the limited diplomatic encounters between Iran and the U.S. in 2009 and 2010 cannot be characterized as an exhaustion of diplomacy.

Acceptance of this narrative would result in limiting Washington's options on Iran to various forms of confrontation—that is, either continued sanctions and containment or military action. In view of the failure of sanctions and containment thus far, that policy option is arguably not stable and will eventually deteriorate into military confrontation as well. This narrative is taking hold at a time when the U.S. is losing its leadership role in the region, and tensions with traditional allies such as Israel and Saudi Arabia are at a height over how to handle the shifts in the region following the Arab spring. I argue in this book that the premise of this narrative is erroneous because opportunities for diplomacy still remain *if* the political will to pursue it exists.

This book is focused on foreign policy and, more specifically, on how the Obama administration handled the many challenges of diplomacy with Iran. It seeks first and foremost to document the events as they occurred. Second, the book aims to explain why talks did not bring about the desired results and why the pursuit of diplomacy ended up being so short-lived. It analyzes the decisions of the two governments and the reasoning behind those decisions, as well as other factors that either distort or in other ways impact the decision-making process, such as lack of information, mistrust of the other side's intentions, and domestic constraints on the governments' foreign policy maneuverability.

The book is predominantly based on primary sources, that is, interviews with decision makers from the U.S., the EU, and Iran, as well as with other key players such as Russia, Israel, Saudi Arabia, Japan, Brazil, and Turkey. This includes interviews with both top government officials as well as the actual negotiators. Other primary sources used are confidential state documents of the parties involved that either were made public through *Wikileaks* or were shared with me by government officials. Secondary sources, such as the writings of other analysts and news items, have also been utilized. The news items are primarily from English-language sources as well as from Iranian newspapers in Persian. Because the book covers a very recent time period, however, the availability of secondary sources is somewhat limited.

More than sixty interviews were conducted with diplomats, negotiators, and decision makers from the involved countries. Their accounts of the events have been crossed-checked, and no information has been included without a caveat when based on just one or two testimonies. The interviewees were selected based on their direct involvement in the decision making of the respective countries and/or as members of the negotiation teams. As a result of the June 2009 presidential election in Iran, access to Iranian diplomats and decision makers has become increasingly difficult. Though I enjoyed valuable access to key Iranian officials and negotiators, less information was available to me from the Iranian side compared with that of the American side. This is due partly to the difficulty of accessing Iranian officials post-2009 elections, and partly to the revelation of the *Wikileaks* documents and my continued contact with American government officials throughout the period in question. While insufficient (or even lack of) access to Iran and Iranian decision makers has not prevented others in Washington from writing books about Iranian foreign policy, one must recognize that the imbalance in data renders more difficult an exhaustive analysis of the decisions, reasoning, and mistakes committed by the Iranians. Still, compared with much of the literature in the West in regard to Iran, this book is based on a greater amount of data from Iran.

Though it is not possible to list all the decision makers who have played a role in making themselves and information about their government's reasoning available, and some of them have chosen to remain anonymous because of their government role, a few of them deserve to be, and can be, mentioned. Israel's Deputy Minister of Foreign Affairs Danny Ayalon, among others, provided invaluable insights into Israel's thinking in regard to the Obama administration's diplomatic efforts. Prince Turki Al-Faisal, former director general of Saudi Arabia's intelligence agency, was among those who generously provided the same information about Saudi strategizing. On the European side, I am very grateful to the insights of David Miliband, then–foreign secretary of the United Kingdom; France's ambassador to the United Nations, Gérard Araud; France's ambassador to the U.S., Pierre Vimont; Germany's ambassador to the United Nations, Peter Wittig; as well as Ambassador Andreas Michaelis of the German Foreign Ministry. The perspectives and accounts of Brazil and Turkey were aptly provided by, among others, then–foreign minister of Brazil, Celso Amorim, and Ibrahim Kalin, Turkish prime minister Tayyip Erdogan's foreign relations adviser. Similarly, conversations with Ataollah Mohajerani, Iran's former minister of culture and adviser to Green movement leader Mehdi Karroubi, and Ardeshir Amirarjomand, spokesperson for presidential hopeful Mir Hossein Mousavi, have provided deep insights into the unfolding of events in Iran around the presidential elections as well as the perspectives of the leaders of the Iranian opposition. In regard to the perspectives of the Iranian government itself, I am grateful to both Iran's UN ambassador Mohammad Khazaee and Ambassador Ali Asghar Soltanieh, who represented Iran in the Vienna negotiations. On the American side, the vast majority of interviewees preferred to remain nameless in the book because of their continued role in the U.S. government.

The book begins by addressing the geopolitical realities that drove the Obama administration toward pursuing the option that the Bush administration had shunned for eight years: direct diplomacy with Iran. The second chapter addresses the many political obstacles the Obama administration's diplomatic outreach faced from some of its own allies, demonstrating the difficulty facing a policy shift of this magnitude both at home and abroad. In chapter 3 I address the Iranian reaction to Obama's election victory and their fears and hopes regarding what Obama's new approach could bring. The fourth chapter goes into greater detail on how the Obama administration devised its new Iran policy once in office, followed by a chapter on how the U.S. and Israel clashed over diplomacy with Iran. In chapter 6 I address the elections in Iran, the human rights abuses that the Iranian government committed and the paralysis this caused within Iran's political elite, and how these conditions affected Obama's willingness and ability to pursue diplomacy. Chapter 7 addresses the tensions between sanctions and diplomacy in the Obama administration's so-called dual-track policy, followed by a chapter recounting the failed negotiations between Iran and the U.S. in October 2009. Chapter 9 addresses the Obama administration's shift toward the punitive track and the diplomacy surrounding the pursuit of sanctions in the UN Security Council. The subsequent chapter gives a detailed account of Brazil and Turkey's mediation and successful negotiations with Iran, and why Washington rejected their intervention. Finally, the last two chapters of the book analyze why diplomacy fell short and why it was abandoned so quickly. They also provide a forward-looking analysis of whether diplomacy can resolve tensions between the U.S. and Iran in the new environment in the Middle East and, if so, whether it can generate the necessary measures to alleviate the enmity ensnaring Tehran and Washington.

Acknowledgments

This project would never have been completed had it not been for the help and assistance of countless friends and colleagues. There is not enough room here to thank everyone who deserves credit, nor can I thank enough the ones I do mention. I am forever indebted to Haleh Esfandiari, who generously provided me the opportunity to conduct the research for this book at the Woodrow Wilson Center for International Scholars in Washington, D.C. And, of course, I am forever indebted to Ruhi Ramazani, the dean of Iranian foreign policy studies. As a friend and a mentor, he gave advice and assistance that have been priceless, and I continue to aspire to study international relations and Iranian foreign policy in accordance with the standard he has set.

I must also thank my agent, Deborah Grosvenor, for the invaluable help she has provided, and Chris Rogers at Yale University Press for his patience and persistence. Stephen Heintz and the Rockefeller Brothers Fund provided generous funding to support my travels during the research phase of the book, as did my friend Allahverdi Farmanfarmaian.

I have had the privilege of working with dozens of research assistants during this past year who have provided me vital help in both editing and research. These include Shawn Amoie, Natasha Bahrami, David Elkins, David Elliott, Natasha Rastegari, Darya Razavi, Shahrzad Safavi, David Shams, Sanaz Talaifar, Samir Tata, and Shawn Vaziri. A special thank-you must be extended to Reza Marashi and Lara Talverdian, whose assistance went well beyond what was required of them. Many of these talented research assistants were provided by my friend Ambassador Wendy Chamberlin and the Middle East Institute in Washington, D.C.

Above all, I must thank my family: my wife, Amina, without whose love, strength, and patience this book never would have come to fruition. And my children, Darius, Jamil, and Yasmine, whose innocence pushes me to strive for a better world. I am to them eternally grateful.

A Single Roll of the Dice

One

A Peace of Necessity

You cannot prevent and prepare for war at the same time.
—Albert Einstein

Tim Guldimann arrived in Washington in early May 2003. As the Swiss ambassador to Tehran, he served as caretaker of American interests in Iran because the United States does not have an embassy there. He visited the U.S. capital every few months to brief American officials on the latest developments in the Islamic Republic. But this was no ordinary visit. In Guldimann's possession was an Iranian document offering something many at the time believed was unthinkable: comprehensive negotiations between the United States and Iran.

Guldimann's visit to Washington came only weeks after U.S. troops had sacked Baghdad and ended Saddam Hussein's tyrannical rule. In less than two years, the George W. Bush administration had defeated both the Taliban in Afghanistan and Iraq's Republican Guard. Iran was encircled. Hundreds of thousands of U.S. troops were now deployed on Iran's eastern and western flank. Tehran could very well be next on the Bush administration's list of targets. Though Washington had shown minimal interest in talking to the Iranians, Tehran made a final effort to get the Americans to the negotiating table. An offer for comprehensive negotiations was prepared by Sadegh Kharrazi, Iran's ambassador to Paris, and it eventually won the approval of Iran's Supreme Leader, Ayatollah Ali Khamenei. The proposal spelled out the contours of a strategic realignment between the United States and Iran based on the resolution of all major points of contention between them. To make sure that Washington understood Iran's seriousness, the negotiation proposal was given to the Swiss ambassador—the recognized and authentic intermediary between the United States and Iran in the absence of direct diplomatic channels—to be hand-delivered to the U.S. Department of State.

The proposal astonished the Americans. The Iranians put all their cards on the table, declaring what they sought from Washington and what they were willing to give in return. In a dialogue of "mutual respect," the Iranians offered to end their support for Hamas and Islamic Jihad, and pressure them to cease attacks on Israel. On Hezbollah, the pro-Iranian Shiite group in Lebanon that Iran had helped to create, Tehran offered to support its disarmament and transform it into a purely political party. The Iranians offered to put their contested nuclear program under intrusive international inspections in order to alleviate any fears of weaponization. Tehran would also sign the Additional Protocol to the Non-Proliferation Treaty and even allow extensive American involvement in the program as a further guarantee and goodwill gesture. On terrorism, Tehran offered full cooperation against *all* terrorist organizations— above all, al-Qaeda. Additionally, Iran would work actively with the United States to support political stabilization and the establishment of a nonsectarian government in Iraq.

What probably astonished the Americans the most was Iran's offer to accept the Beirut Declaration of the Arab League—that is, the Saudi peace plan from March 2002, in which the Arab states proffered collective peace with Israel, recognizing and normalizing relations with the Jewish state. In return, Israel would agree to a withdrawal from all occupied territories and accept a fully independent Palestinian state, an equal division of Jerusalem, and an equitable resolution of the Palestinian refugee problem. Through this step, Iran would formally recognize the two-state solution and consider itself at peace with Israel. This was an unprecedented concession by

Tehran. Only a year earlier, hard-liners in Tehran had dismissed the Saudi initiative, arguing that an Israeli return to the pre-1967 borders would be an unjust solution for the Palestinians.[1] The laundry list of policies that Iran was willing to discuss and amend was nothing short of an American wish list of everything that needed to change about Iran.

In return, the Iranians wanted members of the Mujahedin-e Khalq Organization (MEK), a U.S.-designated terrorist organization of Iranian origin based in Iraq, handed over to them in return for the al-Qaeda operatives Iranian authorities had captured. At a more strategic level, the Iranians wanted to reach a long-term understanding with the United States that involved ending all U.S. sanctions; respecting Iranian national interests in Iraq and supporting Iranian demands for war reparations; respecting Iran's right to full access to nuclear, biological, and chemical technology; and, finally, recognizing Iran's legitimate security interests in the region. The proposal also spelled out a procedure for step-by-step negotiations toward a mutually acceptable agreement.

Guldimann delivered the proposal to the State Department and briefed U.S. officials on his conversations with Iranian officials. To ensure that the proposal would reach the president's desk, the Swiss ambassador also gave a copy of the proposal to Republican congressman Robert Ney of Ohio, who in turn delivered it directly to Karl Rove, Bush's special adviser. Ney, a fluent Persian-speaker who had lived in Iran prior to the 1979 revolution and favored diplomacy with Tehran, received a call from Rove within a few hours. Rove wanted to be sure of the authenticity of the proposal, which he called "intriguing," and promised to deliver it directly to the president. While few had expected the Iranians to initiate such outreach efforts, the response of the Bush White House was even more stunning.

Many in the State Department recognized the proposal for what it was: an authentic offer for negotiations approved by the highest authorities in Iran, partly motivated by America's strength in the aftermath of—at that time—successful military operations in Iraq and Afghanistan, and by Iran's sense of vulnerability.[2] Some senior officials favored a positive response to Tehran, including Secretary of State Colin Powell and his deputy, Richard Armitage. But Vice President Dick Cheney and Secretary of Defense Donald Rumsfeld denied them an opportunity to debate the pros and cons of the issue. Their argument was simple but devastating. "We don't speak to evil," they determined.[3] Not one single interagency meeting was set up to discuss the proposal.[4] "In the end," Lawrence Wilkerson, Colin Powell's former chief of staff told me, in a harsh reference to the neoconservatives, led by Cheney and Rumsfeld, "the secret cabal got what it wanted: no negotiations with Tehran."[5]

The hard-liners in the Pentagon and the vice president's office did not disagree that Iran's decision to make a proposal blatantly opposed to its official ideology was a sign of its weakness and sense of vulnerability. But negotiating with Iran was simply wrong, they contended, because America could get what it wanted for free by simply removing the regime in Tehran. If, on the other hand, talks were initiated and America accepted Iran's assistance, Washington would be put in the awkward situation of owing the ayatollahs.[6] Why talk to Iran when you could simply dictate terms from a position of strength?

An opportunity for a major breakthrough had been willfully wasted. Many former Bush administration officials admit that the nonresponse was a mistake. The proposal had come at an opportune time—Tehran did not yet have a functioning nuclear program, it was not swimming in oil revenues from soaring energy demands, and it was not enriching uranium. In fact, its centrifuges were not even spinning. To those in the administration opposed to the neoconservative agenda, it was difficult to fathom how such an opportunity could have been dismissed. "In my mind it was one of those things you throw your hands up in the air and say, 'I can't believe we did this,'" Wilkerson said.[7]

But merely rejecting the proposal was not enough. The hard-liners in the Bush administration apparently wanted to add insult to injury. Instead of simply turning down the Iranian offer, the Bush administration decided to castigate the Swiss for having delivered the proposal in the first place. Only a few days after its delivery, Washington rebuked Guldimann and the Swiss government for having overstepped their diplomatic mandate. The message to Tehran was clear: not only would the Bush administration refuse Iran the courtesy of a reply, it would punish those who sought to convey messages between the two countries.

Only a few months later, an insurgency erupted in Iraq that simultaneously emboldened Iran and entangled the United States. While Tehran's influence began to rise because of its ties to the Shia in southern Iraq and to the Kurds in the north, Washington's maneuverability began to shrink. With its outreach to Washington rejected, Iran instead opted to pursue a more aggressive policy, challenging U.S. interests and expanding its nuclear enrichment program. Mired in Iraq and Afghanistan, Washington was increasingly incapable of stopping Iran from expanding its influence and reach in the region. With the Bush administration refusing to engage in diplomacy, sanctions failing to change Iran's policies, and military action remaining a deeply unattractive option, the Bush administration had few policy options left beyond issuing various empty threats.

Soon enough, even some of the most hawkish figures in Washington's foreign policy establishment began to recognize the foolishness of this squandered opportunity for diplomacy. But recognizing the mistake was not enough. A new president had to occupy the White House before diplomacy would be given a chance.

The thirty-year-old U.S.-Iran enmity is no longer a phenomenon; it is an institution. For three decades, politicians and bureaucrats in both countries have made careers out of demonizing each other. Firebrands in Iran have won political points by adding an ideological dimension to an already rooted animosity. Shrewd politicians, in turn, have shamelessly used ideology to advance their political objectives. Neighboring states in the Persian Gulf and beyond have taken advantage of this estrangement, often kindling the flames of division.

Israel and some of its supporters in the United States, in particular, have feared that a thaw in U.S. relations with Iran would come at the expense of America's special friendship with the Jewish state.

But the strategic cost to the United States and Iran of this prolonged feud has been staggering. Harming both and benefiting neither, the U.S.-Iran estrangement has complicated Washington's efforts to advance the peace process between the Israelis and Palestinians in the 1990s, win the struggle against al-Qaeda, or defeat the Taliban in Afghanistan and the insurgency in Iraq. Still, the strategic cost of this enmity has oftentimes been dwarfed by the domestic political cost to overcome it. In Washington, the political cost for attempting to resolve tensions with Iran has simply been too great and the political space too narrow to justify starting down a fraught and uncertain path to peace with Iran. Political divisions, in turn, have paralyzed Tehran at key intervals, with vying political factions not wishing to see their competitors define the outcome of a U.S.-Iran rapprochement or get credit for reducing tensions.

The hostility has been institutionalized because either too many forces on both sides calculate that they can better advance their own narrow interests by retaining the status quo, or the predictability of enmity is preferred to the unpredictability of peace making. Thus, over the years, this antipathy has survived—and hardened—because the cost of maintaining the status quo has not outweighed the risk of seeking peace—until 2008, that is.

With the election of Barack Obama, the stars aligned for a radical shift in U.S.-Iran relations. Tensions between the United States and Iran had risen dramatically during the Bush administration, putting the two countries on the verge of war. While the U.S. invasion of Afghanistan and the occupation of Iraq put American troops on Iran's eastern and western borders, respectively, the defeat of the Taliban and the end of Saddam Hussein's reign also removed two of Iran's key regional rivals from the strategic chessboard. Freed from the burden of its long-standing enemies, Iran was now a fast-ascending power that astutely took advantage of America's inability to win the peace in the Middle East. At the same time, Iran's advancing nuclear program added more fuel to the fire. Increasingly, Iran's rise, combined with America's painful predicament in the region, rendered a continuation of the U.S.-Iran rift too costly. Iran and the United States were gravitating toward a confrontation that neither could afford.[8]

Meanwhile, the American public had turned against not only president George W. Bush's invasion of Afghanistan and occupation of Iraq, but also the ideological foundation of Bush's worldview. Previously, Beltway hawks maintained that negotiations and compromise were not mere tools of diplomacy, but rather rewards that should be granted only to states that deserved an opportunity to talk to the United States. Inspired by this philosophy, Bush refused to engage with Iran during his entire presidency, even on issues of such importance as Iraq and Afghanistan (with the exception of episodic instances of brief diplomatic outreach for tactical purposes). Moreover, the neoconservative philosophy, viewing the United States as the source of legitimacy at home and abroad, dictated that talking to the autocratic rulers in Tehran would help legitimize Iran's theocratic and repressive government. But while refusing engagement with Iran upheld a sense of ideological purity for the Bush White House, it did nothing to address the growing challenge that Iran posed to the United States in the region. During the Bush presidency, Iran amassed more than 8,000 centrifuges for its nuclear program while expanding its influence in Iraq, Afghanistan, and Lebanon.

This reality was widely acknowledged in the United States toward the end of the Bush administration. In March 2006 Congress appointed a bipartisan Iraq Study Group to assess the Iraq war and to make policy recommendations. One of the group's key endorsements was direct U.S. dialogue with Iran over Iraq and the situation in the Middle East—a stark refutation of the Bush White House ideology.[9] And in September 2008, only two months before the U.S. presidential elections, five former secretaries of state—Madeleine Albright, Colin Powell, Warren Christopher, Henry A. Kissinger, and James A. Baker III—called on the United States to talk to Iran.[10]

Then-Senator Obama recognized that unprecedented political space had emerged for new foreign policy thinking. So rather than shying away from the issue of diplomacy with Iran, Obama took the unusual step of making engagement with U.S. adversaries a central part of his foreign policy platform during the 2008 presidential election—something that, under normal circumstances in Washington, would have been considered political suicide. In the televised presidential debates, Obama boldly declared that it was "critical" that we "talk to the Syrians and the Iranians," and that those saying that the United States "shouldn't be talking to them ignore our own history."[11]

Finally, the persona of Barack Obama himself was an important factor. He was a most unlikely candidate—and the most difficult one for the Iranian leadership to dismiss or vilify. Born to a Kenyan Muslim father and a American Midwestern mother, Obama spent most of his childhood in Hawaii and, later, in Indonesia, after his mother was remarried to an Indonesian. Having been exposed to both the Muslim and Christian religions, having grown up in a Third World country shortly after it had won its independence from colonial powers, and having the middle name Hussein—the name of one of the most revered figures in Shia tradition—Obama simply did not fit the Iranian stereotype of American, "imperialist" leaders—arrogant, ignorant, and incapable of empathizing with the grievances of Third World states against Western powers.

Clearly, Obama recognized the historic opportunity that lay before him. Only twelve and a half minutes into his presidency, he sought to seize it by extending America's hand of friendship in the hope that Iran would unclench its fist.

Two

With Friends
Like These . . .

We live in a neighborhood in which sometimes dialogue . . . is liable to be interpreted as weakness.

—Israel's foreign minister Tzipi Livni, declaring her opposition to U.S.-Iran diplomacy, November 2008

Millions around the globe were glued to their TVs to watch President Obama's message of hope on Inauguration Day 2009. In Tehran, however, decision makers were looking for a key buzzword in the new president's speech: mutual respect. Obama didn't disappoint. "To the Muslim world, we seek a new way forward, based on mutual interest and mutual respect . . . we will extend a hand if you are willing to unclench your fist," Obama said in his address to the 1.5-million-strong crowd on the Washington mall. "Mutual respect" has become an almost mysterious term in U.S.-Iran relations. The Iranians have repeatedly stated that improved U.S.-Iran relations can come about only when the two countries negotiate with each other as equals, with "mutual respect." The rather ambiguous term has often bewildered U.S. officials who do not understand what exactly the Iranians are demanding of the United States. "What does this 'mutual respect' mumbo-jumbo mean?" an American lawmaker once asked me. "Why don't they just say what they want?" While from the American point of view the U.S.-Iran conflict is rooted in policy differences and opposing visions for the Middle East, to the Iranians it is very much about discarding an uneven relationship—that between a master and a servant. The term "mutual respect" is so critical to Tehran that the Iranians even included it in their 2003 negotiation offer to the Bush administration (see chapter 1).

But the Iranians were not the only ones listening for signals in Obama's articulated vision for U.S.-Iran relations. Washington and Tehran may be the main actors in this drama, but plenty of other states also follow every twist and turn of their dysfunctional relationship. While some of them welcomed the Obama administration's promise of a new approach toward international affairs in general, and its policy toward Iran in particular, most feared what such change could bring about.

Europe's Relief and Anxiety

In Europe the election of Obama was largely welcomed, as was his promise for U.S.-Iran talks without preconditions, in contrast to the Bush administration's insistence that it would talk to Iran only on the condition that Iran first suspend its enrichment program. "The new tone set by the Obama administration engendered hope, not least since many European countries for a long time had identified and propagated a less conditioned approach to negotiating with Iran," a senior non-EU3 (France, Germany, United Kingdom) diplomat explained. Few doubted, however, that the task lying ahead of Obama was daunting. But the opportunity was too great to be missed; the United States was led by a new president with no baggage, giving Washington and Tehran a "chance for a new start." What emerged from Europe was principled support for diplomacy, with realistic expectations of what could be achieved. "For us it was a relief. It was a lot of happiness," a senior EU official told me. The Bush administration's refusal to engage in diplomacy, as well as its militaristic foreign policy, had frustrated the Europeans. There was a strong sense that the nonproliferation objectives of the U.S. and the EU could be better achieved with an American administration "that could be more flexible on modalities" and that "would be ready to meet the Iranians." Even when the United States endorsed the EU-Iran talks in 2006 and agreed to sit down with the Iranians—albeit with a precondition that was widely viewed as self-defeating—Washington still did not want to give the appearance of really engaging with the Iranians. "They were part of the group, but they really wanted to remain in the back," a senior French diplomat said.[1]

But once the diplomacy that Europe officially supported was about to start, fears and apprehensions emerged in some European capitals, despite their official support. What exactly did "direct" diplomacy "without preconditions" mean? Would the Obama administration cut the Europeans out of the process and opt for a bilateral channel with Tehran? If Europe were cut out of the process, would it lose its ability to bring pressure against any eventual military action down the road? "We didn't have many indicators with regard to the shape of the new Obama Iran policy," a senior EU diplomat explained. In France, specifically, there was "unease" and "apprehension" that Washington would go soft on Iran and, in the words of French foreign minister Bernard Kouchner, "ruin the dual-track approach"—the idea that the most effective strategy on Iran would entail an appropriate balance between talks and incentives on the one hand and hard-hitting sanctions on the other.[2]

"Going soft on Iran" would be especially problematic from the perspective of the French, in the event that Washington would amend its redline on the nuclear issue and accept enrichment on Iranian soil. During the campaign, then-Senator Obama had expressed strong opposition to the spread of nuclear weapons and declared that a *nuclear-armed* Iran would be intolerable. "Iran's development of a nuclear weapon, I believe, is unacceptable. And we have to mount an international effort to prevent that from happening," he said at his first postelection press conference on November 7, 2008. But throughout the campaign, Obama, unlike his presidential opponents, avoided making any statements on the issue of *uranium enrichment,* which is a key step in the process of producing nuclear fuel for peaceful purposes, as well as for producing nuclear weapons material. The Bush administration maintained a zero-enrichment objective, meaning that Iran should not only be denied nuclear weapons, it should also be prohibited from gaining the knowledge of the enrichment process. As such, the Bush administration rejected the Iranian claim that, as a signatory of the nonproliferation treaty, Iran had an inalienable right to enrichment. (Article IV of the treaty stipulates that member states have an "inalienable right" to "develop research, production and use of nuclear energy for peaceful purposes without discrimination.") Most states contested the Bush administration's rejection of the right to enrichment on a legal basis, and many U.S. allies also questioned the feasibility of denying Iran knowledge of the enrichment process.[3]

By 2008, an increasing number of influential foreign policy and nonproliferation voices in Washington had begun to question the wisdom of the zero-enrichment policy. In February 2008, former U.S. undersecretary of state for political affairs Thomas Pickering co-wrote an article in the *New York Review of Books* proposing that "Iran's efforts to produce enriched uranium and related nuclear activities be conducted on a multilateral basis, jointly managed and operated on Iranian soil by a consortium including Iran and other governments." At a conference a few weeks later in the U.S. Senate organized by the National Iranian American Council, Pickering defended his position in favor of abandoning the zero-enrichment policy. "We should not let the perfect become an enemy of the good," he said, arguing that, while zero-enrichment may be ideal, it is not the only solution to the Iranian nuclear challenge. At closed U.S. think tank seminars, one could hear even more blunt acknowledgments that the zero-enrichment policy had failed. The challenge was how to discard it without further emboldening the Iranians.[4]

As Washington was ready to move toward diplomacy, the enthusiasm for engagement in parts of Europe was waning. Neither the French nor the British were encouraged by the new mood in Washington and feared that the Obama administration would move the nuclear redlines. "We thought that was wrong, we thought it was bad tactics to signal [abandonment of the zero-enrichment objective]. . . . You shouldn't say that until the full might of U.S. diplomacy had been tested," a senior European official explained. President Nicolas Sarkozy of France was pushing toward a harsher stance that appeared to be closer to Bush's outlook on Iran than to Obama's. Together with the United Kingdom, France pressed the EU to adopt tough new sanctions on Iran in January 2009 at the same time that Obama was taking office. The push reopened divisions within the EU, with several states opposing it, preferring to place the emphasis on dialogue with Tehran instead. The French had several reasons for adopting a tougher stance. There was some resentment that the U.S. was taking over the process, and adopting a more rigid line would increase Europe's leverage and relevance. There was also a fear that Iran would play for time and outmaneuver the Obama administration, which could unravel the momentum for sanctions. Harsher EU measures could also help ensure a more hard-line outcome of the Obama administration's review of its Iran policy. Moreover, there was a general fatigue in Europe when it came to talks with Iran. Although more than two years had passed since the previous United Nations Security Council sanctions resolution had been imposed on Iran, Tehran had nevertheless continued with its nuclear program. It was time for new punitive measures, decision makers in Paris reasoned.[5]

While the French maintained that harsher EU sanctions would strengthen the Obama administration's hand in dealing with Iran, other EU states disagreed and worried that punitive measures at that time would undercut Obama. "Going in hawkish on the European side while Obama was stretching out his hand would certainly undermine the credibility of the outstretched hand," a senior non-EU3 diplomat said. These EU states welcomed Obama's impending outreach since they did not believe that there was a sanctions solution to the Iranian challenge. In the end, the French and British push for sanctions fell flat and the EU decided to wait for Obama to make the first move.[6]

Arab Doublespeak

Concerns about Obama's outreach to Iran were even greater in parts of the Arab world. Many Arab states were vehemently opposed to the policies and approach of the Bush administration in the Middle East—primarily the invasions of Afghanistan and Iraq; the way those military missions helped unleash Iranian and Shiite influence in the region; the neglect of the Israeli-Palestinian conflict; as well as the failure to consult and take into consideration the advice and concerns of the Arab states. There were also "deep concerns" that while the Arabs would be immediately affected by Iran going nuclear, they were not involved or consulted in the nuclear negotiations with Iran.[7]

During a visit to Saudi Arabia in October 2010, many Arab officials complained to me that the United States had "given Iraq to Iran on a golden platter" and that Iran was now in a position to establish hegemony in the region. Some officials could not fathom that these were unintended consequences of the Bush administration's Middle East policy, and rather suspected that the U.S. was secretly colluding with the rulers in Tehran. After all, the Arabs maintained, they had warned the United States about these exact consequences. Others blamed the situation on neglect and incompetence. "The Bush administration policies regarding the region suffered from a lack of consultations and dialogue with its regional friends like Saudi Arabia. We clearly and repeatedly warned them of the potential problems of their original plans in both Iraq and Afghanistan, and explained the geostrategic imbalances they might create, but they were not in the listening mode," Rayed Krimly, a special envoy of the Saudi king, told me. "Only much later did they begin to recognize the inherent contradictions in their policies and became more willing to seek dialogue and cooperation from Saudi Arabia and other allies. But by then it was clear to everyone that Iran was the only side in the region that benefited from U.S. mistakes by expanding its influence in both Iraq and Afghanistan," he continued.[8]

The Saudis and their Sunni Arab allies fear U.S.-Iran diplomacy primarily for three reasons. First, a U.S.-Iran rapprochement could help facilitate and grant acceptance to Iran's alleged ambitions for regional hegemony. Tensions between Iranians and Arabs have historic roots, dating back to the Arab conquest of Iran in the seventh-century AD. For centuries, Iran and Saudi Arabia have viewed each other as regional rivals. In more modern times, the Saudis have feared and resented the idea of the U.S. reestablishing the relations it had with Iran when, under the shah, Mohammad Reza Pahlavi, Iran was considered the custodian of stability in the region. In Arab eyes, the shah enjoyed the blessing of the United States to behave as a regional hegemon, much to the chagrin of Iran's Saudi rival. Any movement back in that direction would inevitably come at the expense of the Sunni Arabs' standing and influence in the region, the Saudis fear. Only days after Obama's election victory, the Jordanian foreign minister, Salah Bashir, told Western diplomats that "the nuclear crisis became a crisis [for the West] but for us the Iranian surge for hegemony has become a crisis." Egypt's then-president Hosni Mubarak told American officials repeatedly that he viewed Iran as the region's primary strategic threat and that its influence must be rolled back. An oft-repeated line by Saudi officials reads, "Engagement yes, marriage no," meaning that diplomacy for reducing tensions was acceptable, but not for a full-fledge rapprochement with American acceptance of Iranian policies and ambitions. "The [Saudi] kingdom's main concern is to prevent any ceding of Saudi-Arab interests for the sake of what has been termed by some Iran lovers as 'The Grand Bargain,' " Prince Turki bin Faisal Al Saud, the former director general of Saudi Arabia's intelligence agency, told me. "This term, generally, means that anything to do with the Middle East has to pass by Iranian doors," he argued.[9]

To the Americans, these concerns were generally viewed as exaggerated and unrealistic. The idea that the Americans would betray the Saudis if "the Iranian price is right" seemed removed from reality since a U.S.-Iran rapprochement was neither likely nor necessarily desirable to many American officials. "There's probably some concern in the region that may draw on an exaggerated sense of what's possible," said Robert Gates, secretary of defense in both the Bush and the Obama administrations, while on a visit to Saudi Arabia in May 2009. To reassure America's Sunni Arab allies, Gates added that "building diplomacy with Iran will not be at the expense of our long-term relationship with Saudi Arabia and other Gulf states that have been our partners and friends for decades."[10]

Second, even if improved U.S.-Iran relations would not grant Iran a hegemonic position, they could still enhance Iran's ability to "meddle in Arab affairs." Describing Iran not as "a neighbor one wants to see" but as "a neighbor one wants to avoid," King Abdullah of Saudi Arabia impressed on Obama administration officials early on that "Iran's goal is to cause problems." Many Arab states are particularly sensitive to Iran's penetration of the Israeli-Palestinian conflict, which has provided Tehran with ample opportunities to extend its influence in the Sunni Arab world. By taking a tougher stance against Israel than that of Washington's Arab allies, Tehran has increased the divide between these regimes and their populations. This bewilders Sunni governments, which despise being outflanked by Iran and having their inability—or unwillingness—to safeguard the rights of the Palestinians revealed. According to classified State Department cables, King Abdullah told Iran's foreign minister, Manouchehr Mottaki, in a heated exchange in March 2009 that "you as Persians have no business meddling in Arab matters," referring to Iran's involvement in the situation in the Palestinian territories.[11]

According to some analysts, Arab anxiety over Iran's rising influence has created new fault lines in the region. The old fault line of "Israel versus Arabs and Muslims" has been replaced with one that divides the region between states aligned with or opposed to the West. In this new Middle East, if given a choice between fighting Israel or opposing Iran's increased influence, the Sunni Arab dictatorships will choose the latter. This view of the region gained credence during Israel's bombing campaign of Gaza in late 2008.

Operation Cast Lead began on December 27, 2008, with surprise air strikes by the Israeli air force against the Gaza Strip, followed by a ground invasion on January 3, 2009. The assault continued for twenty-one days and resulted in seventeen Israeli and more than 1,400 Palestinian deaths. Images of the war and the Goldstone Report findings of Israeli war crimes brought anger in the Arab world to a boiling point. What was perhaps most problematic for America's Sunni Arab allies, however, was the information that emerged suggesting that some of them had been colluding with Israel in order to bring down the Hamas government in Gaza as a means to counter Iran's growing influence. Hamas's ties to Iran had provided Tehran with credibility among Arabs and a dangerous entrance to the heart of Arab politics, they argued. A defeat for Hamas would also be a defeat for Iran.[12]

That objective never materialized, but the war did impose a major cost on all actors in the region. The Egyptian government's alleged support for the Israeli operation, particularly its refusal to allow a general opening of the Rafah Crossing into Gaza, earned it much criticism in the Arab world. In a speech on al-Manar TV, the leader of Hezbollah singled out Egypt and echoed Hamas's condemnation of the leadership in Cairo. According to the *Jerusalem Post*, the Iran-aligned Hezbollah leader appeared to be calling for an open revolt against the Egyptian government as part of the fight against Israel. Iran's hard-line president, Mahmoud Ahmadinejad, further pounced on the Mubarak government in Egypt. "Today it has been heard in some of the West's political meetings that the Egyptian government is a partner in crimes in Gaza and they are after breaking Hamas as part of the resistance and bring it under their own influence," the semiofficial Mehr News Agency quoted Ahmadinejad as saying. The Egyptians, faced with demonstrations at home against the government's position on the Gaza war, in turn accused Iran and Hezbollah of provoking a conflict in the region to advance their own interests. "[They tried] to turn the region to confrontation in the interest of Iran, which is trying to use its cards to escape Western pressure . . . on the nuclear file," then-Egyptian foreign minister Ahmed Aboul Gheit said. Whether or not there are new fault lines in the region, the Gaza war did reveal the extent to which Sunni Arab dictatorships fear Iran's rising influence and the lengths they are willing to go to contain it.[13]

The third, and perhaps most important, reason that the Saudis and their Sunni Arab allies fear U.S.-Iran diplomacy is because such a dialogue, and the continued spread of Iranian influence that the Arab states assume it would entail, could constitute a direct threat to the survival of the Sunni Arab autocracies. The Islamic Republic is viewed as a twin threat because it embodies the idea of political Islam, which, prior to the Arab spring, was believed to be the primary domestic political threat to these autocratic and monarchial regimes. And during the first decade after the Iranian revolution in 1979, the Islamic Republic openly sought to export its revolution to its neighboring Arab states with the aim of replacing their governments with Islamic regimes. In addition, Iran challenges the U.S.-dominated order in the region—an order under which the United States seeks to guarantee the survival of its allied Sunni Arab dictatorships. The collapse of this order would constitute a direct threat to the survival of the current autocratic political systems in key Sunni Arab states.

Though leaders of these states publicly oppose a U.S.-Iran war, classified U.S. State Department cables that recently have come to light reveal that some Arab states have pushed the U.S. to go to war with Iran. In February 2007, Mohammed bin Zayed Al Nahyan, the crown prince of Abu Dhabi, urged the chief of staff of the U.S. Air Force, General Teed Moseley, to "delay their program—by all means available." He added: "I am saying this knowing that I am putting my country at risk and placing myself in a dangerous spot." Moreover, the king of Saudi Arabia had made frequent exhortations to the U.S. to attack Iran, the cables said, asking U.S. officials to "cut off the head of the snake."[14]

The Israel Factor

"We live in a neighborhood in which sometimes dialogue . . . is liable to be interpreted as weakness," Israel foreign minister Tzipi Livni said during an interview with Israel Radio only twenty-four hours after congratulating President-elect Obama on his historic election victory. Asked specifically if she supported discussions between the U.S. and Iran, she left no room for interpretation: "The answer is no," she declared. For decades, Israel has been a key factor in America's relations with Iran. Israel has at times pushed Washington to get closer to Tehran, but in the past twenty years has been a vehement opponent of a U.S.-Iran dialogue. In fact, Sunni Arab apprehension about the Obama administration's promise of diplomacy with Iran has been surpassed by only that of Israel.[15]

When Ahmadinejad began his tirades against Israel, the world appeared to be light-years away from the idea that ideological conflicts had come to an end. It seemed that ideologues had once more taken the reins of power and rejoined a battle in which there could be no parley or negotiated truce—only the victory of one idea over the other. Even before Ahmadinejad pulled Ayatollah Ruhollah Khomeini's poisonous anti-Israel rhetoric from the dustbin of history, the tense relations between Iran and Israel were often seen as one of history's last ideological clashes. On one side was Israel, portrayed as a democracy in a region beset by authoritarianism and an eastern outpost of Enlightenment rationalism. On the other side was the Islamic Republic of Iran, viewed as a hidebound clerical regime whose rejection of the West and aspiration to speak for Muslims everywhere were symbolized by its refusal to recognize Israel's right to exist.

The Israeli-Iranian confrontation is far more complex than an ideology-based understanding would indicate, however. Exclusive focus on the vitriol between the two countries has come at the expense of a deeper understanding of the strategic nature of their conflict and its impact on U.S.-Iran relations. That the conflict is strategic is underscored by the fact of past Iranian-Israeli cooperation. Prior to the overthrow of the shah, the conventional view in both countries was that non-Arab Iran and Israel—both surrounded by a sea of hostile Arabs and at odds with the Soviet Union—enjoyed strong common strategic imperatives, perhaps even a natural alliance. Indeed, as long as Iran and Israel faced common Arab and Russian threats, they forged close clandestine security ties that survived the Islamic Revolution of 1979 and continued for a number of years. It was not just the shah who traded and cooperated with the Israelis; Khomeini had his fair share of dealings with Israel as well. In spite of his frequent calls for Israel's destruction, the Khomeini government was very careful to avoid direct confrontation with Israel. "We never wanted to get directly involved in the fights against Israel," Alavi Tabar, an Iranian revolutionary close to Khomeini, explained to me over tea and cookies at his Tehran office. Iranian passivity regarding Israel had everything to do with Iran's strategic imperatives. Khomeini was careful not to turn Israel into a direct threat to Iran, and he told his associates that, in the event of an agreement between the Palestinians and the Israelis, Iran should lend its support to the agreement by standing behind the Palestinians.[16]

Indeed, the Israelis recognized the difference between Iran's rhetoric and its policy, and treated Iran as a potential regional ally, regardless of the nature of its regime and its oratory. While Khomeini called Israel a "cancerous tumor," the Israelis—particularly Shimon Peres, successively Israel's prime minister and foreign minister— were lobbying Washington to boost Iran's defenses and bring Tehran "back into the western fold." Only three days after Iraq invaded Iran in September 1980, Israel foreign minister Moshe Dayan interrupted a private visit to Vienna to hold a press conference to urge the United States—in the middle of the hostage crisis—to forget the past and help Iran keep up its defenses. In 1982, Ariel Sharon (then Israel's defense minister) proudly announced on NBC television that Israel would continue to sell arms to Iran in spite of an American ban on such sales. Sharon added that Israel provided the arms to Iran because it felt it was important to "leave a small window open" to the possibility of good relations with Iran in the future.[17]

In that period, Iran's strategic imperatives and its rhetorical objectives clashed, and the ideology of the revolutionaries was repeatedly sidelined by realist calculations. As a result, Iran huffed and puffed but did very little against Israel. Similarly, geopolitical factors compelled Israel to seek a revived working relationship with Iran in spite of the Iranian regime's Islamist nature. Israel regarded Iraq's invasion of Iran with great concern since an Iraqi victory would leave Israel in a far more vulnerable position. Baghdad would become the undisputed hegemon over the Persian Gulf, with the world's third-largest oil reserves and an army more than four times the size of Israel's. It would make the threat of the "eastern front" worse than ever before: an Arab alliance with Iraq's full participation could overrun Jordan and quickly place the Iraqi army on Israel's eastern front. Although Iraq was flirting with the United States, and some in the Reagan administration—like Donald Rumsfeld, President Reagan's special envoy to Iraq—were flirting back and toying with the idea of making Saddam their new ally in the Persian Gulf, an Iraqi-Western rapprochement would have little bearing on Baghdad's hostility toward Israel. An Iranian victory, as unlikely as it appeared at the outbreak of the war, did not particularly worry Israel. Because Iran was a thousand miles away, its ability to participate in a war against Israel was minimal, even if it came out of the war victorious. "Throughout the 1980s, no one in Israel said anything about an Iranian threat—the word wasn't even uttered," said Professor David Menashri of Tel Aviv University, Israel's foremost expert on Iran.[18]

At the height of Iran's ideological zeal, Israel's fear of an Iraqi victory, its dismissal of the dangers of Iran's political ideology, and its efforts to win Iran back and revive its periphery alliance with the non-Arab states in the region all paved the way for Israel's policy of arming Iran and seeking to defuse tensions between Washington and Tehran. Stopping Saddam was paramount, and if "that meant going along with the request for arms by the Iranians, and that could prevent an Iraqi victory, so be it," asserted David Kimche, former head of the Israeli Foreign Ministry. But there was more. Inducing Washington to reach out to Iran had the benefit of not only stopping Iraq and reviving its strategic ties with Iran; it would also distance the United States from the Arabs and ultimately "establish Israel as the only real strategic partner of the United States in the region." A majority of senior Israeli officials, including Yitzhak Rabin, simply continued to believe that Iran was a "natural ally" of Israel.[19]

As the war progressed without the fall of Iran's revolutionary government, Israeli thinking increasingly shifted from counting on the Khomeini government's disintegration to seeking the strengthening of moderate elements within it. Though the Israelis began to realize that the Khomeini regime was not going to collapse anytime soon, they still viewed its Islamic nature and extremist views as a historical parenthesis. The real, geostrategically oriented Iran that would resume the shah's strategic cooperation with Israel would soon reemerge, they believed. This made it all the more important for Israel to support Iran in the war because an Iranian defeat would not only embolden the Arab front against Israel, it would also reduce the chances of reviving Israel's alliance with Iran, as the next regime would be weak and dependent on Iraq. Empowering moderates within the Iranian regime could facilitate the process of reestablishing Israel's ties to Iran, and the one element in Iran that could change the situation for the better amounted to the professional officers in the Iranian army. "There was a feeling that if we in Israel could somehow maintain relations with the army, this could bring about an improvement of relations between Iran and Israel," Kimche explained. It was this reasoning that eventually culminated in the Iran-Contra scandal, which was an Israeli initiative to convince the United States to talk to the Khomeini government in Tehran, sell arms to it, and ignore its anti-Western rhetoric.[20]

What changed the nature of Israeli-Iranian relations from a tacit alliance to open enmity was not the Iranian revolution of 1979, but the geopolitical changes that swept through the Middle East in the early 1990s. The defeat of Iraq in the 1991 Persian Gulf war and the collapse of the Soviet Union eliminated the two common threats that had brought Iran and Israel closer to each other since the 1950s. This improved the security environments of both Iran and Israel, but also left both states unchecked. Without Iraq balancing Iran, the Persians would now become a threat, Israeli hawks argued. These new geopolitical conditions necessitated new strategies and policies. This was particularly true for Israel, given that the end of the Cold War had put Israel's strategic utility to the United States under question. During the Persian Gulf war, which drove Saddam Hussein out of Kuwait, Washington had increasingly treated Israel as a burden rather than an asset. And as the United States gravitated toward the Arab position (Washington organized the Madrid conference immediately after the war to pressure Israel to compromise with the Palestinians), and as its need for Israel as a bulwark against Soviet penetration of the Middle East evaporated, how would Israel's standing in Washington fare if the U.S. also sought a rapprochement with Iran?

Drastic actions were needed to adjust to these new realities. Israel needed to make peace with the Palestinians to reduce friction with the United States, and it needed to redirect its resources toward the potential Iranian threat to convince Washington to confront Tehran. In October 1992, the Labor government undertook a major campaign to depict Iran and Shia Islamic fundamentalism as a global threat. Rhetoric reflected intentions, and, having been freed from the chains of Iraq, Iran was acquiring the capacity to turn intentions into policy, Labor argued. And since Tehran was "fanatical and irrational," finding an accommodation with such "mad mullahs" was a nonstarter. While the threat depiction resembled prophecy more than reality, it underlined the link between the Labor Party's intent to secure a peace deal with Israel's immediate Arab neighbors and the new drive to confront Iran. To convince a skeptical Israeli public that peace could be made with the Arab vicinity, it was necessary to bolster the threat portrayal of the Persian periphery. Even though Iran was weak mili-

tarily after the devastating war with Iraq, Rabin told Israel's Knesset
(parliament) in 1993 that Israel's "struggle against murderous Islamic
terror" was "meant to awaken the world[,] which is lying in slumber,"
to the dangers of Shia fundamentalism. "Death is at our doorstep,"
Rabin said of Iran, even though just five years earlier he had dismissed
Iran's rhetoric as inconsequential. A key component of the campaign
to isolate Iran was the effort to prevent a U.S.-Iran rapprochement, in
the words of a former Israeli ambassador to Washington, since improved relations between Washington and Tehran could come at the
expense of Israel's strategic relationship with the U.S.[21]

Soon enough, the Iranian government began hitting at Israel.
Fearing that Israel was pushing the U.S. to build a new regional order
based on Iran's prolonged isolation, Iran started targeting what it
perceived to be the weakest link in that strategy: the peace process.
The new realities in the region had realigned Iran's ideological goals
with its strategic interests, causing Tehran to turn its anti-Israel rhetoric into policy. Now, venomous outbursts against Israel were to be
accompanied with action, primarily in the form of providing material
support to militant organizations targeting the Jewish state. Paradoxically, Tehran had not misperceived American and Israeli intentions.
According to Martin Indyk, a key Middle East hand in the Clinton
administration and an architect of the "dual containment" policy that
wedded peacemaking between Israel and the Palestinians with efforts
to isolate Iran, "The more we succeeded in making peace, the more
isolated [Iran and the rogue states] would become; the more we
succeeded in containing [Iran], the more possible it would be to make
peace. So they had an incentive to do us in on the peace process in
order to defeat our policy of containment."[22]

Initially, the American establishment was skeptical toward Israel's
change of heart on Iran. "Why the Israelis waited until fairly recently
to sound a strong alarm about Iran is a perplexity," wrote Clyde
Haberman of the *New York Times* in November 1992. Haberman went
on to note: "For years, Israel remained willing to do business with
Iran, even though the mullahs in Teheran were screaming for an end

to the 'Zionist entity.' " Eventually, however, the mad mullah argument stuck. After all, the Iranians themselves were the greatest help in selling that argument to Washington. From the Israeli perspective, rallying Western states to its side was best achieved by emphasizing the alleged suicidal tendencies of the clergy and Iran's apparent infatuation with the idea of destroying Israel. As long as the Iranian leadership was viewed as irrational, conventional tactics such as deterrence would be rendered impossible, leaving the international community with no option but to prohibit Iranian capabilities. How could a country like Iran be trusted with missile technology, the argument went, if its leadership was immune to dissuasion by the larger and more numerous missiles of the West?[23]

Israel sought to ensure that the world—Washington in particular—would not see the Israeli-Iranian conflict as one between two rivals for preeminence in a region that lacked a clear pecking order. Rather, Israel framed the clash as one between the sole democracy in the Middle East and a theocracy that hated everything the West stood for. When it was cast in those terms, the allegiance of Western states to Israel was no longer a matter of choice or real political interest. Ironically, Iran too preferred an ideological framing of the conflict, since its desire for Iranian great-power status would gain more support among the Muslim masses if it were projected as an effort to advance Islam and the rights of the Palestinians.

The ideological zeal masking the Israeli-Iranian rivalry contributed to Washington's poor understanding of the root causes of this conflict. While there was some recognition that Israel exaggerated the Iranian threat in order to push Washington to take a harder line on Iran, there was little acknowledgment of Israel's real concerns about Iran. In spite of its rhetoric, Israel views the regime in Tehran as rational (but extremist), calculating, and risk-averse. Even those Israeli officials who believe that Iran is hell-bent on destroying the Jewish state recognize that Tehran is unlikely to attack Israel with nuclear weapons due to the destruction Israel would inflict on Iran through its second-strike capability—a guaranteed ability to retaliate because of its nuclear-equipped submarines. "Whatever measure [the Iranians] have, they can't destroy Israel's capability to respond," Ranaan Gissin, spokesperson for Israel's former prime minister Ariel Sharon told me.[24]

What lies at the heart of Israel's concern is not necessarily the fear of a nuclear clash, but the regional and strategic consequences that nuclear parity in the Middle East will have for Israel. The real danger a nuclear-capable Iran poses for Israel is twofold. First, an Iran that does not possess nuclear weapons but that has the capability to *build* them in short order would significantly damage Israel's ability to deter militant Palestinian and Lebanese organizations. It will damage the image of Israel as the sole nuclear-armed state in the region and undercut the myth of its invincibility. Gone would be the days when Israel's military supremacy would enable it to dictate the parameters of peace and pursue unilateral peace plans. "We cannot afford a nuclear bomb in the hands of our enemies, period. They don't have to use it; the fact that they have it is enough," Israel's former deputy minister of defense, Ephraim Sneh, explained to me. This could force Israel to accept territorial compromises with its neighbors in order to deprive Iran of any justification for fomenting hostility toward the Jewish state. Israel simply would not be able to afford a nuclear rivalry with Iran and continued territorial disputes with the Arabs at the same time. "I don't want the Israeli-Palestinian negotiations to be held under the shadow of an Iranian nuclear bomb," Sneh continued.[25]

Second, the deterrence and power Iran would acquire by mastering the nuclear fuel cycle could compel Washington to cut a deal with Tehran in which Iran would gain recognition as a regional power and acquire strategic significance in the Middle East at the expense of Israel. "The Great Satan will make up with Iran and forget about Israel," Gerald Steinberg of Bar Ilan University and an adviser to Israel prime minister Benjamin Netanyahu said of the Israeli fear. All likely outcomes of U.S.-Iran negotiations are perceived to be less optimal for Israel than the status quo of intense U.S.-Iran enmity that threatens to boil over into a military clash. Under these circumstances, U.S.-Iran negotiations could damage Israel's strategic standing. Common interests shared by Iran and the U.S. would overshadow Israel's concerns with Tehran, thereby leaving Israel alone in facing its Iranian rival. After Obama's election victory, the Israeli National Security Council foresaw two possible Iran-related diplomatic developments that could hurt Israel: a U.S.-initiated dialogue leading to rapprochement between Iran, the United States, and the Arab world, or the U.S. building a wide international coalition against Iran for which Israel might be forced to pay a price. Preventing these scenarios was essential, the Israeli National Security Council argued. Yuval Steinitz, right-wing Likud Party member of the Knesset and aspiring defense or foreign minister, went so far as to compare Obama to Neville Chamberlain, the British prime minister who thought Adolf Hitler could be stopped through diplomacy. Obama "will have to choose in the next year whether to be [Neville] Chamberlain or [Winston] Churchill," Steinitz said.[26]

U.S.-Iran diplomacy could come at Israel's expense due to the risk of diverging American and Israeli redlines on the nuclear issue. To Israel, nuclear know-how is tantamount to a nuclear bomb; once Iran controls the fuel cycle, Israel maintains, it can weaponize at will in spite of its obligations under the nuclear nonproliferation treaty (NPT). Consequently, Israel has insisted that Iran's nuclear program should be halted well ahead of the redline of uranium enrichment, even though enrichment is permitted by the NPT and is conducted by numerous states. Then-Israeli defense minister Shaul Mofaz told U.S. lawmakers in March 2005 that the operation of the enrichment cycle was the "point of no return" for the Iranian program. Meir Dagan, chief of Mossad (Israel's intelligence agency), went a step further, saying that the Iranian program will be unstoppable once it no longer requires outside assistance to complete the enrichment process. Hence, any diplomacy would require as its primary objective a "complete, full, verifiable cessation of the fuel cycle program," which means a full suspension of all enrichment, reprocessing, heavy-water-reactor construction, and related research activities. Israeli Deputy

Foreign Minister Danny Ayalon was categorical about zero-enrichment as an unbending Israeli redline. "Enrichment in Iran is certainly
unacceptable," he told me in October 2010. While the Bush administration maintained an identical objective with regard to enrichment,
there were still concerns in Israel that Washington would compromise
that stance through negotiations. Once Obama took office, those
concerns grew significantly. Confidence in the United States' sincerity in maintaining a zero-enrichment objective plummeted. In the
Israeli view, the Obama administration had made America's redlines
flexible and unreliable.[27]

Although Israel believes that the only way to stop Iran is through
the threat or use of force, Israel itself lacks the military ability to
destroy the Iranian nuclear program. "To our regret, there is no
Israeli military capability that would enable us to reach a situation
whereby Iran's nuclear capabilities are destroyed without the possibility of recovery," former National Security Council chairman Giora
Eiland warned in December 2008. "The maximal achievement that
Israel can accomplish is to disrupt and suspend Iran's nuclear program," he said, adding that Israel "cannot defeat Iran." In an even
more blunt admission contradicting Israel's many warnings that it will
attack Iran unless it stops its nuclear program, outgoing Israeli prime
minister Ehud Olmert told the Israeli newspaper *Haaretz* in October
2008, "What we can do with the Palestinians, the Syrians and the
Lebanese, we cannot do with the Iranians. . . . The assumption that if
America and Russia and China and Britain and Germany do not know
how to deal with the Iranians, we, the Israelis, know—that we will take
action—is an example of the loss of proportion. Let's be more modest,
and act within the bounds of our realistic capabilities."[28]

Israel's inability to take on Iran militarily made it all the more
important for Israeli policy makers to push the U.S. to embark on a
bombing campaign. To that end, serious, concerted efforts were
undertaken by Israel in the spring of 2008, pressing the U.S. either to
attack Iran (the preferred option) or to support an Israeli attempt to
take out the Iranian nuclear facilities. On May 14, during President

George W. Bush's trip to Israel for the sixtieth anniversary of the state's founding, then–prime minister Olmert raised the issue in a one-on-one meeting. But America was already overwhelmed with problems resulting from its occupation of Iraq and Afghanistan. Even the Bush administration, which otherwise was widely viewed as favoring military action, resisted Israeli pressure to go to war with Iran. Bush also refused to give a green light for an Israeli attack at that time.[29]

Israel was deeply disappointed but did not relent. Hoping that Bush would eventually agree to order an American strike on Iran's nuclear facilities before leaving office, Israel's deputy prime minister, Iranian-born Shaul Mofaz, told the newspaper *Yedioth Ahronot* a few days after Olmert's meeting with Bush, "If Iran continues its programme to develop nuclear weapons, we will attack it. The window of opportunity has closed. The sanctions are not effective. There will be no alternative but to attack Iran in order to stop the Iranian nuclear programme." The Bush White House's wariness about Israeli pressure and the risk of Israel acting unilaterally prompted the administration to send a flurry of senior American officials to the Jewish state to implore them to show restraint. Mike McConnell, director of national intelligence, traveled to Israel in early June 2008. Admiral Michael Mullen, chairman of the Joint Chiefs of Staff, followed suit in late June. Both officials reportedly argued against an attack on the grounds that it would retard the Iranian nuclear program without destroying it; rally support for the unpopular government of President Mahmoud Ahmadinejad at a time of growing economic difficulty in Iran; undermine U.S. policy in Iraq and in Afghanistan; and produce unpredictable consequences. A week after his return from Israel, Mullen gave Israel a strong rebuke for its pressure on America. Asked about speculation concerning an Israeli strike on Iran, Mullen responded, "From the U.S. perspective . . . opening up a third front right now would be extremely stressful on us . . . that would really be very challenging." Mullen seemed to indicate that an Israeli strike would inevitably drag the U.S. into war—a war Washington neither wanted nor could afford. "This is a very unstable part of the world and I don't need it to be more unstable," he added.[30]

The military route, however, was not Israel's only option. Rather, it increasingly became the preferred option due to the belief that other tactics had failed. In April 2007, Mossad head Dagan explained to Undersecretary of State for Political Affairs Nicholas Burns that Israel's approach to Iran consists of five pillars: 1) Efforts to isolate Iran internationally; 2) Covert actions; 3) Counterproliferation actions to prevent Iranian access to know-how and technology; 4) Efforts to secure international sanctions; and 5) Promoting regime change through support for political and ethnic groups opposing the Iranian regime. Iran's minorities are "raising their heads, and are tempted to resort to violence," he said. (Iran has long accused Israel of being behind acts of violence and terror conducted by ethnic separatists in Iran.)[31]

With Israel, and, to a certain extent, the powerful Jewish-American constituency in the U.S. already viewing Obama as an unknown entity at best—or, at worst, as suspect—the Israeli appetite for advancing the American president's Iran policy was clearly limited. Though there was some concern among Israeli officials not to be viewed as a spoiler, and though some isolated, careful, and qualified statements were made in favor of diplomacy, Israel predictably became a key obstacle to Obama's engagement efforts.[32]

The hard truth was that the appetite for Obama's outreach to Iran was lukewarm at best among America's most powerful allies in Europe and the Middle East. Many wished Obama well, but few of the key actors wished him success.

Three

"He Is with Us"*

I n a building adjacent to the Iranian embassy in The Hague, high-level representatives of the Iranian government and senior American foreign policy experts—many of them associated with the Obama campaign—met over the course of two days in early spring 2008 to see if the problems between the two countries could be resolved peacefully. It was their second meeting in less than three months; two more meetings would be held before the year's end.

It was neither an official meeting nor an official negotiation. But the high-level representation from both sides signified that this was not an ordinary academic or track-two diplomacy session. The renowned Pugwash Conferences on Science and World Affairs—an international organization that brings together prominent practitioners to work toward solutions to global security threats and reducing the danger of armed conflict—organized the meetings. In 1995, Pugwash won the Nobel Peace Prize for its efforts to "diminish the part played by nuclear arms in international politics and in the longer run to eliminate such arms." Pugwash's strength lies in its ability to talk to all parties involved in a conflict, and to bring the world's top scientists and key officials to the table. In the case of the Iranian nuclear crisis, Pugwash's energetic secretary general, Professor Paolo Cotta-Ramusino, had achieved what no other peace and conflict resolution organization had managed at the time: bringing to-

---

*Direct Persian translation of the name "Obama"

gether current and former American officials with representatives of
the conservative factions ruling Iran.[1]

The American side was represented by top nuclear scientists,
lawmakers, senior Senate staff, and prominent members of the Washington foreign policy establishment, and was led by former defense
secretary William Perry, a member of the Obama campaign's national security working group. Mojtaba Samareh Hashemi, an old
friend and ally of Mahmoud Ahmadinejad, led the Iranian delegation. Samareh had served the Ahmadinejad government in several
capacities, including as senior adviser to the president, vice president, and later director of Ahmadinejad's reelection campaign. His
hard-line views have earned him the sobriquet "Ahmadinejad's Dick
Cheney." Representatives from Iran's national security adviser Saeed
Jalili and the Supreme Leader's office, as well as Ambassador Ali
Asghar Soltanieh, Iran's permanent representative to the International Atomic Energy Agency, accompanied Samareh to the meetings. Other participants included prominent foreign policy experts
from Europe and Canada. With the Iranian officials reporting back
to their national security teams, it was widely believed that Defense
Secretary Perry personally briefed then-Senator Obama on the exchanges.

The piles of emptied Persian pistachio shells grew as the two
sides tested each other's sincerity, strength, and genuineness. Iranian
diplomacy is predicated on patience and endurance, and the Americans' stamina was tested early on. In their more than hour-long
opening statement, the Iranians provided a detailed description of
the principles and sources of Iranian foreign policy under the Islamic
Republic, ranging from Islamic definitions of justice to the role of
spirituality in human nature. Once the conversation turned into
more concrete policy issues, the two sides delved into the details of
the nuclear issue, security in the Persian Gulf, and substantive ways
in which the mistrust between the U.S. and Iran could be shed.
Though some headway was made during the talks, at least in gaining
a better understanding of each other's positions, aims, interests, and

even misperceptions, the most significant value was perhaps the creation of a personal rapport between the key actors from the U.S. and Iran. The importance and utility of this grew considerably in the following months as some of the American participants moved into top positions in the Obama White House.[2]

Two days after Obama's election victory, he received a most unexpected congratulatory note. The letter was from Mahmoud Ahmadinejad, sending the Islamic Republic's first congratulatory message to an American president. While not as harsh as Ahmadinejad's previous letters to President George W. Bush, it nevertheless contained a heavy dose of criticism of America.

> The nations of the world expect an end to policies based on warmongering, invasion, bullying, trickery, the humiliation of other countries by the imposition of biased and unfair requirements, and a diplomatic approach that has bred hatred for America's leaders and undermined respect for its people. They want to see actions based on justice, respect for the rights of human beings and nations, friendship and non intervention in the affairs of others. They want the American government to keep its interventions within its own country's borders. In the sensitive Middle East region, in particular, the expectation is that the unjust actions of the past 60 years will give way to a policy encouraging full rights for all nations, especially the oppressed nations of Palestine, Iraq and Afghanistan.[3]

From the Iranian perspective, the content of the letter was less important than the fact that the letter had been sent in the first place. It was an unprecedented move, the Iranians maintained, aimed at showing Iran's interest in dialogue and its willingness to take political risks to begin engagement with America. "It showed Ahmadinejad's guts," one of Iran's nuclear negotiators told me.[4]

The letter quickly became a political issue in Iran. It had not been coordinated with or approved by Iran's Supreme Leader, which made it easier for Ahmadinejad's political rivals in the Iranian *Majles* (parliament) to attack him for it. Ahmad Tavakkoli, the head of the Majles national security committee and a sworn rival of Ahmadinejad, viewed the letter as indefensible, arguing that American officials have in the past responded poorly to unilateral Iranian efforts to reopen talks. The right-wing daily newspaper *Jumhouri Islami* said that the issue was of a magnitude that only Iran's Supreme Leader was qualified to address. Ironically, it was Ahmadinejad's bitter rivals on the reformist side that expressed support for the letter, calling it "a brave act."[5] While the letter became a hot-button issue in Iran, it made almost no waves in Washington. Discussion as to whether the president should send a formal response was unsurprisingly brief. Obama immediately poured cold water on Ahmadinejad's initiative. When asked by a reporter three days after the election whether he would reply to the letter, Obama asserted, "Iran's development of a nuclear weapon I believe is unacceptable. And we have to mount an international effort to prevent that from happening."[6]

The response and its reference to the nuclear issue did not go over well with the Ahmadinejad faction in the Iranian government. But it did not visibly change the contradicting combination of fascination, hope, skepticism, and fear that the Iranians felt about America's mysterious new president. Several Iranian officials had publicly voiced their preference for an Obama victory due to his comments and positions during the campaign. Ali Larijani, the powerful Speaker of the Majles and staunch opponent of Ahmadinejad, said that he fancied an Obama victory because "he is more rational and flexible, despite our knowledge that U.S. policy will not change much."[7] Obama's vice-presidential pick, Senator Joseph Biden, also received cautious praise in the Iranian media, citing his policy positions on Iran.[8] Moreover, the newspaper *Aftab* viewed a John McCain victory as a continuation of a neoconservative American foreign policy that would increase the risk of war.[9] Even among conservatives, although they publicly denied any difference between Obama and McCain, the general preference was for an Obama victory.[10] Tehran-based foreign journalists reported that the general public in Iran tended to hold similar sentiments. "The Democrats are a people who do not like war. If Obama wins, he will open the way to negotiations with Iran," a prominent merchant told the *Wall Street Journal*.[11] Once Obama secured the presidency, the Iranian public's enthusiasm became even more evident. *Time* reported that Iranians were "relieved" and hoped for improvement in relations. According to the BBC, Iranians were "thrilled" by the election results.[12]

The perspectives of decision makers within the Iranian government, however, were more complicated. Some of the archconservatives expressed disbelief. In their cynical view of the American political system, perhaps reflective of their own political conduct, they never thought that Obama could win, in spite of his popular support. Rather, he won because "those behind the scenes who make presidents and make policies—the puppeteers—decided, and only changed their puppet."[13] But there was also hope.[14] Iranian officials were on the record favoring diplomacy; Ayatollah Khamenei deemed dialogue with the U.S. reasonable, and Ahmadinejad said that Tehran was "ready to have positive dialogue" with Washington. There was also a sense that Obama's background might differentiate him from previous presidents.[15] Amir Mohebian, a prominent conservative figure, argued that Iran should seize the opportunity provided by Obama's election to further Iran's interests through diplomacy, but "without an unreasonable level of optimism or pessimism."[16]

Among the various cross sections of Iranian people and political elite, the reformists most readily harbored a sense of optimism, hoping that Obama could provide long-term change in America's foreign policy. With Iran's own presidential elections less than a year away, the possibility of change coming to Tehran could "bring together historical forces that could finally turn around this very troubled relationship."[17]

But some of the hope quickly transformed into fear and skepticism. While Bush was hardly a popular president on the world stage—thereby complicating America's efforts to isolate Iran—Obama could use his global superstar status to push through new economic sanctions at the UN or amass a coalition of the willing to cripple Iran's economy. "We're afraid someone like Obama would have the diplomatic influence necessary to form a strong coalition against us," a private Iranian banker said.[18] Bush's aggressive and oftentimes clumsy approach made him a convenient target to vilify and demonize, lending the Iranian government an air of reasonability and victimization. Losing this inept nemesis could prove to be costly for the Iranian government. "America was doing a lion's share of the work here, demonizing itself by its actions and . . . loud and incompetent, inept propaganda efforts in the Middle East," said Ahmad Sadri, a prominent Iran expert and professor at Lake Forest College.[19] There was also an ideological dimension. After thirty years of institutionalized enmity between the U.S. and Iran, some elements in the Iranian government believed that the animosity had become an important element of the Islamic Republic's identity. "If we solve it, we will dissolve ourselves," Mohebian said.[20]

Despite the skepticism and cynicism, Obama's posture and interest in engagement did help prompt an unprecedented debate in Iran about relations with the U.S.—an age-old, strictly enforced taboo in the Islamic Republic. Discussions and debates about the relations between the two countries that only months before were unthinkable now took place publicly, including in the media. U.S. diplomats were told by their contacts that members of Tehran's political elite who favor cooperation with the West had become noticeably emboldened. In the words of a reformist strategist, Obama had helped open up the political landscape in Iran.[21] On the other side of the spectrum, a growing number of voices in the Iranian media started questioning Obama and whether America was capable of altering its approach to Iran. Some arguments, such as accusations of Obama putting "on a mask of friendship, but with the objective of betrayal," appeared based on nothing but fear and paranoia, while others pointed to structural factors inhibiting Obama's maneuverability. Pressure from pro-Israel groups in the U.S., which, in Tehran's view, are inherently hostile to Iran, would limit how far Obama could move when it came to Iran, they argued. Even if Obama's intentions were pure, the gigantic foreign policy machinery in the United States would overwhelm and devour him, these skeptics said.[22]

Early decisions by the Obama administration made the Iranian skeptics feel vindicated, particularly with some of the foreign policy personalities Obama decided to bring with him to the White House. His choice for secretary of state, Senator Hillary Clinton, who during the campaign had threatened to "obliterate Iran" if it ever attacked Israel, strengthened the conviction of pessimists and raised doubts among those holding a more optimistic view.[23] Clinton, in turn, appointed Dennis Ross of the Washington Institute for Near East Policy to serve as her envoy to the Middle East. The hard-line *Kayhan* newspaper viewed Ross's pick as an "insult" due to his role as a "pioneer of the American-Zionist lobby." Other, more moderate, elements in the Iranian foreign policy establishment shared the view that the appointment would undermine Iran's confidence in the Obama administration. "It shows that the Americans appointed Dennis Ross by the eyes of the Israelis. It means flying to Tehran by the connecting flight via Tel Aviv," said Sadegh Kharrazi, the co-author of Iran's 2003 negotiation proposal.[24]

These appointments, as well as that of Rahm Emanuel—who had volunteered to serve in the Israeli army during the first Persian Gulf war—along with the mixture of hawkish Clinton-era officials and nonproliferation hard-liners populating the Obama White House, caused Iranian officials to call on Islamic states not to raise their expectations for Obama, and rather "heed the reality of his administration."[25] The Iranian government had also taken notice that the Obama administration publicly argued that diplomacy was needed in order to increase Iran's isolation. If Iran did not respond favorably to diplomacy, Washington would be in a better position to put international pressure on Iran, the argument read. Obama said that he will be "tightening the screws diplomatically on Iran," and getting sanctions in place as soon as possible. "We've got to do that before Israel feels like its back is to the wall."[26]

As the debate in Tehran proceeded, the hard-line view eventually prevailed; Obama's intentions and capabilities were unclear, and as a result Iran could not take a risk by making conciliatory moves toward the Obama administration. Change had to be fundamental and not cosmetic, they argued. Mere words and slogans would not do; concrete evidence of a new policy toward Iran was needed. "The U.S. must prove that their policies have changed and are now based upon respecting the rights of the Iranian nation and mutual respect," said Mojtaba Samareh Hashemi, one of Ahmadinejad's closest advisers. If America's policies toward Iran change, "the distance between Iran and the U.S. will become less. If these promises are acted upon, there will be more chance for closeness between the two nations," he continued.[27] The Iranian line was to signal skepticism, while keeping the door open for a positive surprise. At the same time that the Iranians were cautiously entertaining the possibility of change in U.S. foreign policy, they were increasingly preparing for it not to happen. The unified position among key Iranian officials was instructive.[28] A few days after Obama's inaugural address, Ahmadinejad told reporters that he was waiting patiently to see the Obama administration's next move. "We will listen to the statements closely, we will carefully study their actions, and, if there are real changes, we will welcome it," he said.[29] That same day, at the World Economic Forum in Davos, Switzerland, then–foreign minister Manouchehr Mottaki said that Tehran would take a "cooperative approach" with Washington as long as it saw changes that go beyond words. "We do believe that if the new administration of the United States, as Mr. Obama says, is going to change its policies not in saying but practice, they will find in the region a cooperative approach and reaction," Mottaki said.[30]

Majles Speaker Larijani presented perhaps the most candid assessment. The U.S.-Iran conflict was "serious and not for fun," and could not be resolved through mere "gestures." Denouncing Obama's "carrots and sticks" policy as "savagery" and "cowboy" foreign policy—Iran's national interest could not be compromised through bribes or threats—Larijani went to the heart of the matter: the conflict between the U.S. and Iran is of a strategic nature and can be resolved only through a change in strategy, not tactics. "If the Americans think they can approach Iran instrumentally through tactical change, they are wrong." A "strategic conversation," he pointed out, "is a different matter."[31]

The underlying reason for Iran's insistence on a strategic conversation was its fear that Washington would seek Iranian collaboration to stabilize its predicaments in Iraq and Afghanistan, only to return to the enmity characterizing U.S.-Iran relations, including efforts to topple the Iranian government, once Iran's assistance was no longer needed. In other words, Washington would engage with Iran *tactically* to achieve its own strategic aims, the Iranians feared. At the time, the reformists in Iran sought *strategic* engagement aimed at fundamentally changing the nature of U.S.-Iran relations.

The Iranians' fear was not necessarily rooted in paranoia and suspicion; it also had a basis in Iran's experience dealing with the Bush administration. After 9/11, Washington initiated talks with Iran about Afghanistan, led by James Dobbins, the president's special envoy to Afghanistan. Contrary to the commonly held perception, the U.S. did not assemble a coalition against the Taliban; Washington joined an existing coalition led by Iran. Meeting in Geneva in the fall of 2001, the U.S.-Iranian discussions focused on how to effectively unseat the Taliban and establish an Afghan government. Iran's material help was not negligible. The Iranians offered air bases to the U.S.; they offered to perform search-and-rescue missions for downed American pilots; they served as a bridge between the Northern Alliance and the U.S. in the campaign against the Taliban; and they even used information provided by American forces to find and kill fleeing al-Qaeda leaders.[32] Nowhere was this common interest clearer than at the Bonn Conference of December 2001, where a number of promi-

nent Afghans and representatives from various countries met under
UN auspices to develop a plan for governing Afghanistan. The United
States and Iran carefully laid the groundwork for the conference
weeks in advance. Iran's political clout with warring Afghan groups
proved crucial. Washington and Tehran were on the same side, but it
was Iran's influence over the Afghans—not American threats and
promises—that moved the negotiations forward.

On the last night of the conference, an interim constitution had
been agreed upon and all other issues had been resolved except the
toughest: who was to govern Afghanistan? The Northern Alliance
insisted that, as the winner of the war, the spoils should be theirs.
Though they represented about 40 percent of the country, they
wanted to occupy eighteen of the twenty-four ministries. At around
two o'clock in the morning, Dobbins brought together the Afghan
parties, the Iranians, the Russians, the Indians, the Germans, and
Lakhdar Brahimi of the UN to resolve this final point. For two hours,
the various delegations took turns trying to convince the representative of the Northern Alliance to accept a lower number of ministries, to
no avail. Finally, the Iranian representative took him aside and began
whispering to him in Persian. A few minutes later, they returned to the
table and the Afghan conceded. "Okay, I give up," he said. "The
other factions can have two more ministries." The next morning, the
historic Bonn agreement was signed. America had not only won the
war, but, with the help of Iran, it had also won the peace.[33]

For the Iranians, this was a moment of triumph. Not only had a
major enemy—the Taliban—been defeated, but Iran had also undeni-
ably demonstrated that it could help stabilize the region and that
America could benefit from a better relationship with Tehran. And
yet, only a few weeks later, on January 29, 2002, in his first State of the
Union address, Bush lumped Iran together with Iraq and North
Korea as dangerous and threatening states that formed an "Axis of
Evil." Tehran was shocked. Then-president Mohammad Khatami's
policy of détente and Iran's assistance in Afghanistan had been for
naught. Having seen his domestic agenda fall apart, Khatami's inter-

national standing was now also undercut. He had stuck out his neck and argued against hard-liners in Tehran, whose skepticism about America's trustworthiness appeared to have been justified.[34] "'Axis of Evil' was a fiasco for the Khatami government," said Farideh Farhi, an Iran expert at the University of Hawaii. "It was used by hard-liners, who said: 'If you give in, if you help from a position of weakness, then you get negative results.' "[35] Hard-liners argued that Iran should not have offered the U.S. any help without exacting a price beforehand. Some Iranian diplomats involved in the Afghan talks were later forced to pay for the calamity with their careers, making others think twice before extending a hand of friendship to the U.S.

What the Iranians did not know was that prior to their engagement in Afghanistan with the U.S., Deputy National Security Advisor Stephen Hadley had adopted rules to regulate how Washington should interact with rogue states such as Iran in a meeting of the "deputies committee." The regulations were informally called the "Hadley Rules," and they determined that tactical collaboration with rogue states such as Iran was permissible within the context of the so-called War on Terror, but that this tactical collaboration could never be permitted to translate into a change in the strategic nature of America's relations with these states. In other words, regardless of how fruitful U.S.-Iran collaboration in Afghanistan would be, it simply would not change the definition of Iran as a mortal enemy of the United States. Iran's aim of improving its relations with Washington by demonstrating its utility in Afghanistan was doomed from the outset. Providing assistance to the U.S. would not help Iran achieve its strategic objectives a relationship with America that, at a minimum, eliminates the risk of military confrontation and recognizes Iran's legitimate security interests and regional aspirations.[36]

The experience in Afghanistan negated what little trust existed between Washington and Tehran, and rendered any future cooperation more difficult. Any serious engagement with Washington absent a clarification of its strategic aim became increasingly unlikely, as the Iranians feared that Washington would seek tactical cooperation with the strategic aim of overthrowing the Iranian government the instant Tehran's help was no longer needed. Iran's experience with the Bush administration tainted its perception of the Obama administration's outreach and diminished Tehran's willingness to give Obama the benefit of the doubt. "Our viewpoint is, the U.S. strategy to Iran has not changed, but the tactics have changed," conservative politician Hamidreza Taraghi said. "When the U.S. says to open your fist, our fist has always been in defense. It's the U.S. that has always had its fist clenched."[37]

The mistrust among the conservatives was so grave that they risked missing the opportunity that lay before them. Information that vindicated the mistrust—such as Iranian intelligence reports claiming American support for the anti-Iranian terrorist organization Jundollah, a group tied to al-Qaeda—was magnified, while indications that Obama sought a strategic shift with Iran—such as the inclusion of PJAK, a militant Kurdish organization, on the U.S. State Department's terrorist list due to its violent activity against Iran—was met with disbelief or ignored.[38] This solidified the belief that the conservatives' mistrust was not baseless, reformist politician Ataollah Mohajerani said, and they "concluded that they didn't have the confidence needed to proceed."[39]

Similar mistrust on the American side had caused the U.S. to miss opportunities with Iran, prominent Iran expert Ali Ansari of St. Andrews University in Scotland pointed out. In 1997, the victory of reformist, antiestablishment candidate Mohammad Khatami in the Iranian presidential elections took the world by surprise. The world was unprepared for Khatami and his ideas of détente, and consequently failed to seize the opportunity he represented. America's perception of Khatami in 1997 was a carbon copy of Tehran's later perception of Obama: at the end of the day, the structures of the Islamic Republic of Iran were believed to be incapable of permitting any meaningful change. "The Iranians never really knew what to do," Ansari said. "They weren't prepared for Obama."[40]

Four

The Review

The hybrid option is designed to concentrate the minds of Iranian leaders on what they stand to lose without humiliating them.

—Middle East envoy Dennis Ross, explaining the logic of the dual-track approach, September 2008

For almost a decade, Mohamed ElBaradei, director general of the International Atomic Energy Agency (IAEA), was at the center of the discord over Iran's nuclear program. Yet the former Egyptian diplomat readily recognized that the nuclear issue was not the root problem; rather, it was a symptom of the ongoing dispute between the United States and Iran. As the temperature between Washington and Tehran reached a boiling point under the Bush administration, ElBaradei went beyond just addressing nuclear technicalities and began acting as an indirect mediator between the two capitals. And rather than just seeking to stop an Iranian bomb, he did not shy away from declaring that he also sought to stop Iran from being bombed. In the view of top IAEA officials the two were linked, because a likely consequence of an attack on Iran would be a nuclear-armed Iran. It was a role that won ElBaradei few friends in the Bush White House. But it did win him the Nobel Peace Prize in 2005.[1]

Neither Tehran nor Washington was without blame, in ElBaradei's view. Yet he took particular exception to the Bush administration's approach to Iran, which he argued had exacerbated an already unstable situation. "Anytime you try to isolate a country, the situation gets much, much worse," he said in an interview with CNN, declaring that he had had "zero confidence" in the efforts to isolate Tehran.[2] ElBaradei ascribed this failure to "a combination of ignorance and arrogance," as well as to the unrealistic objectives of hard-liners around Vice President Dick Cheney—or "Darth Vader," as ElBaradei called him. The end result of the isolation policy was that instead of limiting the Iranian program to a few dozen centrifuges, Iran managed to amass thousands of centrifuges, stockpile several hundred kilos of low-enriched uranium, and master knowledge of the nuclear fuel cycle.[3]

These points were not lost on Obama when he took office in January 2009. Clearly, a new approach was needed that centered on diplomacy. But neither the end nor the strategy had been determined. The first measure of the Obama administration was to initiate a comprehensive review of the Iran policy to identify how best to implement the president's promise for diplomacy. Middle East Envoy Dennis Ross and Puneet Talwar, senior director for Iraq, Iran, and the Gulf States at the National Security Council, led the review. Talwar came to the White House from the Senate, where he had been a longtime adviser on the staff of the Senate Foreign Relations Committee and a staunch proponent of engagement. A tightly held and top-heavy process, the review looked at all aspects of America's Iran policy and involved numerous entities within the government, as well as a few outside experts.[4] It also gave the White House an opportunity to demonstrate to its allies that the Obama administration would listen to its friends and take their concerns into consideration, in contrast to the modus operandi of the Bush administration. "We will be consulting with regional leaders and listening. . . . Be confident that you will be privy to our strategy and be consulted," Secretary of State Hillary Clinton reportedly told United Arab Emirates foreign minister Sheikh Abdullah bin Zayed al-Nahayan.[5] Several sessions were held with EU officials, including the EU diplomats who had led Europe's nuclear negotiations with Iran since 2003. American and European officials closely studied past negotiations to identify successful strategies with Iran. "There was a sense of actually listening to the European allies when it came to Iran," a senior EU official told me.[6]

The Obama administration exhibited humility, receptivity, and a visible willingness to learn and to fine-tune its approach, according to foreign and American officials involved in the process. For instance, when it came to their attention that the term "carrots and sticks" translated badly into Persian—both linguistically and culturally—and angered the Iranians rather than make them more open to Obama's extended hand, the phrase was quickly eradicated from the administration's vocabulary.[7] This openness was also appreciated by elements in the bureaucracy who viewed the emphasis on diplomacy with some skepticism. Though most State Department officials were "thrilled" by the Obama administration's new approach, members of the nonproliferation community within the U.S. government felt "some discomfort." There was a concern that the Obama administration would rush to the judgment that all Bush era policies were flawed and reverse them by default. Furthermore, some feared that the desire for a quick deal with Iran was so strong that many interests, including important nonproliferation principles, would be sacrificed in the process. In particular, some hard-line nonproliferation hands in the bureaucracy opposed the idea of dropping the zero-enrichment objective. "There was a fear that the new crowd would seek too quick a deal and make too many compromises," a senior State Department nonproliferation hand told me. But as Obama began assembling his new team, some of these concerns were alleviated. Putting Clinton, Ross, and Gary Samore, a veteran arms control negotiator in the Clinton administration, in charge significantly increased the comfort level of the nonproliferation hawks in the bureaucracy. "These were no softies on Iran," the State Department official continued. Moreover, the very review itself indicated that the Obama team did not have a prepared plan, and no strategy, idea, or tactic was shelved simply because it had Bush's fingerprints on it.[8]

Prior to joining the Obama administration, Ross had recommended secret back channels to the leadership in Tehran to avoid empowering Ahmadinejad or publicly undercutting the ongoing nuclear negotiations. "Keeping it completely private would protect each side from premature exposure and would not require either side to publicly explain such a move before it was ready. It would strike the Iranians as more significant and dramatic than either working through the Europeans or non-officials," Ross wrote for the Center for a New American Security in September 2008. Ross favored a hybrid option that combined tightening the noose of sanctions, including incentives to Russia and China to support the sanctions, while engaging Iran without preconditions. "The hybrid option is designed to concentrate the minds of Iranian leaders on what they stand to lose without humiliating them," Ross wrote. Samore, on the other hand, argued for a more open and comprehensive approach—direct bilateral talks addressing the nuclear program, U.S.-Iranian relations, Iraq, as well as regional security. And talks could begin without Iran suspending its enrichment activities, Samore argued in a paper published by the Brookings Institution. John Brennan, Obama's White House director for counterterrorism, went a step further and called for a presidential envoy to handle negotiations with Iran while publicly recognizing that Iran had significantly scaled back its use of terrorism in the past decade.[9]

The review of U.S. policy toward Iran addressed many different options and strategies. On the diplomacy side, the administration considered a series of measures and the order in which to offer them, including but not limited to: easing sanctions on investment in Iran's decrepit oil infrastructure; establishing a low-level diplomatic presence in Iran; recognizing and aiding a limited civilian nuclear capability for Iran under strict IAEA inspections; opening up a direct channel of communication with Iran's Supreme Leader; and lifting the prohibition on direct contacts between American diplomats and their Iranian counterparts. Simultaneously, much in line with Ross's hybrid recommendation, the administration explored strategies to escalate pressure by significantly strengthening sanctions against Iran. Considerations included sanctions on Iran's purchase of gasoline; sanctions targeting Iran's banking sector; and more extreme measures such as cutting off credit guarantees to European companies that do business with Iran.[10] These sanctions would not be effective unless there was significant international support behind them, the administration believed. Iran had been astute at exploiting divisions within the international community and finding loopholes in the sanctions. Any new sanctions strategy would have to remedy this, it was argued.

The Europeans, whose sanctions would have greater impact by virtue of their extensive trade ties with Iran, would likely not get onboard unless a new UN Security Council resolution was adopted. Such a resolution, however, would in turn require support or, at a minimum, no opposition from Russia and China. Analysts both inside and outside the administration argued that Russian collaboration was essential to any effort to pressure Iran. Rather than giving concessions to Tehran, concessions should be given to Moscow in return for its collaboration in pressuring Iran, the argument read. Such concessions could include cancelling the plan to set up the missile defense system in Eastern Europe and showing greater consideration for Russian concerns regarding potential NATO ascension countries that Moscow views as part of its sphere of influence.[11] At the same time, pressure on Russia was needed to thwart its planned sale of the S-300 long-range air-defense system to Iran. The sale would significantly enhance Iran's air defense capability and make the country more resistant to threats of American or Israeli air strikes against its nuclear sites. In February 2009, only weeks after the review had begun, the Obama administration requested support from several Arab states to press Russia to stop the sale. Saudi Arabia even offered to buy the system from Russia in return for a promise that Moscow would not sell it to Iran.[12]

Securing Chinese support was in some ways a less complicated effort, in spite of the stiff resistance Beijing likely would exert. Two factors dominated China's interests with regard to Iran. First, China did not want sanctions that could impair Chinese economic growth and its priority of moving millions of Chinese out of poverty. China receives approximately 13 percent of its oil from Iran, and any disruption in that trade would have considerable economic and political repercussions for the leadership in Beijing. Second, China is very reluctant to be the odd man out in the Security Council. Beijing's opposition to sanctions was relatively cost-free as long as it could hide behind even stiffer Russian opposition. But if Russia could be brought onboard the American effort to punish Iran, it was believed that China would likely follow suit. Ross had devised a strategy to secure Chinese support prior to entering the Obama administration. In his and David Makovsky's book *Myths, Illusions & Peace: Finding a New Direction for America in the Middle East,* published in 2009 but authored before Ross joined the Obama team, the two wrote that China is more reliant on Saudi Arabia than on Iran. Securing Beijing's support for sanctions could be achieved if the Saudis offered to guarantee replacing Iranian oil sales to China—and threatened to cut their own sales to China if Beijing did not collaborate. "Business is business, and the Chinese have a higher stake in Saudi Arabia than in Iran. Again, the Saudis need not broadcast what they are doing—but they do need to be enlisted to quietly pressure the Chinese to change their approach to Iran lest they lose out on a profitable future with Saudi Arabia," Ross and Makovsky wrote.[13] Later in 2009, Obama sent Ross to Saudi Arabia to seek a guarantee that it would help supply China's needs in the event of an Iranian cutoff. "We'll look for ways to make sure that if there are sanctions, [the Chinese] won't be negatively affected," a senior official told the *New York Times.*[14]

The administration was aware that time, in many ways, was not on its side. The Iranians were amassing more low-enriched uranium; the political space for any elaborate diplomacy would likely shrink once Obama's honeymoon with the U.S. Congress came to an end; and nervousness among U.S. allies, particularly Israel, was growing. At the same time, the White House was also aware that Obama's greatest strength—his novelty and lack of baggage with Iran—would quickly evaporate if the first attempt at diplomacy failed. Obama, it was said, could be a virgin only once. So while America needed to act fast, its first move also needed to be well thought through. In this regard, the upcoming June presidential elections in Iran complicated the administration's calculations. As the Iranians entered their political season, their ability to engage with the United States was compromised. The question was whether to initiate the engagement prior to the elections, or wait for the next Iranian administration to get situated before serious diplomacy began. Initially, the debate within the administration tilted in favor of starting talks before the elections. Ahmadinejad was likely going to win anyway, the argument read, so the concern that engagement could help boost his reelection bid was moot. Moreover, if America engaged with the conservatives and they ended up losing to the reformists in the elections, the conservative camp would have a more difficult time opposing and sabotaging any ensuing reformist-led engagement with the U.S. It would be a way for Washington to show its interest in engaging with the Iranian government as a whole and not with any particular faction within it. After all, time was running out and engaging Iran was important not just to resolve the nuclear issue, but also to help stabilize Iraq and Afghanistan and address regional and global energy security. The administration also considered reaching out directly to the Supreme Leader rather than to Ahmadinejad, which would circumvent the entire issue. Eventually, however, the administration decided to avoid any interaction that could inadvertently end up benefiting Ahmadinejad.[15]

Israeli Opposition

Though the policy review ostensibly addressed America's interests vis-à-vis Iran, a significant portion of the discussions dealt with alliance management—the arduous task of ensuring that America's allies, particularly those nervous about the implications of improved U.S.-Iran relations, would go along with the policy and not sabotage it. This was particularly true in the case of Israel, which possessed both the ability and the history of creating complications for U.S.-Iran diplomacy. Though the U.S. and Israel agreed on the strategic objective of preventing an Iranian bomb, their similarity tended to end there. On tactical matters, Israel's and the Obama administration's perspectives were steadily diverging.

Even on intelligence matters, despite often reviewing the same information, Washington and Tel Aviv's conclusions differed vastly. When the United Nations reported that the Iranians had amassed enough low-enriched uranium to build one nuclear bomb, American and Israeli differences on how to interpret and react to this development were worlds apart. The Israeli press reported that Amos Yadlin, the chief of Israeli military intelligence, had told Prime Minister Netanyahu's cabinet that the crossing of this technological threshold meant that Iran could reach military nuclear capability through a mere adaptation of its nuclear strategy. It would no longer be a question of ability, but of preference. Iran was now no more than one step away from being a nuclear-capable state, Israel maintained. In Washington, however, the perspective was a bit more sober. Admiral Dennis Blair, the new director of national intelligence, told Congress that the Israelis "take more of a worst-case approach to these things."[16] A month earlier he had, in an annual threat assessment delivered to Congress, cast doubt on the assumption that Iran was dead-set on acquiring a nuclear weapon. "Although we do not know whether Iran currently intends to develop nuclear weapons, we assess Tehran at a minimum is keeping open the option to develop them," he said. Though Blair's assessment echoed that of the IAEA—ElBaradei had repeatedly stated that he did not "believe the Iranians have made a decision to go for a nuclear weapon, but they are absolutely determined to have the technology because they believe it brings you power, prestige, and an insurance policy"—it was not appreciated in Israel.[17]

Israel made no secret that it was uncomfortable with Washington's outreach to Tehran, expressing "constant skepticism" to U.S. decision makers. One of Netanyahu's common talking points read that "Persia" was closing in on Israel through its tentacles—Hamas and Hezbollah—and that it could be stopped only through massive economic sanctions, including a naval blockade, and the insistence that America's military option remain viable. Israel did not, he said, oppose diplomacy per se, provided that it was not pursued for more than two months and with fixed results; that is, zero-enrichment as the outcome. Otherwise, Iran would "take you to the cleaners," he told a delegation of U.S. lawmakers in February 2009. Israel's four demands on U.S.-Iran diplomacy were broad and debilitating: tight deadlines, a set outcome for the talks, more sanctions, and persistent reference to the military option. Without a clear time frame and set benchmarks, Washington would fail to stop Iran, according to Strategic Affairs minister Moshe Ya'alon. "I have no doubt that the Iranians will use any dialogue to stall for time if there will not be a clear time frame and clear benchmarks like telling them that they have two months to stop the enrichment," Ya'alon said. "What the West needs to do is stand up against this wave and confront it." Israel believed that Iran had suspended its enrichment program in 2003 and offered to negotiate with the U.S. once it perceived of a credible American military threat. Iran needed to be confronted, the Israelis asserted, because without re-creating that viable threat from 2003 Tehran could not be stopped. Even if diplomacy was pursued, it should be under the "stick of military pressure," according to Israel.[18]

Israel's insistence on the military option at this early stage of the president's outreach campaign undermined the Obama administration's prospects for diplomacy in several different ways. During this initial phase, Washington and Tehran were still testing each other's intentions to determine the other side's sincerity. The long-standing atmosphere of mistrust granted neither side any margin for error. From Tehran's perspective, uncertainty about Washington's intentions during the Bush administration was fueled partly by the insistence of the military option remaining on the table. Iran was wary of negotiations potentially designed to fail, as failed talks could strengthen the case for military action against Iran. Now the Bush administration's tough talk was being replaced by Israeli rhetoric. Iran's inability to appreciate the policy differences between Washington and Tel Aviv resulted in Tehran's shrinking confidence in Washington's intentions whenever Israel explicitly or implicitly threatened military action. Moreover, Iran's threat perception vis-à-vis the U.S. (and, by extension, Israel) is believed to be one of the driving forces of Iran's nuclear program. Whether Iran seeks a weapon or a civilian program that provides a weapons *capability,* the program's existence provides Tehran with a level of deterrence against the perceived U.S. threat. The Obama administration sought to reduce Iran's sense of threat in order to kick-start negotiations. The threat of Israeli military action risked doing the opposite; it would likely fuel Iranian insecurity and shut the window for diplomacy.[19]

The threat of Israeli military action also helped create arbitrary deadlines for negotiations with Tehran, which were combined with exaggerated expectations of what diplomacy must achieve. According to Netanyahu, results that sanctions and confrontation had failed to achieve with Iran over the past thirty years must miraculously now be obtained after only a few weeks of negotiations. Otherwise Israel said it would have no choice but to take military action. This logic arguably served two purposes. First, it sought to bring the U.S. back to the foreign policy approach of the Bush administration, in which diplomacy was treated with suspicion and skepticism, and military confrontation was viewed as a policy option with guaranteed success. Second, it ensured that diplomacy would fail by denying it the time and space it would need to succeed and by setting the bar too high. In short, threats of military action militarized the atmosphere and created an environment that rendered diplomacy less likely to succeed or, worse, prevented it from being pursued in the first place. The Netanyahu government's actions, whether aimed at undermining Washington's outreach or simply born out of Israeli fears and nervousness, deeply frustrated the Obama administration. Israel was "unnecessarily tying the hands of the United States," while failing to recognize how Obama's strategy could greatly benefit Israeli security. As a sign of Washington's growing irritation with the Netanyahu government, Vice President Joseph Biden publicly cast doubt on Israel's readiness to take military action, and he also deemed such a measure "ill-advised."[20]

But the Obama administration did not stop there. By April 2009 U.S. officials began explicitly linking Israel's and America's differences on Iran with the other major point of contention between the Obama and Netanyahu governments: the Israeli-Palestinian conflict. "For Israel to get the kind of strong support it is looking for vis-à-vis Iran, it can't stay on the sidelines with respect to the Palestinians and the peace efforts. They go hand in hand," Clinton said in House testimony given on April 23, 2009.[21] The linkage to the Israeli-Palestinian issue deeply worried the Netanyahu government because it brought forward an idea that Israel had long sought to discredit: that the Israeli-Palestinian conflict is the main source of conflict in the Middle East. Acceptance of this premise would make the Israeli-Palestinian conflict rather than Iran the top priority for Washington and would lead to extensive pressure on Israel to make concessions to the Arabs, Israel feared. Dismissing this causality as "superficial," Ya'alon argued that most major problems in the region had nothing to do with Israel and its conflict with the Palestinians. "The Islamic Revolution [in Iran in 1979] did not erupt because of us. Al-Qaida was not created because of us and even Hizbullah did not rise up because of us," he said.[22]

Instead, Israel favored a different linkage between the two issues. Recognizing the weight the Obama administration put on mending fences with the Muslim world, and the centrality of the Israeli-Palestinian issue to that relationship, the Netanyahu government declared that it would not move on peace talks with the Palestinians until it first saw progress in America's efforts to stop Iran's nuclear program and limit Tehran's rising influence in the region. "It's a crucial condition if we want to move forward," said Deputy Foreign

Minister Daniel Ayalon. "If we want to have a real political process with the Palestinians, then you can't have the Iranians undermining and sabotaging."[23]

For the Obama administration, devising a new Iran policy and conducting a comprehensive review was very much about balancing America's relationship with Israel with its aspirations for a new relationship with Iran. The diplomacy gamble could lead to a fresh start for U.S.-Iran relations, but it could also lead to a crisis with Israel, or both. "I could draw you a scenario in which this new combination of players leads to the first real talks with Iran in three decades," a senior Obama official told the *New York Times.* "And I could draw you one in which the first big foreign crisis of the Obama presidency is a really nasty confrontation, either because the Israelis strike or because we won't let them." Whatever limitations existed for compromise between the U.S. and Iran, finding an acceptable compromise between Israel and Iran was even more complex. It was difficult to imagine the Iranians willing to give up enrichment entirely. And it was equally inconceivable that the Israelis would accept anything short of that. For the Obama administration, this was a dilemma with no solution. The result of the policy review was a strategy that, until the end, sought to avoid addressing this central issue.[24]

Obama Adopts Ross's Hybrid Option

By April, the review ended and a final strategy was presented. A paper listing Dennis Ross and Puneet Talwar as the primary authors was circulated within the relevant government departments, and the administration's focus turned from strategizing to implementation. The review produced a policy eerily similar to the hybrid approach presented by Ross months earlier: a strategy of simultaneously offering Tehran engagement without preconditions while ratcheting up sanctions in case Iran did not yield to American demands. The State Department called it the dual-track strategy—the idea that the diplomacy and sanctions tracks went hand in hand, and could be effective only when pursued jointly. The long-standing American precondition that Iran suspend enrichment before any negotiations could begin was dropped. This would allow Iran to continue enriching uranium as the talks progressed, before a final status arrangement would be addressed. During this period, focus would shift to inspections and verification of Iran's nuclear sites. "We have all agreed that [the suspension precondition] is simply not going to work—experience tells us the Iranians are not going to buy it," said a senior European official. "So we are going to start with some interim steps, to build a little trust." But the suspension requirement was not eliminated; it just ceased to be a precondition. At some point, Iran would be required to suspend its enrichment activities, according to the strategy.[25]

The review also concluded that Washington's language and tone should change dramatically. Detoxifying the atmosphere was a necessary step to establishing an environment conducive to diplomacy. Otherwise, Tehran would not appreciate Washington's intent to resolve the conflict constructively through diplomacy, the administration believed. This decision would hold even if the Iranians continued their demonization of the U.S. This was a win-win for the U.S. If the Iranians reciprocated and toned down their rhetoric, chances of resolving the conflict would increase. If the Iranians refused to cool their rhetoric, Washington would score points in the international community and further push Iran into isolation.

On the specifics of the diplomatic strategy, the review stipulated that diplomacy with Iran would be centered on the nuclear issue. This was a point of contention within the administration, particularly among those working on the Afghanistan file. Many administration officials recognized that significant common interests existed between the U.S. and Iran in Afghanistan, and that diplomacy might get off to a better start if these common interests were addressed early on. Both Admiral Mike Mullen, chairman of the Joint Chiefs of Staff, and NATO secretary general Jaap de Hoop Scheffer publicly stressed the importance of Iranian involvement in resolving the conflict in Afghanistan, and they said that the United States and the Islamic Republic shared mutual interests that could offer possibilities for cooperation. "We need a discussion that brings in all the relevant players: Afghanistan, Pakistan, India, China, Russia—and yes, Iran," said de Hoop Scheffer. This assessment was widely supported by independent experts and by the Afghan government, which feared that Afghanistan would suffer from increased U.S.-Iran tensions. "If the relationship between the U.S. and Tehran stabilizes, things will be much better for us in Afghanistan," said Davood Moradian, senior policy adviser at the Afghan foreign ministry. The Iranians had also indicated some willingness to collaborate in Afghanistan, knowing very well that they held many cards in that arena and that Washington was in need of Tehran's help. "We have a lot to contribute on the issue of Iraq and Afghanistan and if the U.S. shows a genuine desire to talk to us, we will certainly negotiate," Iran's deputy foreign minister told the *Wall Street Journal.* But engaging on Afghanistan, where Iran's help was needed, could put Washington in a position of owing the Iranians. The administration feared that creating such linkages between regional issues and the nuclear issue would only increase the likelihood of the Iranians extracting nuclear concessions from the U.S.[26]

Yet it was Afghanistan that provided the first direct diplomatic contact between the U.S. and Iran under the Obama administration. Clinton invited diplomats from Tehran to attend an international conference on Afghanistan on March 31, 2009, in The Hague, Netherlands. Ambassador Richard Holbrooke, the president's special envoy to Afghanistan and a proponent of enlisting Iranian support to stabilize that country, held a brief but cordial meeting with Ambassador Mohammad Mehdi Akhoondzade in what was the first official face-to-face interplay between the Obama administration and the Iranian government. Besides exchanging pleasantries, Holbrooke delivered a carefully written letter to the Iranians, aimed at testing Tehran's willingness to take larger steps. Though no discussions on substance were held, the Obama administration was encouraged by Tehran's decision to partake in the conference and by the cordial tone in their limited discussions. "We will look for ways to cooperate with them and I think the fact that they came today, that they intervened today, is a promising sign that there will be future cooperation," Clinton said.[27]

Concurrent with this outreach, the review stipulated that the pressure track should be prepared and that Tehran should have no doubt that sanctions would follow if diplomacy failed. The Iranians needed to know that Washington was ready to activate the second track and to impose "crippling sanctions," aimed at fundamentally changing Iran's nuclear cost-benefit analysis. The review also gave in to some of the demands of those who opposed dialogue. In a move partly meant to reassure the Israelis and some of America's Arab allies, a target of early October was set for diplomacy to bear fruit.[28] Moreover, Obama kept a key political appointee of the Bush administration who had led its sanctions track since 2006. The undersecretary for terrorism and financial intelligence at the Treasury Department, Stuart Levey, constructed American efforts to put the squeeze on Iran by cutting it off from international banks. The idea was to pressure the private sector, starting with the world's banks, to join the effort to sanction Iran regardless of the sanctions legislation in their respective countries. Banks were only as reputable as their clients' practices, and the reputations of banks that did business with Iran were at risk as long as Iran pursued nuclear technology, the argument read. Unlike previous U.S. sanctions on Iran, Levey's efforts turned out to be surprisingly effective in quickly harming Iran's ailing economy—though the pressure failed to change Iran's nuclear policies. Levey succeeded in getting major banks in Britain, France, Germany, Italy, and Japan to curb business with their long-standing Iranian clients. "They're not happy with what's happening," a European diplomat told American journalist Robin Wright. "They complain about U.S. pressure, but accept it. They hope it will pass soon." Levey was kept at the Treasury Department to ensure that the sanctions efforts did not relent, and to send a signal to Tehran that it had much to lose if diplomacy failed. The decision was not popular in all quarters of the U.S. government. Some U.S. officials feared that the Iranians would get the wrong message; rather than interpreting Levey's reappointment as a warning of what would ensue if talks failed, Iranians might instead conclude that the Obama administration was not serious about diplomacy in the first place.[29]

A Journey with No Destination?

The most important part of the review, however, was not what it stipulated but rather what it kept ambiguous, unstated, or undecided. Israel demanded clarity on the issue of enrichment and insisted that the Bush administration's zero-enrichment objective be kept in place. "The Israelis were concerned every time there was a hint that that might have changed," a State Department nonproliferation hand pointed out to me. While Israel pushed the Obama administration to demand a complete cessation of Iran's enrichment activities, Washington increasingly viewed that objective as unachievable. "There were enough people that came into the Obama administration who understood that zero-enrichment was just not possible," a mid-level State Department official told me. Even some former Bush administration officials joined the chorus of voices calling for a negotiations-based solution predicated on limited enrichment, since "having a stockpile of enriched uranium is not the same as having a bomb." Richard Haass, who served in the Bush administration and who currently heads the Council on Foreign Relations, expressed doubt that Iran would simply give up enrichment and suggested that Washington accept Iran's right to enrich. "I believe then the negotiations would need to focus on whether Iran is allowed to have some enrichment capability. Or put another way, how the right to enrichment is defined —what is the scale, what is the degree of transparency, what is the degree of IAEA access," Haass said.[30] Though European diplomats note that Obama administration officials did not go into detail with them on whether enrichment would be off-limits, the general impression was that the Obama administration was preparing for an outcome with limited enrichment on Iranian soil. In a move aimed at nudging the Obama administration to explicitly embrace a non-zero solution, the head of the Senate Foreign Relations Committee, John Kerry (D-MA), told the *Financial Times* that "the Bush administration's [argument of] no enrichment was ridiculous." The Massachusetts senator deemed the policy "bombastic" and "wasted energy." "They have a right to peaceful nuclear power and to enrichment in that purpose," he said. Kerry sought to create political space for the administration to become bolder in its outreach to Iran and to pave the way for a compromise solution down the road. But the administration did not appreciate his help. The White House quickly contacted Kerry after the interview had been published and impressed on him not to repeat any such statements—even though Kerry's point did not contradict the White House's new policy. The unambiguous zero-enrichment redline of the Bush administration had been altered under Obama to read that Iran would be treated no differently than any other nuclear nonproliferation treaty (NPT) state. As such, if Iran restored the international community's confidence, the possibility of enrichment on Iranian soil down the road did exist. The problem was that, for several reasons, the Obama administration did not want to signal this publicly. First of all, there was no consensus on this point between the U.S. and its allies. The Israelis were not the only ones opposing the new redline. Within the EU the French also rejected the existence of "a right to enrichment." In order to maintain a unified front vis-à-vis Iran, it was important to keep the new position ambiguous until consensus could be found. Second, the Iranians would likely interpret the move as a major victory. Rather than meeting the U.S. halfway, the move risked emboldening the Iranians and hardening their stance in the negotiations, the White House feared. Any change on this issue was best presented to the Iranians at a later stage in the negotiations rather than as an opening to the talks.[31]

The ambiguity surrounding America's desired nuclear endgame was closely linked to the lack of clarity in the review on the larger endgame with Iran—what end state in U.S.-Iran relations was Washington seeking, and what form would it have to take to be acceptable to both countries as well as to Washington's regional allies? What role would Iran have in the region, and in what ways would Iran's behavior have to change in order for U.S.-Iran relations to improve? If Iran did change its behavior, how long would the warm-up period in relations last, assuming that Iran was equally interested in seeking more positive relations? What end state was Iran seeking? Was there any overlap between Washington and Tehran's endgames, and would that potential overlap be acceptable to Israel? If such an overlap did not exist, what could diplomacy realistically achieve?

The difficulty of finding satisfactory answers to these fundamental questions had made the topic taboo in deliberations with Washington's EU allies. Rather than thinking hard about the strategic options, the conversations tended to be tactical in nature. The U.S. and the EU "were not looking at the endgame" in this phase; there was no search for "a defined political or diplomatic state." Instead, the discussions centered on "What is our next step in the UN? What is our next step in Vienna?" according to senior EU officials involved in the conversations. "It just wasn't the point in time where you would look at the endgame," the officials explained. Officially, the West rejected the idea that the lack of clarity made negotiations riskier and more difficult. "But how do you want to know before starting the negotiations what the end result of the negotiations will be? So why do you negotiate?" a senior EU official asked rhetorically. Inside the bureaucracy, however, as well as within the foreign policy establishment, there were fears that ambiguity, combined with the atmosphere of mistrust, would only play into the paranoia of the two sides and diminish the inclination to pursue diplomacy in earnest. The Iranians in particular would be disinclined to embroil themselves in a process that they suspected was aimed at denying what they considered to be their rights under the NPT. Instead, Washington's approach under the review was that the destination of the diplomatic journey was a function of the journey itself. If the journey went well, few limits would exist during the warm-up in relations. If, however, the negotiations were difficult and produced few results, Washington would adjust its ambitions accordingly.[32]

The Obama administration's approach did not lack critics at home. Elements on the right opposed talking to the government in Iran and feared that the Obama administration's investment in diplomacy would only enable the Iranians to gain more time to enhance their nuclear program. But experts with greater political proximity to the Obama administration itself also expressed discomfort with the dual-track policy recommended by the review. Former national security adviser Zbigniew Brzezinski, who advised Obama during the presidential elections, expressed sharp criticism of many aspects of the policy in testimony to the Senate Foreign Relations Committee in March 2009. Brzezinski argued against preconditions and timelines for the negotiations; threats of sanctions; mentions of the use of force or regime change; or accusations of terrorism. "It seems to me that we run the risk of . . . wanting to have our cake and eating it too at the same time, of engaging in polemics and diatribes with the Iranians while at the same time engaging seemingly in a negotiating process," he told the committee. "The first is not conducive to the second."[33]

Moreover, senior administration officials seemed at times doubtful as to whether the strategy would work. During a visit to Egypt in early March 2009, Clinton told Arab officials that she was "doubtful" that Iran would respond positively to U.S. overtures of engagement. The secretary of state reportedly told the foreign minister of the United Arab Emirates that she did not expect that diplomacy would stop Iran's nuclear program, but that it would set the stage for stiff international sanctions. Similarly, Secretary of Defense Robert Gates, a holdover from the Bush administration, seemingly contradicted Obama's vision when he told the Fox News network in late March 2009 that Iran was more likely to heed sanctions than diplomacy. "I think frankly from my perspective the opportunity for success is probably more in economic sanctions in both places (Iran and North Korea) than it is in diplomacy." These expressions of uncertainty—or outright opposition—toward the engagement strategy raised questions about the Obama administration's sincerity with regard to diplomacy or about whether Obama had surrounded himself with advisers who did not share his foreign policy vision. While Obama's extended hand to Iran had encountered outside opposition, the last thing the president could afford was opposition from his own immediate circle of advisers.[34]

Obama's New Year's Greeting

Prior to the conclusion of the policy review, the Obama administration made an unprecedented outreach to the Iranian people and government on the occasion of the Iranian New Year. Obama taped a three-and-a-half-minute statement congratulating the Iranians on their new year and expressing his wish for a better future for the two nations. "I would like to speak directly to the people and leaders of the Islamic Republic of Iran," the president said as he praised the contributions of the Iranian nation to art, music, and literature over the centuries and reminded the Iranians of the humanity that binds nations together. Addressing the differences between the nations, Obama sought to clarify America's genuine interest in diplomacy. "My administration is now committed to diplomacy that addresses the full range of issues before us, and to pursuing constructive ties among the United States, Iran and the international community. This process will not be advanced by threats. We seek instead engagement that is honest and grounded in mutual respect," the president said.

"You, too, have a choice," Obama continued. "The United States wants the Islamic Republic of Iran to take its rightful place in the community of nations. You have that right—but it comes with real responsibilities, and that place cannot be reached through terror or arms, but rather through peaceful actions that demonstrate the true greatness of the Iranian people and civilization. And the measure of that greatness is not the capacity to destroy, it is your demonstrated ability to build and create." The president concluded by making clear that the path forward would be hard and demanding. But citing one of

Iran's most famous poets, he emphasized again the common humanity between Iran and the U.S. "I know that this won't be reached easily," Obama said. "There are those who insist that we be defined by our differences. But let us remember the words that were written by the poet Saadi, so many years ago: 'The children of Adam are limbs to each other, having been created of one essence.'"

There was nothing ordinary about Obama's initiative. The outreach was unprecedented, as were the content and tone of the message as well as the medium through which it was distributed. The video was released at midnight, March 20, 2009—with Persian subtitles—on youtube.com and on the White House's own website. It immediately went viral in Iranian circles and dominated conversation in Iran the next morning. By putting the video online, the White House ensured that the president could address millions of Iranians directly without the interference of Iranian government censorship or editing. The thoughtful message was the product of several weeks of drafting between the State Department and the National Security Council. The process was very tightly held, and very few people outside of government were involved or aware of the initiative. The overarching purpose was to signal the Iranian government that the desire on the part of Washington to change the dynamic of the relationship between Iran and the United States was sincere. "We weren't trying to pull the wool over their eyes," a State Department official told me. At the same time, Obama was also making it clear to the Iranian people that engagement with the unpopular rulers in Tehran would not come at their expense. Obama was saying, "We're not trying to sell you down the river by reaching out to a government you don't like."[35]

The statement was remarkable in the extent to which it was signaling the administration's willingness to alter America's approach to Iran. As prominent Iran expert Farideh Farhi of the University of Hawaii pointed out, Obama did not try to drive a wedge between the people and government of Iran. Unlike his predecessors, he addressed them both and he also did not try to increase

cleavages between various political factions within the Iranian government. He did not entangle himself in the endless debate in Washington about whom to talk to in Iran or how talks could be used to
strengthen one faction against another. Moreover, his statement that
the growing problems between the U.S. and Iran could not be resolved through threats indicated a sharp departure from the approach of the Bush administration and could be interpreted as a
dismissal of the military option on Iran.[36] And by referencing the
official name of the Iranian government—the Islamic Republic of
Iran—the president indicated that the days of actively seeking U.S.-
sponsored regime change in Iran were past. Perhaps most important,
Obama signaled his strategic intent with Iran—"We seek instead
engagement that is honest and grounded in mutual respect"—and
gave a hint of what the endgame of the engagement could be if
diplomacy succeeded by stating that the U.S. wants Iran to "take its
rightful place in the community of nations." The phrase appeared to
indicate American willingness to grant Iran a greater role in regional
and global affairs—a key demand of the Iranians who were deeply
frustrated by their belief that their accepted role in regional affairs
was not on par with their geopolitical weight.

Though the statement caught the Iranians off guard—not only
because of the content of the message but also because of its level of
cultural sophistication—their official response was swift. Within a
day, Iran's Supreme Leader, Ayatollah Ali Khamenei, gave a speech
in his hometown of Mashhad, directly addressing Obama's New
Year's message. The fact that Khamenei himself gave the first response, and that he did it so quickly, was significant. By swiftly
responding, he made it clear who has the final word on determining
Iran's positions and actions, while also setting the tone and approach
toward the U.S. He essentially shut down any debate in Iran on how
to respond to Obama—Khamenei's line on Obama and the U.S.
would be Iran's only line. This was arguably itself a sign of the
success of Obama's move, because no other U.S. president had
managed to compel Iran's Supreme Leader to act in this manner.[37]

Khamenei's speech primarily dealt with domestic matters; the only foreign policy issue he addressed was Obama's statement, and he devoted roughly twenty minutes to it. Following what had become a typical pattern of the Islamic Republic's responses to U.S. overtures, he dedicated the majority of the time to revisiting the many grievances Iran had with the U.S., followed by a small and qualified opening at the end of the speech. Letters between U.S. lawmakers and Iranian officials regularly followed a similar pattern, oftentimes causing the American decision makers to miss the veiled opportunity the Iranians would present. Khamenei covered Iranian suffering due to sanctions; freezing of assets; his belief that Washington gave Saddam Hussein the green light to invade Iran in 1980; American support for Iranian opposition groups; and his belief that the U.S. supported the Baluchi terrorist and secessionist group Jundollah. He did not call for an apology, however, and cited these grievances not as reasons why dialogue with the U.S. should be avoided, but rather to reinforce his skepticism about the Obama administration and why a change of tone and vocabulary was not enough to reconcile the differences between the two countries.[38]

His response to Obama centered on three interrelated points, followed by a cautious opening to the U.S. First, he expressed his doubts about Obama's ability to change U.S. foreign policy, arguing that the real decision makers in Washington were unknown. This response echoed the speculation in Tehran that even if Obama were serious, structural factors would overpower him. Khamenei rhetorically said, "I do not know who makes decisions for America, the president, the congress, behind the scene elements, but I would like to say that we have logic. Since the beginning, the Iranian nation has moved with logic. Regarding our vital issues, we are not sentimental. We do not make decisions based on emotions. We make decisions through calculations."

Second, he categorically rejected the notion that Iran—or any respectable nation—would respond positively to a combination of engagement and pressure—that is, the dual-track policy. "If you go on with the slogan of discussions and pressure, saying that you will negotiate with Iran and at the same time impose pressures, threats and adaptations, our nation will not like such words," Khamenei said. Sanctions and diplomacy did not go hand in hand, Khamenei indicated, because the former undermines the sincerity of the latter. Third, and perhaps most important, the Supreme Leader questioned Obama's sincerity by arguing that change thus far had only been a slogan with no follow-up. He said:

> They have the slogan of change. Where is the change? What has changed? Clarify this to us. What has changed? Has your enmity towards the Iranian nation changed? What signs are there to support this? Have you released the possessions of the Iranian nation? Have you removed the cruel sanctions? Have you stopped the insults, accusations and negative propaganda against this great nation and its officials? Have you stopped unconditional support for the Zionist regime? What has changed? They talk of change but there are no changes in action. We have not seen any changes. Changes in words are not adequate; although we have not seen much of a change there either. Change has to be real.[39]

Real change could not be a mere change of tactics while pursuing the same old strategic aim, Khamenei continued. "This is not a change. This is deceit," he declared soberly. But right there Khamenei also offered a small and cautious opening to the U.S. Admitting that the Obama administration did not carry the baggage of previous administrations when dealing with Iran, it would be too early to pass a conclusive judgment on the new American president. Moreover, Khamenei declared that Iran would change its policy toward the U.S. if Obama followed through with his promise and delivered real change in America's approach to Iran. "We do not have any experience with the new American president and government. We'll see and judge. You change and we will change as well,"

Khamenei said. According to veteran Iran-watcher Rasool Nafisi of Strayer University, Khamenei was signaling that Iran "will start afresh, without prejudice, and will evaluate the policy of the U.S. according to its actions rather than its rhetoric."[40] And if those actions involved concrete measures to show America's goodwill—as opposed to mere words—Iran would reciprocate. The Supreme Leader was saying, "Stop tightening the noose. Give me some hints that you are thinking in terms of an alternative policy," Farhi argued. So despite Obama's unprecedented outreach, the ball was still in America's court, Khamenei insisted.

The "change for change" mantra was not limited to Iran's hard-liners. Even the reformists—though they tended to be more open to the possibility that Obama was sincere and seemed deeply impressed by the thought behind the New Year's message—agreed that it did not address the real grievances between the two countries. The reformist-leaning *Asr-e Iran,* for instance, argued that the measures that would reveal a real change of attitude in Washington would be the release of Iranian assets and lifting of sanctions. Pointing out that the U.S. was already preparing new sanctions on Iran, the reformist newspaper deemed Obama's gesture insufficient.[41] More conservative and centrist figures in Iran's political elite quickly endorsed Khamenei's position and offered a united front on this issue. According to Booz Allen Hamilton's Persia House News Brief, these figures all gave speeches and presentations following the same formula: initial questioning of the sincerity of Obama, followed by a stern warning that Iran would not be moved by anything other than substantive change, and concluding with a laundry list of items Iran would seek from any dialogue. Hashemi Rafsanjani, the chairman of the Expediency Council and the Assembly of Experts, said that the Obama administration must "show goodwill" by releasing Iranian assets frozen by the U.S. government since the 1979 hostage crisis. If such measures were taken, sincerity would be established and a new relationship could emerge because Iran didn't wish to have enmity with the U.S. "We don't have any enmity with the American people.

We won't have any enmity with the American government if it treats us fairly and acts in line with international norms," Rafsanjani said.[42] Iran's hard-line president Ahmadinejad reiterated the same points in his public comments, repeating the mantra that change must be real. Otherwise, Iran would respond to Obama as it did with Bush. Ahmadinejad, however, did take the unusual step of referring to Obama as "the honourable president of America"—a rather remarkable departure from the usually bombastic and belligerent rhetoric of the hard-line Iranian president.[43]

From the Iranian perspective, calling for a goodwill gesture beyond symbolic statements was justifiable, mindful of previous failed attempts at U.S.-Iran engagement. The Iranian request was moderate, Tehran argued, because it was not calling for difficult measures such as the lifting of sanctions. Rather, the Iranians were looking for much smaller measures such as the establishment of direct flights between the two countries or the unfreezing of Iranian assets in the U.S.[44] The Iranians were content with the fact that Obama had taken three important symbolic steps toward improving relations between the two countries. He had adopted a more respectful tone that recognized the Islamic Republic and signaled that U.S.-sponsored regime change was no longer an American objective. He had welcomed Iran's involvement in resolving issues of common concern such as Afghanistan. And he had declared Washington's intent to participate in nuclear negotiations with Iran under the auspices of the UN Security Council.[45]

But the Iranians wanted more. Though many Iran experts viewed Khamenei's response as ultimately positive—Iran would change if America changed—the irony was that Iran was seemingly emulating the Bush administration's policy. From Washington's perspective, the Iranian government essentially put a precondition for engagement to take place. The Iranian government famously said during the Bush presidency that they had only one precondition for diplomacy, and that was that there should be no preconditions. Now, as Washington dropped its precondition, Iran seemingly adopted its own.

Five

Israel and Obama Clash

It cannot be that the money is invested in enriched uranium and the children are told to remain a little hungry, a little ignorant.

—Shimon Peres' New Year's greeting to the Iranian people, March 2009

As Obama was preparing his Iran strategy and laying the groundwork for diplomacy, opponents and skeptics of engagement worked diligently to close the president's political space for any sustained outreach. In what many analysts viewed as attempted sabotage, Israeli president Shimon Peres released his own Persian New Year greeting only hours after learning of Obama's unprecedented video recording. Peres' predecessor, Iranian-born Moshe Katsav, had sent New Year's greetings in Persian to the Iranian people on the Voice of Israel radio for a few years. But this was the first time Peres spoke to the Iranians.

Peres did not mince his words, blasting the Ahmadinejad government and the many failures of the Islamic Republic while challenging the Iranian people to rid themselves of the ruling theocracy. "I urge you, the noble Iranian people, on behalf of the ancient Jewish people, to reclaim your worthy place among the nations of the enlightened world, while contributing a worthy cultural contribution," Peres said. "Things in Iran are tough," he continued. "There is great unemployment, corruption, a lot of drugs, and a general discontent. You can't feed your children enriched uranium, they need a real breakfast. It cannot be that the money is invested in enriched uranium and the children are told to remain a little hungry, a little ignorant." The Israeli president also issued a warning, reminding the Iranians of the Jewish people's success in overcoming obstacles to their survival. "We've heard, over the 4,000 years of our existence, many speeches, many anti-Semites, many people who wanted to destroy us—we survived and they did not." Peres concluded by predicting that the Iranian people would soon topple their government and once again befriend Israel. "I think that the Iranian people will topple these leaders, these leaders who don't serve the people," he said.[1]

The Israeli newspaper *Haaretz* wrote that the contrast between Obama's and Peres' messages revealed the increasing distance between the U.S. and Israel on Iran. "While the Americans are actively seeking a way to start a dialogue, Israel is preaching confrontation and the toppling of the government in Tehran," the *Haaretz* editorial said. "It is clearly in Israel's interest to halt Iran's nuclear program, but it is no less in our interests to have close ties and a coordinated policy with the United States. The new government should give Obama's diplomatic initiative a chance."[2] A former Israeli peace negotiator called Peres' message a "sabotage attempt," and Marsha Cohen, a scholar of Israeli-Iranian relations, wrote that "nothing would make any Israeli politician happier than being considered personally responsible for preventing rapprochement between the U.S. and Iran." Recognizing the diluting effect Peres' statement could have on Obama's message, the Obama administration quickly clarified that there had been no coordination between the U.S. and Israel on this matter.[3] In fact, rather than coordination, Israel and America were heading toward a major political clash over Iran, as well as the Palestinian issue.

Showdown at the Oval Office

A showdown between the U.S. and Israel had been brewing ever since Obama entered the White House. Obama's diagnosis of and vision for the region fundamentally clashed with Israel's views. Obama favored diplomacy with Iran, opposed Israeli settlements on Palestinian territory, and wanted to renew America's relationship with the Muslim world. Israel feared abandonment—that diplomacy would leave Israel facing the Iranian threat alone, that American opposition to settlements would lead to greater international pressure on Israel, and that Washington would sacrifice its relationship with Israel to improve ties with the Islamic world.

On May 18, 2009, Israeli prime minister Benjamin Netanyahu came to Washington for a visit that both sides hoped would dispel fears of a crisis in their relationship, but neither side was in a compromising mood. Netanyahu did not have the appetite for either American diplomacy with Iran or American pressure against Israeli settlements. Going up against the American president, however, would be a dangerous gambit. Obama was an immensely popular president, both nationally and internationally, who enjoyed the political latitude American presidents usually experience only during their first year in office. The president's party also controlled all three branches of government and, on top of that, enjoyed a supermajority in the Senate. Clashing with Obama under these circumstances could be very damaging. Still, that was the path Netanyahu chose. In the weeks prior to his visit to Washington, he intensified the Israeli campaign to weaken Obama's ability to move forward with his vision on Iran. The strategy centered on four key areas: securing a tight deadline for diplomacy; tightening sanctions before any diplomacy began; securing American commitment to zero-enrichment; and keeping the military option on the table. Working in tandem with pro-Likud (Israel's right-wing political party) interest groups in Washington and lawmakers sympathetic to the Israeli perspective, Netanyahu hoped to outflank Obama and confine his room for maneuverability. That was easier said than done, as Netanyahu suffered two quick setbacks as he sought to take on Obama over Iran.

To Sanction or to Dialogue?

The first setback was on sanctions. On April 6, 2009, only a week after he assumed office, Netanyahu met with a bipartisan delegation of U.S. lawmakers led by Senator Jon Kyl (R-AZ). Adopting a "forceful stance," Netanyahu pressed the American delegation on what the U.S. planned to do if engagement failed to stop Iran's nuclear program. While Kyl concurred in his skepticism of diplomacy and support for sanctions, Democratic lawmakers pushed back, arguing that engagement needed to be tried. Not impressed, the Israeli prime minister told the American lawmakers that engagement should be given only four to twelve weeks, with the explicit objective of putting an end to the Iranian nuclear program—a near impossible task.[4] A week later, Senator Evan Bayh (D-IN) announced on the Fox News network that he and Kyl would be introducing a new sanctions bill targeting Iran.[5] The bill was introduced just a week before the annual conference of the American Israel Public Affairs Committee (AIPAC) in Washington, D.C., during which more than six thousand citizen lobbyists flock to Congress to push for legislation favored by the hawkish pro-Israel lobby. AIPAC argued that additional sanctions would give Obama the tools to pressure Iran if diplomacy failed. Also, imposing sanctions before talks began would increase the incentives for Tehran to be flexible in the negotiations. "The threat of a popular sanctions bill wending its way through Congress while U.S. officials negotiate outreach might help spur Iran toward allowing expanded U.N. monitoring of its uranium enrichment," a pro-Israel insider told the Jewish Telegraphic Agency.[6] Opponents of sanctions, on the other hand, argued that they did nothing to enhance diplomacy but would rather undercut the president's diplomatic message. Moreover, they pointed out that even those who supported punitive measures admitted that more sanctions would lead to the deaths of Iranian civilians. "Look, we need to be honest about this," said Fred Kagan, resident scholar at the American Enterprise Institute (AEI) at a conference hosted by the AEI. "Iranians are going to die if we impose additional sanctions."[7]

Though Israeli officials and supporters of the Netanyahu government struggled to strike a tone that would not directly undercut Obama's push for diplomatic engagement—claiming that engagement "should be backed with tougher sanctions to enhance the probability of success"—the White House was not impressed and rejected their calls.[8] When the six thousand AIPAC supporters reached Capitol Hill to push for the sanctions bills to be passed within the first week of May, just a month before the Iranian presidential elections, they were met with surprising resistance. "Tomorrow is the day the rubber meets the road," AIPAC president David Victor told the conferees before they descended on Capitol Hill. "This is a moment of danger. We are the only constituency in America making this case [against Iran]." To their amazement, even some stalwart supporters of AIPAC in Congress refrained from supporting the sanctions measure. Howard Berman (D-CA), chair of the House Foreign Relations Committee, who introduced the sanctions legislation in the House and whose committee oversaw it, took the extraordinary step of declaring that he had no intention of moving the bill forward. "I fully support the Administration's strategy of direct diplomatic engagement with Iran, and I have no intention of moving this bill through the legislative process in the near future," Berman said. "However, should engagement with Iran not yield the desired results in a reasonable period of time, we will have no choice but to press forward with additional sanctions—such as those contained in this bill—that could truly cripple the Iranian economy."[9]

The unusual setback prompted Andrew Glass of the news organization Politico to write that AIPAC faced some "challenging times." AIPAC's failure resulted from the "rough consensus that had formed in Congress to give the Obama administration time and space" to pursue diplomacy, a senior Senate staffer told me. Lawmakers wanted the threat of sanctions to be very real, as a "sword of Damocles" if engagement did not succeed. But they were at that time willing to give Obama the opportunity to try diplomacy first.[10] A few weeks later, Secretary Clinton told a congressional committee what the administration had until then only privately indicated to lawmakers: that the White House did not favor any new sanctions at that point. "I am not sure that adding new unilateral sanctions is really that helpful," Clinton told the lawmakers.[11] Tensions were also mounting between the Obama administration and Netanyahu's government on the Palestinian issue. Vice President Biden used his keynote address at the AIPAC conference to convey the Obama administration's insistence on a number of policies directly conflicting with those of the government in Israel, including the need for a two-state solution, cessation of settlement expansion, the dismantling of existing outposts, and provisions for enabling freedom of movement for the Palestinians.[12]

The Deadline Debacle

The Netanyahu government's second tactical setback was over the issue of a deadline for diplomacy. The argument for tight deadlines was first raised in public in December 2008 at a conference hosted by the Institute for National Security Studies in Tel Aviv, Israel. In an interview after addressing the conference, Berman said U.S.-Iran talks should last no longer than twelve weeks. Deadlines were needed in order to ensure that Tehran would not drag out the talks indefinitely, while simultaneously continuing its nuclear advances. Under such circumstances, Iran would eventually present the West with a nuclear fait accompli, having developed its nuclear weapon under the guise of negotiations. Furthermore, since talks were aimed at testing Iran's sincerity, after which sanctions and pressure would follow if Iran showed a lack of earnestness, this test period could not be permitted to be too long in duration. Israel's foreign minister, Avigdor Lieberman, said in a statement on May 6, 2009, that "it is important that the dialogue with Iran be limited in duration and that if after three months it will be clear that the Iranians are playing for time and not ceasing their nuclear program, then the international community will have to take practical measures."[13]

Opponents of deadlines argued that the U.S. focus should be on making diplomacy succeed rather than on debating when to declare it a failure or to position the U.S. for other steps after an eventual breakdown. A conflict that has remained unresolved for three decades could not possibly be resolved after only a few weeks of talks. Rather than achieve success, deadlines would signal America's insincerity and contribute to the failure of diplomacy, opponents argued. After all, tight deadlines set by the Bush administration on the Iraqi government in 2003 helped ensure war rather than a negotiated settlement.[14] Throughout spring of 2009, recurring rumors surfaced regarding various deadlines for the talks, and each time the Obama administration resisted committing itself to any deadline. "Let me just say that we're not setting any deadline," a State Department spokesperson said on May 14 after reports emerged in the Israeli press that the administration had committed itself to an early fall deadline for talks. "We're not interested in setting any kind of specific or even notional timeline. We are, of course, monitoring very closely what the Iranians are doing, assessing progress. But it—we don't have any timeline forward."[15]

The real showdown over deadlines came a few days later, though, during Netanyahu's visit to the White House. The two leaders met for two hours—one full hour longer than scheduled—and this was followed by a joint news conference in the Oval Office, at which neither man appeared comfortable. The extended meeting, as well as their failure to issue a joint statement summarizing the talks, revealed the depth of their disagreements, according to former U.S. ambassador to Israel Samuel Lewis.[16] Indeed, each man's talking points and body language were at odds with the other's. With Netanyahu at his side, Obama explained the rationale for diplomacy and why it needed time to succeed:

We didn't expect—and I don't think anybody in the international community or anybody in the Middle East, for that matter—would expect that 30 years of antagonism and suspicion between Iran and the United States would be resolved in four months. So we think it's very important for us to give this a chance. Now, understand that part of the reason that it's so important for us to take a diplomatic approach is that the approach that we've been taking, which is no diplomacy, obviously has not worked. Nobody disagrees with that. Hamas and Hezbollah have gotten stronger. Iran has been pursuing its nuclear capabilities undiminished. And so not talking—that clearly hasn't worked. That's what's been tried. And so what we're going to do is try something new, which is actually engaging and reaching out to the Iranians.[17]

Obama refused to commit to an arbitrary deadline but accepted that a timetable was needed in order to prevent talks from proceeding indefinitely.

It is important for us, I think, without having set an artificial deadline, to be mindful of the fact that we're not going to have talks forever. We're not going to create a situation in which talks become an excuse for inaction while Iran proceeds with developing a nuclear—and deploying a nuclear weapon. My expectation would be that if we can begin discussions soon, shortly after the Iranian elections, we should have a fairly good sense by the end of the year as to whether they are moving in the right direction and whether the parties involved are making progress and that there's a good faith effort to resolve differences. That doesn't mean every issue would be resolved by that point, but it does mean that we'll probably be able to gauge and do a reassessment by the end of the year of this approach.

Obama also linked the Israeli-Palestinian issue to Iran, but with the causality reversed from that preferred by Israel. "To the extent that we can make peace . . . between the Palestinians and the Israelis, then I actually think it strengthens our hand in the international community in dealing with the potential Iranian threat," he said. Netanyahu's response evaded an explicit embrace of a two-state solution, contrary to what Obama had hoped. "I want to make it clear that we don't want to govern the Palestinians; we want to live in peace with them," said Netanyahu. And he challenged Obama by reinterpreting the president's remarks as an explicit acknowledgment that the military option remained in play. "I very much appreciate, Mr. President, your firm commitment to ensure that Iran does not develop nuclear military capability, and also your statement that you're leaving all options on the table," Netanyahu told Obama in front of the reporters.[18]

The disagreements between Obama and Netanyahu on Iran were decisive but were more about tone than substance. During their conversation prior to the news conference, Obama told the Israeli prime minister that the success or failure of diplomacy would be determined by the end of the year and that the military option remained on the table, according to leaked State Department cables recounting Netanyahu's version of the meeting.[19] The differences were in the public presentation and the volume of the rhetoric. The military option is always on the table, regardless of whether the president of the United States refers to it on a regular basis. But for the U.S., this line of thinking should not be expressed openly. It should be made explicit only if it serves a direct function. From Obama's perspective, reiterating the phrase would undermine the credibility of his outreach and fuel Iranian suspicions. From Netanyahu's viewpoint, however, Iran would respond to diplomacy only if faced with a credible military threat. A disconnect between the three states, their strategies, and their leaders seemed almost complete. "There's a three-way race going on here," one of Obama's strategists told the

New York Times. "We're racing to make diplomatic progress. The Iranians are racing to make their nuclear capability a fait accompli. And the Israelis, of course, are racing to come up with a convincing military alternative that could plausibly set back the Iranian program."[20]

In the end, all of Israel's pressure against the diplomacy it so feared was for naught. The Iranians, it turned out, would do far more damage to diplomacy than Israel ever could.

Six

Fraud

Where is my vote?

   —Iranian protest sign in the aftermath of

   the 2009 presidential election

Journalists at the Press TV headquarters in Tehran were eagerly monitoring the country's June 2009 election results late into the evening. Though the English language station was set up during Mahmoud Ahmadinejad's presidency to convey his government's perspective on global affairs to an English-speaking audience outside of Iran, a "Green Wave"—the movement behind Mir Hussein Mousavi's presidential campaign—had swept most of the station's employees. The mood was jubilant as many of the employees predicted a strong showing by Mousavi. The polls had been closed for just an hour, and the results were starting to trickle in slowly.

The phone rang, and one of the producers answered. The caller was Press TV director Mohammad Sarafraz, who said sternly, "Announce that Ahmadinejad is ahead in the elections with a significant margin." The producer responded in anger and disbelief, asking, "But how?" It was impossible for the handwritten ballots to be counted this fast. "Is there a detailed vote count I can refer to?" he asked. "I repeat," Sarafraz fired back, "run headlines that Ahmadinejad is ahead. Details will be presented later." Shortly thereafter, Iranian state TV shocked the Iranian nation—and the world—with the announcement that Ahmadinejad was heading toward a landslide victory. In the meantime, Mousavi's campaign headquarters were attacked and taken over by security forces. Dawn had yet to break when Facebook profile pictures began morphing into icons of a green square with the words "Where Is My Vote?" A few days later, several journalists at Press TV resigned in protest. The 2009 Iranian election scandal had begun, and Iran, the world, and the Obama administration all were caught off guard.[1]

Mousavi and the Green Wave

Few presidents in Iran have been as polarizing as Ahmadinejad. His persona and unpopularity among his many opponents guaranteed that the 2009 presidential election would be a nail-biter. Iranian elections are neither free nor fair. The Guardian Council, an unelected body of twelve clergymen, decides which candidates are permitted to run—a process that has been as political as it has been undemocratic. In 2004, for instance, sitting reformist members of the parliament were not approved to stand for reelection. And yet, Iranian elections have been competitive and have yielded surprising results. In 2009, the four candidates permitted to run were all insiders of the Islamic Republic: Mehdi Karroubi, the former Speaker of the parliament who ran on a reformist platform; Mohsen Rezaii, the former head of the Iranian Revolutionary Guards Corps; former prime minister Mir Hossein Mousavi; and Ahmadinejad. The candidate who would steal most of the limelight and pose the greatest challenge to Ahmadinejad was Mousavi and his Green Wave. His campaign had a slow start and initially ran into tensions with former president Mohammad Khatami, who withdrew his candidacy once Mousavi threw his hat in the ring.[2] But that changed about two to three weeks before the election. Suddenly, a groundswell of support for Mousavi emerged, beginning on the university campuses and then spreading like wildfire. Ahmadinejad, whom many Western governments thought would be comfortably reelected, was in trouble, as his many critics were energized and had found a candidate around whom they could rally.

The son of a tea merchant, Mousavi was born March 2, 1942, in Khameneh in the East Azerbaijan Province of Iran. He studied Islamic architecture in Tehran and became politically active against the Shah's regime during his student years. After the revolution, Mousavi joined with Mohammad Beheshti to found the Islamic Republic Party and eventually became the chief editor of its official publication. A distant relative of Iran's current Supreme Leader, he served as Iran's prime minister from 1981 to 1989 and was largely credited with the successful stewardship of the economy during the tumultuous Iraq-Iran war. But relations between Mousavi and then-President Khamenei were ridden with tension; they clashed repeatedly in their respective capacities as prime minister and president. Their conflict reached a peak in September 1988, when Mousavi tendered his resignation. Ayatollah Khomeini refused to accept it at first but, less than a year later, the post of prime minister was eliminated entirely to create a stronger presidency. Mousavi's defeat, together with the 1989 death of his patron, Ayatollah Khomeini, pushed him to withdraw from public life. He still remained an insider within Iran's political elite, and he advised presidents Hashemi Rafsanjani and Mohammad Khatami while serving on the Expediency and Discernment Council. Mousavi refused to run in the 2005 presidential election but had by this time become a popular figure in reformist circles.[3]

In many ways, Mousavi was an unlikely candidate. He is not especially charismatic, and he lacked the political organization that both Ahmadinejad and Khatami enjoyed. While many reformists respected him, he was also viewed with some suspicion because of his conservative leanings. Others were skeptical about his ability to get back into the political game after a two-decade absence, or disagreed with his "outdated views" on economic and cultural policies.[4] And for much of Iran's young population, Mousavi's legacy as prime minister—his strongest political card—had little or no resonance. But one main point of attraction outweighed all of these factors: as an Islamic Republic insider with both conservative and reformist credentials, and with a reputation of being an effective manager, Mousavi was believed to be the only candidate who could defeat Ahmadinejad at the polls.

From the American perspective, Mousavi brought little change in substance but offered a much-welcomed change in rhetoric and persona. Washington knew that Mousavi "was not going to revolutionize the dynamic," an American diplomat told me. "He would just make it easier, he was digestible."[5] Indeed, on the hot-button issues that had made Ahmadinejad so politically toxic in Washington, Mousavi offered a very different approach. He condemned the killing of Jews in the Holocaust, in complete contrast to Ahmadinejad, who in 2005 called the Holocaust a myth.[6] Both his and Khatami's foreign policy teams resented the confrontational foreign policy Ahmadinejad had pursued. Tensions with the United States did not serve Iran's interests, Mousavi believed, and Ahmadinejad had pursued an extreme policy that had raised tensions without bringing Iran any dividends. "It was *taghamol* against *taghabol*," one of Mousavi's campaign workers told me. Mousavi "would have switched from a confrontational [*taghabol*] approach to constructive interaction [*taghamol*]." A recurring theme in his campaign was denouncing Ahmadinejad's extravagant and adventurous foreign policy. "I have said that our foreign policy is extreme. Sometimes we have gone to an extreme and then found ourselves backpedaling," said Mousavi.[7]

Mousavi favored a softer approach centering on improved ties with the entire international community. "We want to have relations with all countries," he said, "whether they are in the West or the East." One of his campaign slogans was "A New Greeting to the World," indicating that he intended to bring about a new era in Iran's relations with the outside world. He continued: "The diplomacy of the new government coming in must be to create calm and lower tensions. It is important for us that our government develops friendship with others." "Others" included the United States, which the Mousavi camp hoped would show greater flexibility toward an Iran that had discarded the controversial image and rhetoric of Ahmadinejad. But much like the conservatives, Mousavi insisted that negotiations would hinge on President Obama's willingness to change America's policies toward Iran in practical terms. "Holding talks with America is not a taboo for me. If America practically changes its Iran policy then we will surely hold talks with them," Mousavi said two weeks before the election. Mousavi had praised Obama's New Year's greeting but also expressed reservations based on Iran's past experience with the U.S. "Despite America's meddling in our affairs, whenever working with America was in our interest, like in the case of Afghanistan, we did it," he said. "However, as soon as these incidents are over, America returns to its old rhetoric and once again we've fallen down the same path. Of course, Obama's language differs from Bush's language. If he [Obama] effects real change, we will definitely negotiate with America. Otherwise, we will not."[8]

On Iran's redlines, however, Mousavi did not stray too far from the Ahmadinejad government. He insisted that enrichment was Iran's inalienable right and differentiated between the peaceful use of enrichment and building weapons. "It is our right and we have no right to backpedal or there will be dire consequences," the candidate said, insisting Iran was not aiming to produce nuclear weapons. "A right to have technology is different from deviating to weapons building," he continued. While refusing to abandon the Iranian nuclear program, Mousavi did offer greater "assurances" to the international community in the form of greater transparency and access for the International Atomic Energy Agency (IAEA).[9] But Mousavi was not inclined to accept a suspension of the enrichment program as demanded by the UN Security Council. Mousavi had overseen Iran's nuclear program during his term as prime minister in the 1980s and was well versed in its details, and he held "strong, principled views" on the matter, according to one of his advisers. In 2003, when Iran agreed to suspend the program during the course of negotiations with the EU, Mousavi opposed the decision. "I don't think he would have under any circumstances given up Iranian enrichment," one of Mousavi's advisers told me. "We would keep our enrichment capability, however, with safeguards and enough credible inspection regimes that would make it difficult for diversion [toward military use]."[10]

Although the foreign policy positions of the election challengers mattered greatly to Washington, this was not a top issue for Mousavi's campaign. He had a team of about a dozen foreign policy advisers who met on several occasions and drew up the larger themes of his policy. But the discussions would not deal with matters in great detail and were "very, very few" compared, for instance, with the meetings on economic affairs.[11] While the Obama administration's focus was turning toward Mousavi and his challenge to Ahmadinejad, Mousavi was fixated on Iran and not on America.

All Against Ahmadinejad

Ten days before the election, Iranian state TV introduced a new feature to Iran's political system: televised presidential debates. For the Iranian populace, which was not accustomed to the country's problems and policies being openly discussed on live TV, the debates were yet another indication that the political system seemed to be moving toward greater openness. The Islamic Republic, after all, prides itself in its recurring elections and the legitimacy that high voter participation injects into the system. The Iranian hard-liners walk a fine balance on this matter. On the one hand, they welcome high voter participation due to the legitimacy it lends the system. On the other hand, they fear very high participation since conservative candidates likely will not fare well if the masses cast their ballots. The decision to air live debates between the candidates was likely a product of this balancing act. But from the perspective of the hard-liners, it was a mistake, as the unprecedented confrontations on live TV energized primarily the anti-Ahmadinejad voters. Moreover, the debates showed that there was a real contest in the election and that every vote could matter. Consequently, many of those who had planned to boycott the election changed their minds.

Accusations flew in all directions when Ahmadinejad and Mousavi faced each other. Ahmadinejad attacked all of his predecessors and accused them of corruption. Severe accusations were leveled against key figures within the Islamic Republic—a strategy Ahmadinejad hoped would win him many of the antiestablishment votes. He brought up the wealth of former president Hashemi Rafsanjani and his family and noted that his own ministers were humble and pious. He accused the reformists of weakness on the international stage and argued that suspension of enrichment, acceptance of intrusive inspections, and other goodwill gestures had not brought Iran any benefits. Instead, Iran was branded by President George W. Bush as part of the "Axis of Evil." By contrast, Ahmadinejad asserted, his own uncompromising stance had brought the United States to its knees. Mousavi, who otherwise displayed few emotions in their exchange, heatedly derided Ahmadinejad's foreign policy and argued that his ferocity against Israel had aided the Jewish state's efforts to isolate Iran. Mousavi accused Ahmadinejad of causing instability in Iran with "adventurism, heroics and extremism." The hard-line president had "undermined the dignity of our nation" with his acidic anti-West, anti-Israel, and Holocaust-denying remarks, he added.[12] The most memorable—and decisive—moment in the debate, however, came when Ahmadinejad launched a series of personal attacks against Mousavi's wife, Zahra Rahnavard. To many Iranians, regardless of their political leanings, Ahmadinejad had crossed a line. The debates, and Ahmadinejad's miscalculation, shifted the momentum unambiguously in Mousavi's favor. In the end, the shift may have mattered little to the Ahmadinejad camp; their strategy for victory was ultimately not based on securing votes.

Takeover on Election Day

Whether the election in Iran was rigged, whether the votes were ever counted, and whether the fraud was unnecessary—some argue that Ahmadinejad would have won even without any cheating—will be debated endlessly. And no universal consensus will likely ever be reached—the issue has so polarized the two sides that any agreement on an objective reality is unlikely for the foreseeable future. What can be concluded, however, is that the Ahmadinejad camp had a plan. Three days before the election, Ahmadinejad's Interior Ministry secretly issued arrest warrants for key people within the Mousavi and Karroubi campaigns. The Interior Ministry and the intelligence services of the Iranian Revolutionary Guards Corps (IRGC) had for months prior to the election subjected top reformist officials to extremely intrusive monitoring. Later in September, Major General Mohammad Ali Jafari, the commander of the IRGC, admitted in a speech that his forces had monitored reformist politicians to check their presumed efforts to undermine Iran's Supreme Leader, Ayatollah Ali Khamenei. Jafari claimed that the decision to target the reformists was in response to a secret statement by Khatami that defeating Ahmadinejad in the election was necessary in order to eliminate the office of the Supreme Leader.[13]

Around four in the afternoon on election day, ten security officers stormed the headquarters of the Mousavi campaign in northern Tehran. The security officers claimed that they were ordered to shut down the TV station broadcast out of the campaign headquarters, citing lack of proper permits. In reality, there was no TV station, just a media center operated by the campaign to upload videos onto the Internet. The reach of these videos was very limited, but the larger objective of the security officers seemed to have been to shut down Internet access in the building and disrupt the operations of the Mousavi campaign. The campaign staff resisted, however, and a fight broke out. The security officers fled; some managed to escape, but the campaign staff disarmed and locked several in the basement of the building. The campaign officials then contacted Hashemi Shahroudi, the head of the Iranian Judiciary, who advised them not to release the security officers. Instead, he recommended, they should be handed over to the police. The campaign did so, but rather than arresting the security personnel the police took them outside and let them disappear into the crowds that had gathered.

The ordeal completely disrupted the campaign's operations. Along with the shutdown of cell phones and text messaging, the main lines of communication within the campaign became compromised, including the campaign's method for reporting the accuracy of the votes from the different precincts nationwide. A few hours later, a second wave of security officers stormed the headquarters. This time, rather than shutting down the Internet, they arrested Mousavi's campaign officials. The polls had not even closed yet. Within forty-eight hours, most of the first and second circle of officials around Mousavi and Karroubi were arrested. Those who escaped arrest went into hiding. By arresting the mid- and top-level officials of the Mousavi campaign, the Ahmadinejad camp managed to disconnect Mousavi from his grassroots supporters. This was a devastating—and perhaps decisive—blow to his ability to lead and direct his movement.[14]

The reformists had expected some degree of foul play. A few days before the election, Mousavi and Karroubi wrote a joint letter to the head of the Guardian Council, Ayatollah Jannati, warning about the possibility of electoral manipulation. They estimated that the conservatives could manipulate up to five or six percentage points of the vote. But this manipulation would be neutralized if voter turnout was high enough. As election day neared, the fear of voter fraud grew more intense. Mohammad Ali Abtahi, Khatami's former chief of staff, sparked an intense discussion on his Facebook page the night before the election. His status line said *Negaranam*—"I am worried"—and, in the ensuing discussion, he explained that there were grounds to be concerned about massive fraud. Emergency meetings were held at the Mousavi headquarters, debating how to react to any attempts to steal the election. But the reformists never expected that their headquarters would be ransacked on election day and that the campaign officials would be arrested en masse. Even if Khamenei preferred an Ahmadinejad victory, the reformists calculated that he would appreciate the legitimacy that high voter turnout would bring to the system. He would see the benefits for his own rule and, as a result, prevent the Ahmadinejad camp from overturning the vote. "We were always of the view this is going to be too sweet for him to make it bitter," one of Mousavi's advisers told me. But just as the reformists had underestimated the extent to which the Ahmadinejad camp was willing to go to retain power, the hard-liners underestimated the Iranian people's determination to have their votes count.

Where Is My Vote?

The election was rife with irregularities.[15] According to the official count, Ahmadinejad had won a landslide victory, securing 62.63 percent of the vote, with Mousavi gaining only 33.75 percent. The vote was immediately contested. After first having declared himself the winner, Mousavi accused the Ahmadinejad government of stealing the vote through "disgusting measures." In a letter to the Guardian Council, Mousavi listed some of the irregularities his campaign workers had reported:

> The number of mobile ballot boxes was increased significantly, and there were no monitors present at those stations. Our representatives were not allowed to be present at the mobile ballot boxes during transportation. Considering the fact that there were 14,000 of those, that gave them the ability to carry out any violation of any sort. The ballot boxes were sealed before we could verify that they were not filled up before election day. . . . There were 45.2 million eligible voters, and 59.6 million voting slips with serial numbers were printed. A day before the elections, there were millions more printed without serial numbers. The fact that there were so many extra voting slips itself is questionable. There is no way we could have run out of voting slips so early into the elections.[16]

Millions of Iranians, dressed in green to support Mousavi, spontaneously took to the streets and demanded an answer to their question: Where is my vote? But Iran's Supreme Leader would not budge. On June 14, two days after the election, he gave his blessings to Ahmadinejad, endorsing the results. The next day, up to three million Iranians came out to rally in support of Mousavi—the largest demonstration in Iran since the 1979 revolution. The protest spread to other cities, and eight protesters were reportedly killed in clashes with the police. The Ahmadinejad government showed no mercy, unleashing both riot police as well as the armed paramilitary group, the Basij, on the protesters. Using cell phones and video cameras, demonstrators documented the brutality of the Iranian security forces. The videos were promptly uploaded onto Facebook and other social media websites, quickly reaching international audiences. Moreover, hundreds of Western journalists who had traveled to cover the election were now caught in the midst of the demonstrations and reported instead on the election fraud and the Iranian government's brutal reaction to the protests. By the fourth day, the Iranian authorities restricted all journalists working for foreign media from firsthand reporting on the streets. But every protester with a cell phone had already morphed into a citizen journalist, and the footage and eyewitness accounts continued to slip out of Iran.[17]

The protesters were not limited to a young and restless Facebook generation. The schism in Iran was not reducible to social class, ethnicity, region, or generation, as witnessed by the makeup of the crowds that had congregated in the streets. For example, the protesters included women in black chadors as well as women wearing makeup. Indeed, Mousavi's support ranged from the urban middle class to students to the intellectuals, all of whom had previously brought the reform movement to power after garnering the attention of many people from humble backgrounds. For many in the lower classes of Iranian society, Ahmadinejad's triumphal economic claims simply did not ring true. They knew the economy had gotten worse on his watch because they had been the most vulnerable to its downturn. While Ahmadinejad went on TV and cited statistics to prove that things were getting better economically, the less fortunate classes were the ones who were unable to marry because they would never be able to afford to have their own homes.

Ahmadinejad also had a political base, primarily consisting of those who felt alienated from the political establishment and who believed that they had been cut out of the spoils of the Islamic Revolution. Ahmadinejad had assiduously courted these constituencies by recklessly throwing money at them through infrastructure projects and social spending with no oversight. Some government employees had doubled their income during Ahmadinejad's time in office. And, of course, many Iranians were so resentful of the regime that they enjoyed Ahmadinejad's naming and shaming of members of the political establishment whom he accused of corruption. Many felt that most of the leaders of the Islamic Republic had betrayed the revolution that propelled them to power and had made it harder for its foot soldiers to get ahead. In Mousavi, Ahmadinejad's supporters saw the epitome of the parasitic political class the president had railed against.

Despite the intensity if this schism, the political contest playing out in the election was, in fact, among rival factions of the same regime. Ahmadinejad represented a conservative element that believed the established political class had hijacked the revolution. Mousavi was not really a reformer so much as a pragmatic, moderate conservative who had campaigned with the backing of the reform movement because it recognized that he had a better chance of unseating Ahmadinejad than did one of their own candidates. Both political camps contained stalwart members of the political establishment, and both claimed to be trying to hold the Islamic Republic to the promise of the revolution that created it in 1979. Still, many of those in the streets demanding their rights nevertheless had a significant stake in its outcome: if the system could not be changed peacefully through the ballot box because of the hard-line establishment's unwillingness to heed popular demand for change, then what peaceful means for change did people have? And if the struggle at the top led people to conclude that working within the limits of the system was hopeless, both factions would lose, since, at the end of the day, they were in the same boat. Neither side could afford a complete collapse of the system because that would be the end of all of them. The question, then, was, who would blink first?[18]

On June 19, a week after the election, Khamenei had the opportunity to declare his intent to accommodate the reformists and to compromise. He delivered a televised sermon at the Friday prayers, watched by millions of Iranians. Many of the protesters hoped he would adopt a soft tone, elevating the image of the Supreme Leader above the election dispute by guiding the nation toward reconciliation. Instead, he endorsed Ahmadinejad's victory, rejected any notion of fraud, and warned against continued demonstrations. By issuing the warning, he put his own credibility and authority on the line; any continued protests would be an act of direct defiance against the Supreme Leader. Khamenei had raised the stakes, but, once again, he had miscalculated.[19]

The next day, thousands of Iranians took to the streets. Clashes between riot police and protesters ended with 450 people detained, and 10 more dead, including Neda Agha Soltan, a twenty-six-year-old student who would become a symbol of the Green movement when her tragic death was captured on film. The intense divisions within the Iranian government were out in the open, with Khamenei backing Ahmadinejad and endorsing a violent clampdown against the protesters, with Mousavi urging his supporters to continue demanding their rights peacefully, and with Ali Larijani, the powerful Speaker of the Iranian parliament (*Majles*), declaring that a significant number of people believed the election was fraudulent and that their opinion should be respected.[20] Former president Hashemi Rafsanjani, a sworn enemy of Ahmadinejad, echoed that sentiment in his Friday sermon later in July. "Doubt has been created [about the election results]," he said. "There is a large portion of the wise people who say they have doubts. We need to take action to remove this doubt."[21] Reports of massive human rights abuses began to surface, including rape and killings in Iran's overcrowded jails. One killing in particular shook the Iranian establishment, that of Mohsen Rouhol-Amini, the son of a senior IRGC commander and an adviser to conservative presidential candidate Mohsen Rezaii. Rouhol-Amini died due to "repeated blows and severe physical injuries" and other mistreatment at Tehran's Kahrizak prison, the semiofficial Mehr News Agency reported. Initially, officials said Rouhol-Amini had died from illness.[22] His murder at the hands of Iran's security forces served as further evidence that the struggle in Iran was not a traditional conservative-reformist political battle. Rather, the entire Iranian power establishment was literally at war with itself.

By August, the internal war within the Iranian elite reached a new level. The protests continued, the clampdown became more ruthless, the death toll grew, and the human rights abuses became more intense and widespread. The Iranian judiciary launched the Revolutionary Court's televised trials of well-known reformers and former government officials such as former vice president Mohammad Ali Abtahi and Mohsen Mirdamadi, leader of the Islamic Iran Participation Front, as well as demonstrators, human rights defenders, political scientists, academics, nonpolitical businessmen, and even Iranian employees of foreign embassies. They were accused, in what was broadly viewed as a kangaroo court, of fomenting unrest in collusion with foreign powers as well as other antigovernment activities. The prisoners looked disheveled and dazed. They sat in the front row of the courtroom wearing gray prison pajamas, in what was an apparent attempt to humiliate them in public. Unshaven, many had lost weight and seemed to have been drugged. Mousavi and Khatami blasted the show trials and accused the authorities of having tortured those on trial. "They have been stepped on so severely that they would have confessed to anything else, had they been instructed to do so," Mousavi said in his Ghalam News website. Khatami blasted the trials as an "insult" to Iran and Islam.[23]

The five show trials lasted into the fall and created, together with

the killings of prodemocracy activists and the acts of repression by
the Ahmadinejad government, next to irreparable divisions within
the Iranian elite and massive resentment among the general population. The Iranian regime had never been shaken like this; two indis-
pensible pillars of the regime were at risk. Many within the clergy
itself were turning against the government, and whatever popular
support that existed for the regime within its ranks was quickly
evaporating, a former Iranian diplomat said to me. At the outset, the
postelection protests were not a revolt against the system. Rather,
they were about the demand on the part of the millions of participants that their votes, cast for one of the more managerially compe-
tent and pragmatic stalwarts of the regime, be counted. Those who
sought to overthrow the system entirely had routinely advocated
boycotting the polls. But as the brutality of the Ahmadinejad government grew, the demands of the protesters on the streets changed. In
the following months slogans of "Where is my vote" became "Down
with the dictator"—unambiguous references to either Ahmadinejad
or Khamenei and finally to "Down with Khamenei" and "Down
with the Iranian Republic," that is, a direct challenge to Khamenei
and a call for regime change. Increasingly, it appeared as if Mousavi
and Karroubi—the figureheads of the Green movement—and some
elements in the grassroots of the movement were drifting apart.
Rather than coalescing around a few set objectives, the Green movement had lost its central control and was going in different directions. "It became more difficult to manage the constituencies because people were getting killed" and so many of the original leaders
had been arrested, one of Mousavi's advisers explained to me.[24]

America Caught Off Guard

The U.S. government had prepared itself for several outcomes of the
Iranian election. But none of these scenarios included massive fraud
followed by months of demonstrations, violent clampdown, and a
virtual civil war within the Iranian elite. Within the government,

there was little doubt that Ahmadinejad had stolen the election. "Everybody knew the fix was in," a State Department official explained. "But nobody knew what the response was going to be. Nobody knew what the response to the response was going to be. So there were a lot of questions."[25] But beyond questions and concerns that the instability in Iran would further delay the president's diplomatic strategy, the unrest and political paralysis in Iran could also offer the U.S. an opportunity, some in the government believed. Several other factors had already increased the Obama administration's confidence in dealing with Iran, such as Hezbollah's narrow defeat in the Lebanese elections, Syria's interest in engaging with Washington, the Arab states' enthusiasm for America's reengagement in the Israeli-Palestinian peace process, as well as the "reset" with Moscow, which was aimed at depriving Tehran of Russian support in the Security Council. "From 2003 to 2009, Iran was on a roll," one senior administration official said. "Expanding its sphere of influence, benefiting from a changed balance of power in the region, and generally optimistic about its world. Many said it was not possible to engage because Iran was so strong and thus disincent[iviz]ed to do so. I do not think any credible analyst would say now that Iran feels that way anymore." But the geopolitical benefits Washington could reap from a weakened Tehran had to be balanced with the political risks associated with the difficulty of handling the unfolding of events in Iran.[26]

Washington initially reacted timidly in public. The Obama administration carefully eluded taking sides, aiming to keep the U.S. from becoming an issue in the election dispute. "There was a real calculation that said the less we say, the better because this is an issue . . . between the Iranian people and their government," explained Michael Ratney of the U.S. State Department's Near East Affairs Bureau. "This is not about the United States. This is not about US-Iranian relations." Rather, the administration's initial reactions focused on withholding comment and judgment while expressing doubts. Two days after the election, Vice President Biden said on

NBC's *Meet the Press* that he had "doubts" about the election results but that "we're going to withhold comment" until a more intensive review takes place. "There's an awful lot of question about how this election was run. I mean we're just waiting to see," he said. Obama addressed the concerns of the protesters and framed them as a human rights issue but stopped short of condemning the government-sponsored violence against the demonstrators. "For those people who put so much hope and energy and optimism into the political process, I would say to them the world is watching and inspired by their participation regardless of what the ultimate outcome of the election was," Obama said during a June 15 Oval Office meeting with Italy prime minister Silvio Berlusconi. He added that many Iranian voters "now feel betrayed" and "the ability of people to peacefully dissent" is a "universal value that needs to be respected," so the world is "rightfully troubled."[27]

The Obama administration informally coordinated with the Europeans in its response to the Iranian election. While the EU supported Obama's approach—as a result of the many "blunderbuss public diplomacy interventions by the U.S.," the Europeans were "basically grateful that [the Americans] weren't putting their foot in their mouths"—many EU actors were also surprised by the mild American reaction to what the Europeans perceived to be "a deeply rigged election." But overall, the Europeans largely agreed, "the net benefit was actually in [the Americans] staying silent."[28]

The administration's critics on the Republican side derided Obama's initial reaction, calling for the president to side squarely with the protesters. "What has occurred is that the election is a fraud, the results are inaccurate, and you're seeing a brutal repression of the people as they protest. The president ought to come out and state exactly those words," said former Massachusetts governor Mitt Romney, adding that it is "very clear that the president's policies of going around the world and apologizing for America aren't working." House Republican whip Eric Cantor criticized "the administration's silence in the face of Iran's brutal suppression of democratic rights" and labeled it "a step backwards for homegrown democracy in the Mideast." Senator John McCain, Obama's 2008 election rival, said that the United States should make clear that it backs anti-Ahmadinejad demonstrators in their battle against "an oppressive, repressive regime." On June 19, 2009, the House of Representatives voted 405–1 to condemn Tehran's crackdown on demonstrators and the government's interference with Internet and cell phone communications. Despite a Democratic-controlled Congress, Republicans were able to initiate and pass the nonbinding resolution as a veiled criticism of Obama.[29]

The debate in Washington was disconnected from the realities on the ground in Iran and the wishes of the prodemocracy forces. Indeed, none of the critics of the Obama administration who called for direct support of the Green movement had asked the leaders of the prodemocracy forces in Iran whether they would welcome such support. First of all, contrary to the perception in Washington, neither the U.S. nor Obama was a major factor in the deliberations of the Mousavi camp. "There was rarely ever, I would say, talk of what is Obama thinking of, what is Obama going to do. We were thinking about how are we going to save ourselves," one of Mousavi's advisers told me. Washington's influence over developments in Iran was minimal— with neither trade, diplomatic relations, nor an embassy on the ground, the United States had few avenues of influence with Iran.[30]

Second, the leaders of the Green movement did not want, did not trust, and did not view American support as helpful. As one of Mousavi's allies said, "Mousavi himself never asked for that endorsement." After thirty years of mutual demonization and enmity, American endorsement of an Iranian politician would be as damaging in Iran's political landscape as an Iranian endorsement of a U.S. politician would be in America's political world. The Green movement leadership did not want to come across as the stooges of a foreign power—and certainly not of Washington. "The Iranian reformers don't want to be perceived as the running dogs or as the agents of some kind of a colored revolution in Iran," said Professor Ahmad

Sadri, who is close to the Karroubi faction of the reformists. "They do not want to appear as if the Americans are supporting them." There were hopes within the Mousavi camp as well that Obama would remain silent out of fear that a higher American profile would benefit the conservative strategy of portraying the Green movement as a foreign-supported-and-controlled force. "We had hoped he would say nothing actually," a Mousavi strategist explained. "They didn't want anyone to play into the hands of conservatives. We were worried that [the Obama administration] might say something stupid. That they would make life more miserable for us."[31]

The fact that Obama refrained from taking sides deprived the conservatives of the ability to convincingly argue that the Mousavi camp was working for foreign agents. It countered efforts by Ahmadinejad to accuse the protesters of being part of a foreign plot carried out by "subversives."[32] The approach was critical, because any hint that the movement was antirevolutionary in nature or could bring about instability risked costing it much valuable support. This was not because discontent with the regime was not widespread but because a significant portion of Iranians feared instability and did not want to repeat the mistake of the 1979 revolution in which one dictatorial regime was replaced—after much upheaval—with another dictatorial regime.

The reformist leadership appreciated Obama's restraint, even though they did not think it would have a major impact on developments in Iran. The reformists were also impressed by Obama's ability to resist pressure from the Republicans on this matter and by his administration's ability to understand the important nuances of the political battle lines in Iran. "I think that was a good move from Obama because he took the position that wasn't detrimental to the movement," one of Mousavi's campaign workers told me. "He was standing at a good distance from the movement, not too close and not too far. That's the position that I think would be ideal." Moreover, the reformists were quite suspicious of U.S. intentions, fearing that Washington would be quick to sacrifice human rights and the democratic aspirations of the Iranian people for the sake of securing a nuclear deal with Ahmadinejad. Even if the U.S. came out in support of the Green movement at the moment, it could easily reverse its position. "An American administration would accept internal suppression [of] human rights inside Iran if Ahmadinejad, Khamenei, and their courts promise the Americans that they're going to suspend nuclear enrichment and cooperate with the Americans in Afghanistan and Iraq," *Newsweek*'s Maziar Bahari told me.[33]

Moreover, the Obama administration's proengagement, anti-confrontation posture had likely contributed to the Green movement's ability to challenge the Iranian government. President George W. Bush sought to destabilize and bring about regime change in Iran for eight years through isolation, threats, and financial support for anti-Tehran groups. For all its labors, the Bush administration failed. The Iranian elite closed ranks, and hard-liners used the perceived threat from the U.S. to clamp down on human rights defenders and prodemocracy activists. Obama's diplomatic outreach and removal of this threat perception did not necessarily create fissures among the Iranian elite in and of itself, but it did weaken the glue that united Iran's many political factions. If the Bush administration still governed and continued to issue threats and provoke confrontation with Iran, Mousavi would probably not have disputed the voter fraud and called on his supporters to take to the streets. Due to the perceived national security threat, Mousavi probably would have swallowed his pride and anger, and would have asked his followers to do the same. The absence of an external threat enabled existing internal differences to come to the surface and bring about an unprecedented political standoff. Internally driven political change could neither have been initiated nor come about under the shadow of an American military threat. If America's posture had returned to that of the Bush administration, the forces of fear and ultranationalism might have swiftly quelled these indigenous forces for change.[34]

The "Iranian streets"—the grassroots of the Green movement— also appreciated Obama's position at first. "The U.S. shouldn't interfere, because a loud condemnation isn't going to affect Iranian domestic politics one way or the other," one of the protesters told Iranian-American journalist Azadeh Moaveni. This view was partly motivated by the desire of many in Iran to resolve the tensions with the U.S. and by the fear that any U.S. interference would jeopardize this opportunity to end the enmity and improve the Iranian economy. "In the end, a dictatorship that doesn't face U.S. sanctions is better off than one that does. Now that after 30 years it seems that we have a chance to negotiate with America, it would be a shame if we lost the chance," another protester said.[35]

To Condemn or Not to Condemn

However, as the Iranian regime's violence against its own citizens became increasingly brutal and the human rights abuses intensified, frustration with Obama's careful approach grew accordingly in Iran, the EU, and the U.S. Obama waited until June 23, 2009, to condemn the violence in Iran. Prior to that, all statements expressed criticism but did not condemn the actions of the Iranian government. The statement came only days after the video of the killing of Iranian student Neda Agha Soltan on the streets of Tehran began airing, over and over again, on American TV stations. Iranian-American academics and policy experts in the U.S. who had been invited to advise the White House had also pressed the administration to condemn the violence and human rights abuses while remaining impartial in the election dispute. "The violence perpetrated against them is outrageous. Despite the government's efforts to keep the world from bearing witness to that violence, we see it and we condemn it," Obama said during a nearly hour-long White House news conference dominated by the unrest in Iran. "As I've said before, the Iranian people will be the ultimate judge of their government's actions, but if the Iranian government desires the respect of the international community, it must respect the rights and heed the will of its people," he continued. Having been advised on the importance of the concept of justice in the Iranian culture, Obama also cast his criticism against the Iranian regime in terms of justice. "No iron fist is strong enough to shut off the world from bearing witness to peaceful protests of justice," Obama said. "Those who stand up for justice are always on the right side of history."[36]

Yet, even after this statement, condemnations of the human rights violations in Iran were few and far between, even though Amnesty International described the human rights situation in Iran to be as poor as at any time in the past twenty years.[37] Obama's reluctance to act and speak more forcefully and frequently on this matter was rooted in several complex calculations. On the one hand, due to Washington's lack of influence over Iran, there were few courses of action the administration believed it could pursue that would actually have an impact. On the other hand, with the experience of the Bush administration in mind, there was a fear that Washington's actions could end up hurting the very people it intended to help. But, perhaps most important, the administration was seeking to avoid a scenario in which a strong profile on the human rights issue would undermine the prospects for diplomacy on the nuclear issue. "We didn't want to affect negatively the possibility of the negotiation on the nuclear issue. So it was calculated that we should rather give the priority to the nuclear negotiations," said a senior European official who was part of the discussions coordinating Washington and Brussels' posture on this issue.[38]

The Obama administration had invested a lot of political capital in testing diplomacy with Iran, and the White House knew that time was not on its side. Shortly after the completion of the policy review and away from public view, Obama had sought to establish a direct channel of communication with Iran's Supreme Leader. A letter had been sent to Khamenei via the Swiss embassy in Tehran—the caretakers of American interests in Iran in the absence of a U.S. embassy there. The first letter had spelled out U.S. interest in direct dialogue with Iran on a broad range of issues with the aim of establishing a qualitatively different relationship between the two countries. Within two weeks, Khamenei sent a reply to Obama. According to several Obama administration officials, the response was mixed but sufficiently positive to warrant a second letter from Obama. But there would be no second reply from Khamenei, as the correspondence between the two got caught in the election crisis. Still, the unprecedented exchanges raised the expectations in the White House that a substantive dialogue could begin after the election, addressing not only the nuclear issue, but regional security, Iraq, and Afghanistan as well. By early June, the White House's mindset was to prepare for diplomacy with Iran—not crisis management over Iran's election fraud and human rights abuses. "They were caught flat-footed by the way [the Iranian] elections turned out. . . . They thought they had a game plan and suddenly they realized everything we prepared for is completely upended," a Senate ally of the White House commented.[39]

The decision to focus on the nuclear file at the expense of the human rights situation was neither easy nor friction-free. In some quarters in Europe, there was both surprise and disappointment in the Obama administration's zero-sum view of the relation between human rights in Iran and the nuclear issue, but little if any pressure was brought on the White House to reconsider its decision. There were also tensions within the Obama administration on this issue. In retrospect, however, both senior U.S. and EU officials concede that the balance struck between the nuclear issue and human rights tilted too far in the direction of the nuclear talks and tended to neglect the gravity of the human rights abuses in Iran. "In retrospect, speaking out stronger against the human rights abuses would have been better, it would have been the right thing," a top Obama official told me.[40]

The split between the formal leadership of the Green movement and its grassroots elements partly centered on the desired reaction of the outside world and the United States. Whereas the leadership initially preferred that the U.S. stay out and stay silent, the streets grew disillusioned with Obama and increasingly leaned toward a more vocal American profile. But even the senior leadership soon began feeling frustration over Washington's relatively weak reaction to the human rights crisis and its singular focus on the nuclear issue. "The main disappointment I think is in the area of continuing to harp on the nuclear issue, which is a real non-issue for the Iranian reformers," Professor Sadri explained. The White House's reluctance to get tough on the human rights issue, either on its own or by acting multilaterally, played into the fears of the Green leaders who viewed the U.S. with great suspicion, particularly the fear that reform and human rights would be sacrificed by the U.S. for a nuclear deal. "It was quite clear that they just were moving all over the place, but their priority was the nuclear issue. Whatever happens to the reform movement, they do not care," an adviser to Mousavi said. This fear had already colored the reformists' view of the Obama administration prior to the election, when there were concerns that Obama would give Ahmadinejad a boost at the polls by starting the talks before June.[41]

The Obama administration did not want to discount or betray the prodemocracy movement, but it grew increasingly doubtful of the Green movement's ability to topple the Ahmadinejad government. "The Green movement never seemed to be a cohesive single political body," Ratney said. "Even the cohesiveness that got them through those demonstrations in the aftermath of the elections started to splinter and it became more and more apparent that you're not talking about one cohesive national resistance movement."[42] Still, administration officials met with several individuals formally or informally associated with the Green movement and sought to accommodate them on matters such as human rights, Internet freedom (U.S. sanctions had significantly aided the Iranian government's efforts to censor and close down the Internet and, consequently, target the Green movement's means of internal and external communication), and diplomacy. Events in Iran had caused the administration to lose both momentum and much of its ability to set the agenda. Soon, developments in Washington would also challenge the White House's ability to set the parameters of its Iran policy.

Seven

Sanctions Versus Diplomacy

After the elections, skepticism in Congress against our strategy turned to outright hostility.

—Senior Obama administration official, October 2010

The election fallout in Iran created an opportunity for opponents of diplomacy to minimize the Obama administration's political space for maneuvering. The images on CNN of the Iranian regime's paramilitary groups shooting pro-Mousavi protesters provided strong impetus to revisit the issue of sanctions in Congress, even though most recognized that sanctioning Iran prior to the commencement of talks could make diplomacy dead on arrival. But a combination of several forces—those seeking sanctions to upstage diplomacy, partisan efforts to undermine Obama, and those who felt that Congress had to take some type of action to demonstrate its opposition to Tehran's nuclear policy and the government's clampdown on protests—ensured that the push for sanctions would be formidable. The violent response to the election protests gave Congress a sense that the Iranian government was wounded and, for some members of Congress, created an opportunity to hit it hard—perhaps even to get rid of it. "The idea of changing the regime has never gone away [in Congress]," a senior congressional staffer said.[1]

The pressure from hawkish pro-Israeli groups for sanctions was particularly intense. The influential lobbying group American Israel

Public Affairs Committee (AIPAC) argued that turmoil in Iran presented an opportunity to ratchet up sanctions. "The world cannot wait for the political situation in Iran to unfold before dealing with the threat of a nuclear-armed Iran. In the chaotic aftermath of the recent disputed presidential election, Iran has not put its nuclear weapons pursuit on hold," its website stated. "A crippling sanctions regime would force Iran's leaders to confront a real choice: continue the nuclear program or face the collapse of Iran's economy and possibly the loss of their own power." In meetings with U.S. lawmakers, Israeli prime minister Benjamin Netanyahu pushed for quick action on gasoline sanctions targeting Iran, placing added pressure on U.S. policy makers. According to a senior Senate staffer deeply involved in legislating sanctions, Israeli lobbying efforts were a direct cause of Congress's decision to shift its focus from divestment to oil and gasoline sanctions.[2]

The pressure from AIPAC, Israel, and other entities on U.S. lawmakers translated into congressional pressure on the White House to act quickly and decisively. From Congress's perspective, it was less about the actual decision over whether to impose sanctions and more about timing. Skepticism over what diplomacy could produce was so great that it was often treated as an item that needed to be cursorily checked off solely to strengthen international support for a new sanctions regime. "Only by making a good-faith effort to engage Iran can we build the support we need from the international community to impose the crippling sanctions necessary should engagement fail," said Howard Berman (D-CA), chairman of the House Foreign Affairs Committee, at a hearing on Iran sanctions in late July 2009. "But while it is important to pursue engagement, it is also critical that these efforts be time-limited, and that the administration be prepared to try a different approach if Iran is not cooperating. I agree with the President's timetable. If by autumn the Iranians are not responsive to U.S. efforts to engage them, it likely will be time to move on, hopefully in close coordination with our allies and other key countries."[3]

The pressure from Congress hardened the Obama administration's approach toward Iran and inhibited the White House's maneuverability. "We were setting important parameters that would shape the final product in key ways," a senior Senate staffer explained. The Obama administration's timetable had already been turned upside down by the election mayhem; congressional efforts to insert itself into the process and set the parameters for discussions further complicated Obama's strategy. "Room for movement shrunk significantly after the June elections," a senior Obama official told me. "It wasn't that great to begin with."[4]

Timing of Sanctions

The dispute between the Obama administration and Congress centered primarily on the timing of sanctions—whether they would be imposed before or after diplomacy and whether Congress should wait for the UN Security Council to act first. Disagreements also existed regarding the extent of sanctions; the Iranian people's courageous struggle for their rights caused the Obama administration to develop greater sensitivity toward the way sanctions would impact the general population in Iran. The term "crippling sanctions," originally favored by Secretary of State Hillary Clinton, had been dropped from the administration's talking points by the summer of 2009. Instead, "targeted sanctions" became the favored concept. The Obama administration sought to communicate to the Iranian people that sanctions were targeting not them but rather the Iranian government. The idea was that the intent and design of sanctions needed to be clearly conveyed to the Iranian masses in order to ensure that the effects of sanctions would not cause the population to turn against the U.S. and rally around the Ahmadinejad government.[5]

The State Department sought to convince Congress to go along with this approach but had limited success. "It's a difficult argument to make because all these sanctions in the end have some effect on the people. And you can't completely insulate them from it," a State

Department official said. Whereas Congress, reacting to pressure from Israel, focused on gasoline sanctions targeting the entire Iranian economy—AIPAC argued that discontent with the Iranian government was so great that the population would blame the effect of sanctions on the Ahmadinejad government and not on the U.S.—the Obama administration was increasingly turning toward sanctions that targeted the Iranian Revolutionary Guards Corps (IRGC) and other institutions of the Iranian regime. The shift toward focusing on the IRGC and lifting some of the sanctions that had inhibited Iranian civilians' access to the Internet constituted the "major philosophical change that we had to demonstrate that we weren't targeting the people," the State Department official said. The argument that the Iranian people should be spared from the impact of sanctions did not find much receptivity on Capitol Hill. And even if it had, it did not seem to matter. "The attitude was, 'Look, if the Iranian people are harmed by this, so be it,'" a senior congressional staffer told me. Some lawmakers stated blatantly that targeting the Iranian people was the aim. "Critics [of the sanctions] also argued that these measures will hurt the Iranian people. Quite frankly, we need to do just that," wrote Congressman Brad Sherman (D-CA) in an op-ed article.[6]

Beyond the risk of harming the Iranian people, the administration considered the Iran Refined Petroleum Sanctions Act to be problematic for several other reasons. Issues arose over the actual implementation of sanctions and the feasibility of monitoring international trade sufficiently enough to identify, track, and prohibit the export and import of targeted petroleum products. There were also concerns over the Iranian government's ability to find and exploit loopholes that would inevitably exist in such a comprehensive sanctions package. Perhaps more important, the gasoline sanctions actually could end up benefiting the Iranian government.

The economics of gasoline in Iran constitute a unique system. Iran had been importing roughly 40 percent of its domestic gasoline consumption at world prices and then selling it, along with domestically refined gasoline, at a government-subsidized price of only forty cents per gallon—far below the actual market price. Over the past ten years, this policy has cost Iran in the range of 10 to 20 percent of its gross domestic product annually, depending on world prices and the government-mandated pump price. In need of additional revenues, successive Iranian administrations have sought to eliminate this subsidy, but all have been paralyzed by the specter of domestic backlash. If gasoline sanctions were imposed, and if they curtailed Iran's ability to buy gasoline on the world market, domestic consumption would decline by 40 percent and government revenues would go up because no payment would be needed for gasoline imports. If Tehran allowed the reduced supply of gasoline to be sold at a price that equated demand with supply, the price would increase to a level that would eliminate the subsidy, meaning no subsidy for imported gasoline and no subsidy for domestically refined gasoline. If the political leaders could weather the domestic backlash, the subsidy headache would be resolved and the Iranian government would end up with more cash on hand to spend elsewhere. In the intense deliberations that took place throughout the summer and fall between the State Department and Congress, this argument "hit home with a lot of staff members." But ultimately the lawmakers just "stopped caring about that argument" and focused only on getting the bill passed. "I don't know what the political marker was, but at some point those arguments stopped having much of an effect," said a State Department official negotiating with the congressional leadership.[7]

The administration's concerns about sanctions also focused on its recognition that what had caused the Iranian people to rise up against the government after the June elections was not economic hardship. While the Iranian economy was badly mismanaged, Iranians had seen much worse times. During the Iran-Iraq war, they faced unprecedented economic hardships, which did not ignite a popular uprising. What did cause Iranians to rise up was not economic suffering but rather dashed hopes and anger over the fraudulent election. If the backbone of the Iranian economy was broken through "crippling" gasoline sanctions, the first casualty would be hope. Economic misery could kill people's faith in a better future. The result would likely be political apathy, which ultimately would benefit the government and not the prodemocracy movement. Congress could be throwing the Ahmadinejad government a lifeline by imposing these sanctions, it was argued. What the administration preferred instead on the energy side was "a European ban on investment in the energy sector, a European ban on selling high-tech."[8]

On the issue of the timing and order of various measures, the State Department argued that sanctions would be more effective if they were multilateral and had substantial international support, preferably through a new UN Security Council resolution. But the administration's ability to mobilize the international community in favor of sanctions would take a huge hit if Congress acted first, particularly if Congress enacted sanctions that would target non-American companies. A multilateral route through the UN would both secure a global response to the Iranian nuclear program and avoid distracting U.S. allies with the bilateral sanctions Congress was weighing. While the State Department argument for multilateralism did carry water, the real disagreement was the pace with which the Obama administration proceeded with the sanctions agenda. Congress pressed for much swifter action, anticipating that diplomacy would inevitably fail. "After the elections, skepticism in Congress against our strategy turned to outright hostility," a senior Obama official said.[9]

White House Skittishness

The State Department's failure to push back against congressional pressure was because of not only the force behind the congressional push—with both the Netanyahu government and hawkish pro-Israeli groups playing a key role—but also the mixed messages that the White House was sending Congress. The White House leaned away from sanctions but for several reasons did not muster a real push against the developments on Capitol Hill. For starters, the White

House was not unified in its position on this issue. Particularly after the June elections, voices of skepticism about diplomacy grew louder, both from senior Obama officials as well as from some of the holdovers from the Bush administration. Second, a distinct line of thinking by some in the White House posited that a visible and growing sanctions threat would compel the Iranians to be more responsive to offers of diplomacy. As such, the noise coming out of Congress could be helpful as long as it did not get out of control. "I have no doubt that there were people in the White House and elsewhere in the administration that saw sanctions as a positive tool," a senior Senate staffer told me. In some cases, senior White House officials privately expressed cautious support for sanctions, contradicting both the White House and the State Department's public stance. Some lawmakers sought clarification from the White House on this matter but did not receive a clear-cut answer.[10]

The pushback from the administration tended to be lackluster and came primarily from lower-level officials. There was "some background noise of 'Why are you pushing us' from the White House, but it was not loud and did not come from senior people," a senior Senate staffer told me. In fact, more criticism came from the State Department, which Congress tended to take less seriously, particularly due to the unusual contrast between the State Department's objections and the White House's relative silence.[11]

The confusion about the White House's position on this matter became even more apparent when the Obama administration's allies in Congress offered to give the president political cover. Several senior Democratic lawmakers spoke out against sanctions and held off cosponsoring the sanctions bills with the intent of helping Obama. These lawmakers were frustrated that the sanctions push had begun so early, disregarding the president's diplomatic strategy. "Supporting Obama meant not supporting sanctions," a senior Democratic staffer told me. These House representatives and senators "stuck out their neck for Obama," but their offers of help were not accepted. "They didn't take advantage of us," the staffer continued. Moreover, the White House did not proactively reach out to lawmakers to seek their assistance on this matter. After a while, congressional offers stopped because the White House offered no clear indications that it appreciated the assistance. Even though congressional supporters of diplomacy recognized that sanctions would create major problems for the administration, they did not want, as one senior Senate staffer said, to "be more Catholic than the Pope" and take on a fight that the White House itself was not willing to support. "If they're falling on their swords and they don't want to get involved, then there is zero political upshot for us," the staffer explained. Because the chances of success in stopping the sanctions push were minor at the outset, and even though fighting the good fight for the administration and for a policy they believed in did have some value, the effort was not worth it if the White House did not even signal its appreciation and support. "If we were going to get rolled, at least doing it as a loyal soldier is one thing," the staffer continued. "But if we were going to get rolled and kind of discarded, there's no upside to that."[12]

Beyond divisions within the White House regarding the utility or consequences of sanctions, two other factors contributed to the administration's indecisive stance on this matter. The divisions within the White House were not necessarily over policy, but rather over politics. Some policy makers favored a stronger stance against sanctions and welcomed the offer of support from senior Democratic lawmakers. But Obama's political advisers were more skittish. Opposing sanctions might have been good policy, but it was bad politics, they argued. It would cost the president tremendous political capital in Congress and could come back to haunt the administration in the midterm elections. Taking a public stance against new sanctions on Iran in the midst of the Iranian regime's televised human rights abuses was not a winning card, the argument read. Moreover, the administration wasn't cognizant of the tsunami-like momentum that the post-election turmoil in Iran gave the sanctions bill. The administration was, at first, somewhat dismissive of the sanctions developments in Congress, thinking that it would not be able to muster the strength to challenge Obama's diplomatic strategy. By the time the White House recognized this impetus, the dismissive mood almost immediately turned into resignation. While many first thought that no action was needed because the sanctions bill was unlikely to pass, many of the same people later felt that no action should be taken because nothing could stop the sanctions. "The die was cast on the sanctions bill" during the summer of 2009, a Senate staffer said. "It was basically understood that sanctions were going to go through. It was just a matter of time. If [the administration] had made a serious push then, it's possible we could be in a slightly different place now."[13]

The Greens and the Sanctions

The collapse of the Mousavi camp's communication capabilities created a leadership vacuum. As the distance grew between the formal leadership and the streets, it became increasingly difficult for Mousavi's staff to maintain their authority and control the message. This communications collapse created challenges for Mousavi and the Green movement's formal leadership on many levels, including their positioning on the pending U.S. sanctions.

Two months into the protests, frustration within the movement was reaching the boiling point. The grassroots were aggravated by the lack of leadership and Mousavi's increasingly moderate stance in comparison to the street's increasingly hardened demands. While Mousavi and Karroubi were framing their struggle as a civil rights movement—meaning a struggle for rights within the existing system —a sizable and vocal segment of the streets was increasingly calling for the overthrow of the system. Mousavi, in turn, was frustrated with the growing number of figures—both inside and outside Iran—who were claiming to speak for the movement. "Things were sort of getting out of control and people were getting emotional, bitter, and angry," an adviser to Mousavi explained. The figureheads outside of Iran's borders were using their freedom of expression mostly to assist in conveying the movement's message and pleas to the international community since the leaders inside Iran either could not or would not speak with foreign media. But the Mousavi camp provided no clear talking points, so outside voices increasingly improvised or presented their personal views as that of the movement. Inevitably, this created contradicting messages that further exacerbated the anger and frustration among the Greens.[14]

This was particularly true on the issue of sanctions. The top leaders within the Green movement vehemently opposed sanctions on several grounds: sanctions stifle the independent entrepreneurial middle class in Iran while strengthening the black market and economic stake controlled by the Revolutionary Guards, they argued. The middle class is the economic backbone of the reformist movement, so why should they support a measure that directly undermines the economic and political health of their base, they asked rhetorically. However, in the name of the Green movement, a few voices on the outside—some of whom had no direct link to the reform movement and had even urged the Iranian people not to vote in the elections—began calling for the U.S. and international community to impose massive sanctions on Iran. In their view, absent such harsh measures from the outside, the Green movement would get crushed. Sanctions could succeed in Iran as they had in South Africa, they argued. Sanctions were viewed as chemotherapy; while they would increase the suffering of the Iranian people, they were nevertheless necessary in order to beat the cancer of the regime. Inside Iran, only a small minority of the top Green movement leadership held these views. Outside of Iran, however, these arguments were advanced by loud voices claiming to speak for the Greens.[15]

Mousavi sought to distance the Green movement from these external arguments by stating that the movement did not have any official representatives or spokespersons outside of Iran. The statement specifically targeted some of the more hard-line figures in the Iranian Diaspora claiming to speak for the Green movement or for Mousavi himself, according to a Mousavi adviser. At first Mousavi resisted commenting on the sanctions issue. He feared that mere commentary on the potential actions of the U.S. would give the impression that the Green movement coordinated its actions with the U.S. government. In addition, the chaotic situation in Iran consumed most of his energy and focus, and neither he nor other leading reformists felt ready to fight both Supreme Leader Khamenei and exiled opposition figures at the same time. Moreover, Mousavi did not want to add to the growing disunity within the Green movement.[16]

But as it became increasingly clear that the U.S. might impose harsher sanctions on Iran, Mousavi realized the danger of not being on the record regarding this matter. The hope was that a statement by him against sanctions would, at best, halt the sanctions push and, at a minimum, make clear that the U.S. did not impose sanctions on Iran due to pressure from the Green movement. "We are against any sanctions against our nation," Mousavi said in a statement posted on a reformist website in late September 2009. Sanctions "will impose agonies on a nation who suffers enough from miserable statesmen," he continued. "We might have simplistically thought this is an advantage for our green movement, but it is not," Mousavi concluded. A few weeks earlier, Karroubi had also rejected sanctions. In an interview with the *Los Angeles Times,* Karroubi said he did not "agree with any outside pressure on any government, as at the end of the day the ordinary people will suffer."[17]

Mousavi's and Karroubi's clarifications of their opposition to sanctions may have created greater understanding in the White House of the desires and priorities of official Green movement leaders. But in Congress it was too little, too late. The Green movement had not generated the push for sanctions, and Iran's prodemocracy forces could not stop it.

Eight

The Confidence-Building Measure

We tried very hard to think of a win-win. Not because we wanted to
do Iran a favor, but because there was no other way to get a deal.

—Senior Obama administration official, July 2010

The Iranian election mayhem turned the Obama administration's timetable and plans for diplomacy upside down, but it did not stop the nuclear clock. Iran's nuclear program was progressing, as were the Obama administration's strategic efforts to bring it to a halt. A critical factor was Iran's growing stockpile of low-enriched uranium (LEU). If the LEU is reenriched to a level of 85 percent or more (from 3.5 percent at the LEU level), it may be converted into high-enriched uranium (HEU) that can be used to build a nuclear warhead. A simple nuclear warhead can be manufactured from approximately 25–50 kilograms of HEU, requiring the reenrichment of approximately 1,300 kilograms of LEU. By summer 2009, Iran had amassed more than 1,500 kilograms of LEU.[1]

Finding a way to get the LEU out of Iran was an important immediate objective of the Obama administration. The further away Iran was from a breakout capability—that is, the technical point at which Iran would have all essential components needed to build a nuclear weapon—the more time there would be for diplomacy. Moreover, there would be less pressure from Israel, as well as from the Republicans and the Saudis, to take military action against Iran. The

Obama administration would have the maneuverability and the leverage vis-à-vis Tehran to be able to negotiate. If, however, the LEU
continued to amass, Washington's bargaining position would weaken
and the voices for more radical measures would be strengthened.

Already in the spring of 2009, several high-level officials in the
State Department's nonproliferation bureau and their counterparts
at the National Security Council got together to brainstorm ways to
begin engagement with Iran and address the nuclear issue. Experience had shown that starting the process by demanding a suspension
of Iran's enrichment activities would not work. Instead, the focus
turned to smaller, confidence-building measures—interim steps that
would be useful to the United States and acceptable to Iran. "We
wanted to break the ice," a senior State Department official explained. "We had a whole variety of ideas, a dozen or so ways of
breaking the ice, establishing some basis of trust and mutual confidence." Many of these ideas addressed the Iranian LEU stockpile.
Part of the challenge was to find a legitimate reason for persuading
the Iranians to ship out their LEU. One State Department official
envisioned the Iranians sending their LEU to Russia for fabrication
of fuel for the Bushehr nuclear power reactor in southern Iran.[2]

Then, suddenly, an unexpected opportunity arose. On June 2,
2009, the Iranian ambassador to the International Atomic Energy
Agency (IAEA), Ali Asghar Soltanieh, sent a letter to the agency
requesting to buy fuel pads for the Tehran Research Reactor (TRR),
a medical research reactor. The forty-year-old U.S.-supplied nuclear
reactor produces medical isotopes for an estimated 850,000 kidney,
heart, and cancer patients. Fuel for the reactor was estimated to run
out by the end of 2010. With a significant shortage of medical isotopes on the international market, these patients would face severe—
even lethal—risks once domestic production dried up. "We have
thousands of patients a month at our hospital alone," said Gholam-
reza Pourmand, a specialist at a Tehran hospital that employs tech-
netium-99, a nuclear medicine used diagnostically by body scanners.
"If we can't help them, some will die. It's as simple as that."[3]

Rather than forwarding Iran's request to all the potential suppliers of fuel, Mohammad ElBaradei, director general of the IAEA, informed just the U.S. and Russia. The Obama administration immediately realized an opportunity. "All of a sudden the IAEA comes to us with this letter and said the Iranians need fuel for the Tehran Research Reactor. And we said, 'Hey, this is similar to an idea we've been working on,'" a senior State Department official commented. Iran was requesting fuel, which made it easier to propose a swap: the supplier countries would use Iran's own LEU to produce the fuel pads. The Obama administration devised a plan in which 1,200 kilograms of Iranian LEU would be shipped out to a supplier country, preferably Russia, where it would be reprocessed to 19.75 percent enriched uranium and subsequently turned into fuel pads. The swap had numerous benefits. The whole process could conceivably be completed in twelve months and would be mutually advantageous: Iran would get fuel for its research reactor before running out of medical isotopes, and the U.S. would get the LEU out of Iran, thereby creating a window of opportunity for more serious negotiations. "Getting 1,200 kilograms [of LEU] out would get you six months of time, and a lot of political space. We could tell the Israelis and the Congress to relax," a State Department nonproliferation official told me. Washington would gain up to a year of "relatively tension-free time of seeing whether we could work something out" on the larger nuclear issue, the official stated. The implementation of such a confidence-building measure might result in an atmosphere that was more conducive to addressing the trickier parts of the nuclear challenge. The TRR swap could provide the West with "not only [a] time-out, but an opportunity to transcend the entrenched positions," according to Germany's UN ambassador, Peter Wittig.[4]

Moreover, time was running out on several other fronts. If the Iranians did not get the fuel, they could begin enriching the LEU themselves to 19.75 percent and, in doing so, creep closer to mastering the nuclear fuel cycle. "If we don't respond to this, somehow they're going to use this as a pretext to enrich to 20 percent. And that was a big issue," a European diplomat explained. (The Iranians argued that the request to *purchase* the fuel pads showed that Iran did not have the intention to enrich at 20 percent.) There was also a need to find a creative way around the precondition of suspending enrichment. Demanding suspension up front had failed, but if the swap could build some confidence between the parties, Iran might be more amenable to a verifiable suspension. "The Tehran research reactor was in a sense a device that would allow us to finesse the suspension point," according to a diplomat involved in the U.S.–EU strategy efforts. In addition, the Obama administration believed the swap had all the hallmarks of a win-win deal. Without entailing too great a risk, both sides would obtain something they desired without giving up too much. This delicate arrangement was necessary because both sides had veto power over the final outcome; either one could walk away from the deal, so it had to be compelling. "We tried very hard to think of a win-win," a senior Obama administration official said. "Not because we wanted to do Iran a favor, but because there was no other way to get a deal."[5]

Legitimizing Iranian Enrichment?

The main win for Iran would be the implicit recognition of its enrichment activities. After all, Iran's own LEU would be used for the fuel pads, and as such, a certain level of recognition, legitimacy—and perhaps legality—of Iran's enrichment activities would be granted. The Obama administration and its allies believed that Iran could view this arrangement as a great victory—a victory that they "could have sold to their public as a breakthrough." But precisely because Iran could consider it a win and claim some "bragging rights," the proposal raised concerns in Washington and Europe that the TRR deal could be too big of a concession. "This is even worse than saying that the endgame is not zero-enrichment," a European official said. "This is recognition, official recognition." The TRR swap would grant the Iranians a gift without the West receiving anything in return, this argument read. There was also a fear that the TRR deal, which was meant merely as a confidence-building measure and not as a strategic end unto itself, could become the centerpiece of negotiations and overshadow the more critical parts of the Iranian nuclear challenge.[6]

Consequently, many of America's allies viewed the proposal with some skepticism, some even showing outright opposition. This included EU states, such as France, which preferred to move more quickly toward sanctions rather than negotiations. The French analysis of the June 12 election was that it amounted to a coup, with radical forces taking over the country, thereby further narrowing the likelihood of successful talks. "We were more in favor of going to sanctions," said Gérard Araud, France's UN ambassador. "We were a bit skeptical about this proposal as a distraction." The French viewed the proposal as "extremely dangerous" since it could legitimize Iranian enrichment and be confused with a final settlement on the nuclear program. How could the international community turn the focus back to the enrichment in Natanz if the fuel swap deal was successful, the French asked. To the French, the swap did not have much nonproliferation value, but rather it was motivated by Obama's political constraints at home.[7]

The Israelis also sounded an alarm. Israel had urged the United States to abandon diplomacy with Iran immediately after the elections. "If we had any shred of hope for change in Iran, the reelection of Ahmadinejad demonstrates the increasing Iranian threat," Deputy Foreign Minister Danny Ayalon said. "The election results in Iran are blowing up in the face of those who thought that Iran is built for real dialogue with the free world." The TRR deal carried a lot of risk from the Israeli perspective because Israel's redline demarcated zero-enrichment in Iran as the optimal outcome, Ayalon told me. The reaction and concerns of Israel, as well as those of some key Arab allies, were important to Washington's calculations; significant alliance management was needed to successfully negotiate with Iran. These states were "extremely nervous" that Washington would cut a nuclear deal with Iran at the expense of changing Iran's behavior in the region. According to a senior Obama administration official, extensive and continuous efforts were made to convince the Israelis to go along with Obama's strategy as a whole, including the TRR. "Israel was a very significant factor in our calculations," he said.

In spite of these pressures and objections, the administration ultimately felt that the swap was worth the risk. The White House considered the issue of recognizing Iran's enrichment as an acknowledgment of current realities on the ground, rather than as acceptance of a permanent feature. And if the swap were not pursued, Iran would continue to amass LEU, which in turn would increase the pressure domestically in the U.S. to abandon diplomacy.[8]

There were other time-sensitive factors in pushing for the TRR deal. ElBaradei's term as director general of the IAEA was ending later in the fall. This was his last chance to push for a solution to the Iranian nuclear question. ElBaradei immediately saw the benefits of the swap proposal and was extremely supportive of it. To the director general, this was not just about the nuclear issue but also about ending U.S.-Iran enmity and stabilizing the region as a whole. Iran was the gate toward a more stable Middle East, in ElBaradei's view. The issue of "legitimizing" Iran's enrichment activities was not a concern for him since he disagreed with the view that Iran did not enjoy such a right to begin with. "Legally they have the right to enrich uranium the way Japan, Brazil, Germany, the thirteen, fourteen countries are having the right to enrich," he said on *Charlie Rose* in the U.S.[9]

Reset with Russia

As soon as the swap concept was sufficiently developed, the Obama administration reached out to Moscow to get Russian support. At this point, the pace of events picked up significantly. On August 6, 2009, a small team of officials—led by Robert Einhorn, the State Department's special adviser for nonproliferation and arms control;

Rexon Ryu, assistant to National Security Advisor Jim Jones; State Department special adviser Jim Timbie; and Kurt Kessler from the U.S. Mission to the IAEA—traveled to Moscow and pitched the idea to both the Russian Foreign Ministry and Rosatom, the Russian state atomic energy corporation. After a few phone calls and one additional meeting, the Russians were onboard, and Einhorn and the Russian ambassador to the IAEA, Alexander Vladimirovich Zmeyevskiy, presented ElBaradei with a joint U.S.-Russian response to the Iranian request.[10]

Several factors drove the administration to partner with Russia. For starters, "reset" with Russia was a priority for the White House because it believed that Moscow was needed both for negotiations with Iran and for ensuring that the Russians did not stand in the way of any potential Security Council sanctions down the road. Russia enjoyed significant trade and nuclear cooperation with Iran, and a sanctions regime without Russian cooperation could not be effective, Washington believed. Reset was also needed to diminish Iran's ability to take advantage of divisions within the UN Security Council. By making Russia a partner, the Security Council would be more united and effective. And with Russia onboard, the White House predicted, China would be less inclined to resist America's line of action on Iran. "I would tell you that the rapprochement between Russia and the United States started very early on in 2009, and that Iran was one of the central reasons for that rapprochement," Jones said. Moreover, the Russians were deeply familiar with the Iranian energy system, and could both deal with the contaminated Iranian LEU and replace the LEU if need be due to their own sizable stockpile. And since ElBaradei had sent the Iranian request for fuel pads to Russia and the U.S., it was natural for the White House to coordinate a response with Moscow.[11]

Russia's analysis of the Iranian nuclear program differed significantly from that of the U.S. Moscow did not believe hard evidence existed that confirmed a military dimension to Iran's nuclear program. The Iranian program was also sufficiently transparent to make it easy to detect any resources diverted to military use, according to the Russians. Nor did Russia singularly view Iran as a threat; it was "much more than a country which might cause concern in the international community," Russian foreign minister Sergei Lavrov told Senator Carl Levin (D-MI) at a meeting on April 15, 2009. Russia had a "rich bilateral agenda" with Iran, he said, adding that Tehran wielded a lot of influence in the region, including in Afghanistan, Iraq, Lebanon, and Gaza. When pressed on the need for sanctions, Russia did not hesitate to remind the Obama administration that the Iranian challenge could have been resolved long ago had Washington taken Moscow's advice and pursued robust diplomacy with Iran years earlier. "Iran is a partner that has never harmed Russia in any way," Lavrov said at a press conference in Moscow. Still, the Russians welcomed Obama's willingness to engage with Tehran and were prepared to undertake the "dual-track" approach—that is, first offering incentives to Iran but keeping in reserve punitive measures in the form of economic sanctions. The Obama administration's new approach "give[s] us a much better chance than we had in the past. We will do everything we can to make it work," Lavrov told Levin. The fuel swap proposal also had the added advantage of being a win-win arrangement between Russia and the U.S., which strongly attracted decision makers in Moscow. "They immediately saw the value of working with us on that," a senior U.S. State Department official said.[12]

During the General Conference of the IAEA in Vienna on September 14–18, 2009, ElBaradei met privately with the head of the Iranian Atomic Energy Organization, Ali Akbar Salehi, and Ambassador Soltanieh. He gave the Iranians a one-page general description of the U.S.-Russian idea of the swap. Its key point notes that Iran would receive the fuel pads it requested if it gave up 1,200 kilograms of its LEU. The details of the deal would be worked out, Russia and the U.S. proposed, through direct negotiations. ElBaradei told the Iranians that they had until the end of the month to respond to the offer. A week later, the political directors of the permanent members of the Security Council, along with Germany's political director—

"P5+1"—met in Geneva. Undersecretary for Political Affairs William Burns, Robert Einhorn from the State Department, and Puneet Talwar from the National Security Council led the U.S. delegation and began finalizing a strategy for the anticipated talks with Iran.[13]

From the time it was informed of the Iranian request for fuel pads, the Obama administration worked at a ferocious pace to prepare and launch the fuel swap talks. The process was not held up by the turmoil in Iran over the fraudulent elections, as U.S. intelligence assessments concluded that the Iranian government was not likely to fall. And even if it did, an Iranian nuclear program and LEU stockpile would still exist and would have to be addressed, the intelligence agencies argued. But Iran's willingness to talk and its actual capability to do so were two wholly different matters. Even if the government was not about to fall, it was arguably still incapacitated by the intense infighting among political elites. The British government told the Obama administration that the Iranian government was "in a state of flux" and "not focused." In other words, the political ability to respond to overtures was unlikely. But the administration felt that beginning talks was a "proposition worth testing." There was no conclusive evidence that the Iranian government was fully incapable of negotiating, but time was running out, political pressure against diplomacy was growing rapidly in the U.S. Congress, and the White House felt "it had a leg up" precisely because of the internal crisis in Iran. Still, this was not a small decision. Diplomacy with Iran had, until this point, been purely theoretical. Now it was real, but it would be with a government that had, in the previous months, ruthlessly and repressively cracked down on its own citizens. "This was the first crisis of principles for the Obama administration," one of the American architects of the nuclear swap told me.[14]

Revelation in Qom

Talks between the P5+1 and Iran were scheduled for October 1, 2009, in Geneva. But the revelation of a previously undisclosed nuclear facility in Iran just days before the talks were to begin cast a shadow over the event in advance. During ElBaradei's meeting with Salehi and Soltanieh, the Iranians handed over a confidential letter disclosing the existence of a nuclear site outside the city of Qom in central Iran. The site was under construction and was not yet operational. Once completed, it could accommodate three thousand centrifuges. On September 23, 2009, Soltanieh met with Olli Heinonen, chief of the safeguards department at the IAEA, to begin discussions regarding permission for agency access to the site. Soon thereafter, ElBaradei flew to the opening of the United Nations General Assembly in New York, where he raised the issue with Undersecretary William Burns and Gary Samore, special assistant to the president on nonproliferation and disarmament. ElBaradei asked if the Obama administration already knew of the site. It did. And the U.S. knew that Iran knew that it knew. But the U.S. was not aware that Iran planned to reveal the site's existence prior to the October 1 meeting.[15]

The Iranians described the facility as a "pilot plant." Iran already had a pilot plant in Natanz, so to the West this duplicate effort was highly suspect. It pointed to either a parallel military-run nuclear enrichment program, or an Iranian attempt to reinforce the strategic depth and survivability of its nuclear program in the face of potential U.S. or Israeli military strikes against Iranian nuclear sites. The Iranians, in turn, argued that the threats from the U.S. and Israel had compelled them to keep the facility a secret. "We had to be cautious and show vigilance and to take precautions . . . to make sure that the enrichment process would not be suspended even a second," Soltanieh said. "In the worst case if Natanz is attacked, we will have a contingency." There were questions as to whether Iran violated its obligations under the nuclear nonproliferation treaty (NPT) regarding stipulations that required informing international authorities of a new nuclear facility. Originally, such declarations were not required until six months before fuel was introduced into the facility. As the Iranians had yet to fuel the plant, the Iranians argued, no violation had taken place. However, in 1992 the IAEA amended the rule to require nations to inform it the moment the decision is made to build a facility, before construction begins. The amendment, called Code 3.1, was mandatory. But in 2006 the Iranian parliament decided it would revert to the original treaty and six-month notification—a legally questionable move.[16]

The United States and some of its EU allies had known about the site's existence since the latter years of the Bush administration. The question of whether and when to confront Iran was dependent on the tactical and strategic benefits the U.S. could extract from such a move. One plan was to have Undersecretary William Burns bring up the issue privately with the Iranian national security adviser Saeed Jalili at the October 1 meeting in Geneva. This move carried the benefit of signaling U.S. sincerity by deferring an opportunity to embarrass Iran publicly while providing it with an incentive to come clean. The opposite tack, confronting Iran publicly with such a revelation, could increase domestic pressure for military action.[17]

But the Iranian move to break the news to the IAEA before the U.S. and its allies acted on its intelligence reports stole the initiative from Washington. Instead of risking exposure by the U.S., which would damage the Iranians' claim that they were in compliance with the NPT, the Iranians informed the IAEA themselves and sought to spin it as evidence of Iranian transparency. The U.S. and its allies believed they had to move quickly to question the legality of the facility and put Iran on the defensive. Teams from London, Paris, and Washington traveled to Vienna to present evidence that the Iranians had violated the NPT, and that the small enrichment facility in Qom could serve only military purposes. Within the Western camp, the French argued for an aggressive approach, including a strong denunciation of Iran at the Security Council as well as at the upcoming G20 (international group of twenty finance ministers and central bank governors) meeting in Pittsburgh on September 24–25. The Obama administration opposed the idea of using the G20 meeting to headline this issue since it would take attention away from the declaration for a world without nuclear weapons—Obama's personal initiative. In the end, the U.S., France, and the United Kingdom held a joint press conference on the margins of the G20 after the summit.[18]

Obama opened the press conference with a statement that challenged Iran on its nuclear intentions while keeping the door to negotiations open:

> Iran has a right to peaceful nuclear power that meets the energy needs of its people. But the size and configuration of this facility is inconsistent with a peaceful program. Iran is breaking rules that all nations must follow—endangering the global non-proliferation regime, denying its own people access to the opportunity they deserve, and threatening the stability and security of the region and the world. . . . We remain committed to serious, meaningful engagement with Iran to address the nuclear issue through the P5-plus-1 negotiations. Through this dialogue, we are committed to demonstrating that international law is not an empty promise; that obligations must be kept; and that treaties will be enforced."

French president Nicolas Sarkozy adopted a tougher tone, arguing that past negotiations with Iran produced no success and that, in this severe confidence crisis, if there is not an "in-depth change by the Iranian leaders" by December, sanctions will have to be implemented. Adopting a similar tone, British prime minister Gordon Brown said that "the international community has no choice today but to draw a line in the sand."[19]

Back in Washington, the Democrat-controlled Congress continued to take a harder line than Obama. The revelation of the Qom facility "casts a heavy shadow over the negotiations scheduled for next week," said Howard Berman (D-CA), chairman of the House Foreign Affairs Committee. Iran had been "lying to the international community for years about its allegedly peaceful nuclear intentions,"

Berman continued, declaring that this had reinforced his determination to have the committee consider new sanctions legislation in October. Unlike the West, Russia had been unaware of the Qom facility. While it was angered by the Iranian move, it also felt irritated that the U.S. and its European partners had not shared their intelligence.[20]

The saga around the Qom facility soured the atmosphere before talks could begin. But the prediplomacy posturing had already begun before the Qom revelation. The Obama administration was signaling that it was laying the groundwork for sanctions that would cut Iran's economic links to the rest of the world if the talks failed, a tactic that was in line with the assumptions behind the dual-track policy—that diplomacy would be successful only if it contained a strong coercive component. Rather than undermine diplomacy by eroding confidence, the threat of sanctions would compel the Iranians to move in the right direction, it was believed. Congress echoed the threat of sanctions, and the House of Representatives adopted new sanctions targeting Iran's gasoline sector on the same day talks in Geneva began. The congressional moves came in the aftermath of significant pressure from the Israeli prime minister and Jewish-American organizations. In mid-September more than three hundred Jewish communal leaders converged on Washington to push for increased pressure on Iran. Among the speakers at the gathering were AIPAC executive director Howard Kohr, Anti-Defamation League national director Abraham Foxman, American Jewish Committee executive director David Harris, and Malcolm Hoenlein, executive vice chairman of the Conference of Presidents of Major American Jewish Organizations. The conference organizers lamented Washington's and the international community's lack of urgency on Iran, leaving Jewish-American organizations with no choice but to be at the forefront of this issue. "We do not have the luxury to not lead" on Iran, Foxman said, while acknowledging that the groups' concerns might be dismissed as simply a Jewish issue. The pressure from the Jewish organizations was followed by personal phone calls from Netanyahu to six congressional leaders, including House Speaker Nancy Pelosi, immediately before the Geneva talks, urging the United States to pursue "crippling sanctions" against Iran.[21]

But the prediplomacy posturing included more than threats of pressure. In an unprecedented move, the Obama administration gave the Iranian foreign minister, Manouchehr Mottaki, permission to visit the Iranian consulate in Washington, two days before the Geneva meeting. Although the administration said that there were no plans for the minister to meet with any American officials, his curiously timed visit seemed to have been a small confidence-building measure to help put the Geneva talks on a good footing. At a minimum, some Iranian media interpreted the move as an indication of U.S. sincerity in regard to diplomacy with Iran.[22]

Act I: Geneva

After more than nine months, the first face-to-face meeting finally took place between the U.S. and Iran since Obama assumed office. On October 1, officials from Iran and the P5+1, along with the High Representative for the Common Foreign and Security Policy of the EU, Javier Solana, held a one-day meeting in Geneva. William Burns, Robert Einhorn, and Puneet Talwar led the American delegation. On the other side of the table sat Saeed Jalili and his deputy Ali Bagheri. It was the first opportunity for the Obama administration to directly test Iran's interest in diplomacy in general, and the fuel swap proposal in particular.

From the U.S. perspective, the top agenda item was Iran's nuclear program and the fuel swap proposal. The U.S. did not object to other issues being placed on the agenda as long as the nuclear issue was included and given priority. The nuclear issue constituted "a dimension of Iranian behavior that posed a direct threat to our security and the security of our friends and allies in the region," said Michael Ratney of the U.S. State Department. Some discussions were held with U.S. allies on how to take action on the human rights front without broadening the diplomatic agenda. Some of these ideas were born out of discussions with Iranian prodemocracy elements, including an invitation for Mehdi Karroubi to address the EU parliament; to have the UN designate a special rapporteur on human rights in Iran; and to have Obama grant an interview to an Iranian journalist to directly address the human rights crisis in Iran.

In the end, these conversations lacked sincerity of purpose, and none of these options were pursued in 2009 and no real efforts were made to put human rights on the agenda for the October 1 meeting. For one thing, there was not a lot of fertile ground between the U.S. and the EU, on the one hand, and Russia and China, on the other, to address the human rights issue in Iran through the P5+1 channel. For another, there was a fear that if the agenda were expanded, the other issues could overshadow the nuclear file and render a solution more difficult. The nuclear question was America's top priority and the issue over which it faced the greatest amount of pressure from its friends and allies. "That was the most important issue that the Israelis pressed on," a top Obama official said in explaining the American decision not to pursue these issues.[23] The Iranians, on the other hand, agreed to address the nuclear issue as long as a wide range of other global problems were on the agenda. For Tehran, having the great powers engage with Iran on global matters could be spun as a victory in and of itself.

Once the meeting began, the atmosphere was surprisingly positive. The morning session began with relatively short opening speeches. The brevity of the Iranian opening statement—although it lacked originality in its substance—was nevertheless viewed as a positive sign. In previous meetings Jalili had presented long monologues addressing the many injustices Iran had suffered at the hand of Western powers without going into the nuclear issue. This had earned him a reputation of being an "unbearable person" among the Europeans and Americans. "You were obliged to be very, very patient" when engaging with him, a European diplomat complained. While the first European encounter with Jalili months earlier in

London had been "totally horrible," there was a much more constructive atmosphere in Geneva, and Jalili's conduct was described as "almost normal." Still, in his initial soliloquy, Jalili failed to address the nuclear issue. One of the Western ambassadors pointed this out to him at the end of his talk. Jalili thanked him for calling attention to it, after which he recounted the Iranian position on the global nonproliferation regime—without addressing the Iranian nuclear file itself.[24]

The substantive talks on the Iranian nuclear issue took place in the afternoon. As the morning session wrapped up and the parties broke for lunch, Burns approached Jalili and suggested that the U.S. and Iranian delegations engage in a private discussion. Jalili assented, and Burns, Talwar, Einhorn, Jalili, and Bagheri went aside for a bilateral session. Burns opened by presenting the Obama administration's approach and genuine desire for a better relationship with Iran. Common interests existed between the two countries, and, while those should be explored—and the U.S. was willing to discuss these issues—the nuclear issue was a major concern for the United States that needed to be addressed as well. Burns emphasized that Obama was seeking new ways and mechanisms to address a whole range of issues, and that the president was entering this process with pure intentions. The U.S. had ideas about a number of long-term solutions to the problem, Burns explained, but believed that starting the process with the fuel swap would be an important confidence-building step.[25]

The U.S. delegation went over the swap concept again: that 1,200 kilograms of Iranian LEU would be shipped to Russia for reprocessing and then sent to a third country to turn it into fuel pads, after which the fuel would be sent to Iran for the Tehran Research Reactor. Jalili responded that, in principle, the Iranians agreed to the concept and were open to discussing it in greater detail. The U.S. then moved on to other issues. First, Burns explained, having episodic encounters was not productive. Rather, the two countries should meet more frequently and regularly to resolve their tensions—

both nuclear and nonnuclear. Burns proposed that the parties meet again before the end of October to hold substantive, detailed discussions on the swap idea, to which Jalili agreed. Next, the Americans expressed their concerns about the Qom facility. Jalili quickly corrected Burns, stating that the facility was called not Qom but Fordu. Apparently, the Iranians did not want it to be associated with the holy city of Qom, so they insisted on a change of terminology. But Jalili did accept the American request to have the IAEA inspect the site within two weeks. Burns also broached the issue of human rights, in particular the detention of three Americans accused of spying. Jalili raised Iran's concerns, including the need for a world free of nuclear bombs and access to peaceful nuclear energy for all. The meeting lasted less than an hour but was viewed as a success because an understanding had been reached on three critical points: that a second meeting would be held by the end of October to finalize the swap; that through the swap Iran would hand over 1,200 kilograms of its LEU; and that Iran would fully cooperate with the IAEA and grant access to the Qom facility. Both sides were cordial and played it fair, according to a top Obama administration official. (Burns asked Einhorn to stay behind and go over the details once more with Bagheri to ensure that there was a common understanding on these points.)[26]

The rest of the day was primarily spent on negotiating the statements of the two sides to the press. Though no joint statement was issued, detailed negotiations took place on the individual statements that would be made by the various parties. "Even the language was negotiated," said an EU official involved in the talks, "word by word, comma by comma." At the conclusion of the talks, a joint press conference was held by the two sides—Iran and the P5+1 represented by Solana—at which their statements on the talks were delivered. Solana first declared that the two sides had "agreed to intensify dialogue in coming weeks" and that progress was expected in regard to an additional meeting at the end of October. The agenda for that meeting would be worked out through diplomatic channels, he said.

"It will focus on nuclear issues, including proposals previously put forward by both sides. It will also deal with global issues that any of the parties wish to address." Second, Iran would cooperate fully and immediately with the IAEA on the new enrichment facility near Qom. Third, the statement described the agreement "in principle that low enriched uranium produced in Iran would be transported to third countries for further enrichment and fabrication into fuel assemblies for the Tehran Research Reactor, which produces isotopes for medical applications." Jalili, in turn, called the discussions "good talks that will be a framework for better talks," and expressed satisfaction that the world had engaged with Iran's global agenda.[27]

Back in Washington, Obama expressed cautious optimism later that day about the talks, while emphasizing what the world expected from Iran. "This is a constructive beginning, but hard work lies ahead," Obama said. "We've entered a phase of intensive international negotiations, and talk is no substitute for action. Pledges of cooperation must be fulfilled. . . . We've made it clear that we will do our part to engage the Iranian government on the basis of mutual interest and mutual respect, but our patience is not unlimited." Despite the president's stern tone, it was clear that the administration was satisfied with the outcome. This was further reinforced by the initial triumphant tone in Iran, which strengthened the administration's belief that the Iranian government could go through with the agreement. Senior hard-line cleric Ayatollah Ahmad Khatami described the Geneva talks as a victory for the Islamic Republic of Iran. "Prior to the talks, [the West] used to speak of suspension and sanctions against Iran but after the talks, there has not been any word of suspension or sanctions. Rather, Iran's package of proposals was the axis," he said in his Friday prayers sermon a week after the Geneva talks. High-ranking Iranian officials, including Ahmadinejad, Iranian parliament (*Majles*) Speaker Ali Larijani, and other influential members of parliament, all expressed support and measured optimism regarding the talks.[28]

If the subsequent talks were successful and Iran agreed to the swap, it would be a major accomplishment that would set back Iran's breakout capability while creating more space and promise for additional diplomacy, which in turn could lead to significant positive reverberations in Iraq and Afghanistan. "At the end of the Geneva meeting, everybody thought that maybe we were at a turning point, maybe this was the beginning of a new process," an EU diplomat involved in the talks said.[29]

Act II: Vienna

The optimism after Geneva lasted only a few days. Shortly after the October 1 meeting, Annalisa Giannella and Robert Cooper from the High Representatives of the Council of the European Union met with Ali Bagheri in Geneva to determine the date and the agenda for the next (political-level) meeting between Jalili and Solana. (The follow-up meeting agreed upon in Geneva was a technical-level discussion.) No agreement could be reached, as essentially the Iranians wished to discuss any matter other than the nuclear issue. This development had a deep impact on the European assessment of Iran's sincerity. In the European view this was a tactic of delay; by raising expectations, a pending negative response from the international community is delayed because of an increased fear that mounting pressure could squash a potential opportunity. "It delays the new Security Council resolution. It delays a bad reaction. They always do that. This is what they have done since 2003," a European official complained.[30]

At the same time, in spite of the success in Geneva, both Congress and the White House proceeded with their respective sanctions plans. One week after the Geneva meeting, ten key allies of the United States convened at the Department of Treasury in Washington under the guidance of Daniel Glaser, deputy assistant secretary of the Treasury, to build consensus on new economic sanctions. But while the Obama administration focused on *multilateral financial sanctions* targeting Iran's economic links to the outside world, Congress continued to push the White House for *unilateral gasoline sanctions*. At a Senate hearing just a few days before the gathering at the Treasury, Congress pressed the administration to move faster on the sanctions track, in spite of the initial diplomatic success in Geneva.[31]

The administration's line against the congressional push focused on three key arguments: the effectiveness of multilateral sanctions versus unilateral sanctions; the need to minimize impact on the general population (on whom gasoline sanctions would be less targeted); and timing of sanctions. "It's very critical that we get the support of the Security Council if we can because that really strengthens the effectiveness," Deputy Secretary of State James Steinberg told the Senate. "I do think we always have to worry about the humanitarian impact and the political impact [of proposed sanctions] because we want to take advantage of the dynamic there and not to undercut the opposition, not to hurt those who are being courageous." At the same time, Steinberg and other administration officials raised questions about the gasoline sanctions that were favored by Congress and the Israeli prime minister. "I think we have not reached a firm conclusion about whether the net benefits [of gasoline sanctions] and the net costs would have the [desired] effect," Steinberg said.[32]

By the start of the second round of negotiations, which were held under the auspices of the IAEA in Vienna on October 19, 2009, expectations had already dampened. The configuration of the talks had also changed. Whereas in Geneva the talks were between the P5+1 and Iran, the Vienna discussions were at a technical level between the parties who would be involved in the proposed fuel swap, the so-called Vienna Group—the U.S., Russia, France, the IAEA, and Iran. ElBaradei and his team of deputies led the meetings. The Iranians were represented by Ambassador Soltanieh, who frequently consulted with Ali Akbar Salehi, head of the Iranian Atomic Energy Organization, back in Tehran. Deputy Secretary of Energy Daniel Poneman led the U.S. delegation, which also included Robert Einhorn, Puneet Talwar, and Mike Hammer from the National Security Council. The Americans hoped that their high-level delegation would prompt Tehran to send Salehi, the principal negotiator in Iran on technical matters, to Vienna. Instead, he adopted the role of a shadow negotiator who conducted his own talks with ElBaradei on the side by phone. The talks lasted three full days, with negotiations taking place during the day and deliberations with colleagues and superiors back in the participants' respective home countries at night. Even on the third day, when the negotiators were reaching a point of exhaustion, the atmosphere remained respectful and constructive.

ElBaradei, who had only weeks left of his term as director general of the IAEA, led the meeting with focus and determination, knowing full well that this would be his last chance to find a solution to the Iranian nuclear challenge. The meetings started with a more detailed presentation on the swap proposal. Though it did not differ from the U.S.-Russian proposal from September, except for its greater level of detail, it had now been adopted by ElBaradei and was referred to as the ElBaradei proposal—a development that did not please the Iranians. The additional details specified that 1,200 kilograms of Iranian LEU would be transferred to Russia in one shipment. The Russians would enrich the uranium to 19.75 percent, after which it would be sent to France for fuel production. After approximately nine to twelve months, the first batch of fuel pads would be delivered to Iran. The full amount of fuel would not be delivered until two years after Iran had handed over its LEU to Russia. Whether the LEU would be shipped in one or more batches had not been specified in Geneva, nor had the exact timeline for the delivery of fuel been set. "The terms of the understanding [in Geneva] were that 1,200 kilograms would be exported quickly," an EU official involved in the talks explained. According to the U.S., however, Jalili understood in Geneva that Washington was looking for the LEU to leave Iran in a single batch even though this was not explicitly specified. Still, what Jalili thought he was agreeing to in Geneva was not the single-batch request, but rather a discussion of the proposal in Vienna, a top Obama official explained.[33]

The Iranians opened by questioning the very principle of the swap proposal. They argued that the motivation for the precondition during the Bush administration was to prevent Iran from increasing its LEU stockpile. By requiring Iran to give up its LEU in order to get fuel pads for a research reactor that carried no proliferation risk, the West had changed only the manner in which this precondition was put forward, rather than eliminating it altogether. For the Iranians, the principle behind the fuel swap was unfair. Iran had purchased fuel for the reactor on the international market before, so there was no basis for forcing Iran to pay for the fuel with its own LEU, they argued. Soltanieh opened his presentation by reminding everyone that it was he who had made the request to purchase fuel pads for the TRR in the early 1990s from then–director general of the IAEA, Hans Blix. The IAEA notified all suppliers at the time and Iran ended up purchasing the fuel from Argentina. "We paid for it and we got it," Soltanieh told me. "Now we wanted the same thing. . . . We were ready to have a contract, agreement, and pay for it." Moreover, even if the idea of using Iran's own LEU to produce the fuel pads was to be accepted, the calculations of the U.S. and Russia were questionable, the Iranians said. With advancements in technology, the Iranians maintained, 800 kilograms of LEU was needed to provide the same amount of fuel Iran had received from Argentina decades earlier. This amount was 400 kilograms less than the U.S. calculation, which the Iranians argued was politically rather than technologically motivated.[34]

Iran also took aim at France's involvement in the deal, which immediately became a point of contention. Because of the political situation in Washington, the U.S. did not want to produce the fuel pads for the Iranian government, so it had to search for states willing and technically able to conduct that part of the swap. Already by October 1 the U.S. had secured France's agreement to participate in the swap. The Iranians, however, claimed that they were not informed of France's involvement in the Vienna Group until just a few days before the second round of talks. The Iranians argued that past business dealings with the government of France had left Tehran distrustful. This feeling was largely, but not exclusively, due to the bitter legal dispute between Tehran and Paris over Eurodif, a multinational enrichment facility based in France that Iran had helped fund. France's refusal to deliver enriched uranium from the plant to Iran—even though Iran held a 10 percent share of the plant—had fueled Iranian mistrust of outside nuclear suppliers and, consequently, its belief in the need for achieving energy independence by supplying all elements of the nuclear fuel cycle itself.[35]

After revisiting the Eurodif dispute, Soltanieh pointed out that France was also holding on to fifty tons of uranium concentrate powder—yellow cake—that belonged to Iran. He argued that rather than using Iran's LEU, France should return the yellow cake to Iran so that a portion of it could be used for the fuel swap. "Roughly about ten tons of it could be converted to this fuel," Soltanieh calculated. Alternatively, if France did not wish to send it back to Iran, it could send the yellow cake to Russia. The Russians could use the remaining forty tons for Iran's nuclear energy plant in Bushehr. The French delegation refused both suggestions. The Iranians capitalized on the French rejection to push France out of the deal. Soltanieh argued that if the French would refuse to deliver natural uranium to Iran or Russia, how could Iran trust it to deliver uranium enriched to 19.75 percent?[36]

But the Iranian suspicion of France was not based solely on past experience with Eurodif or the refusal to return Iran's yellow cake. According to one of the Iranian nuclear negotiators, Tehran had received information from another P5 state that the French had joined the Vienna Group to ensure that the fuel pads would not be delivered to Iran until Tehran suspended its enrichment program. "This made us very suspicious," a member of the Iranian negotiating team told me. Both the French and the Americans rejected the Iranian account. "I would be extremely surprised," Ambassador Araud explained to me, adding that this "did not sound right." One of the American negotiators told me that he had been involved in all aspects of the swap proposal but never heard anything from the French regarding an intent to violate the agreement.[37]

ElBaradei pointed out to the Iranians that they did not need to trust France for a deal to be successful. They needed to trust only the IAEA. Nevertheless it was trust that was in short supply. The structure of the swap prompted the Iranians to fear that most of the risk would be placed on them—that the Iranian LEU would leave Iranian soil and, for a period of nine to twelve months, be under the control of two states (Russia and France) that Iran neither trusted nor had leverage over, before it would receive the fuel pads. Asking Tehran to put its faith in the French once again, the Iranians argued, was difficult. Moreover, if the Iranian LEU constituted a proliferation risk, then it also arguably served as a deterrent against an Israeli or American attack. By shipping it out, Iran would increase its vulnerability to such attacks, Tehran argued.[38]

At this point the Russians interceded and pointed out that if the issue of trust was rooted in French-Iranian tensions, eliminating France as a party to the deal and instead making it a subcontractor to Russia could resolve this issue. That way, France would be Russia's headache, not Iran's. This proposal resolved one of the disputes, at least temporarily. The second draft of the swap agreement involved only four parties: Iran, the IAEA, Russia, and the United States. France was not a party to the agreement, nor was it mentioned. (In a later third draft of the proposal, a compromise was reached in which France was mentioned by name and included as a signatory, but as a subcontractor to Russia rather than as a party to the agreement.)[39]

With the French factor addressed, the negotiations zeroed in on Iran's main concern. At the end of the day, the Iranians could live with the idea of shipping out the LEU and conducting a swap, as it could be a "move towards collaboration and away from confrontation." The real issue was Iran's need for a guarantee that the fuel pads would be delivered, and that the Vienna Group would live up to its end of the bargain. Since Tehran would make the first move and give up its strategic asset—the LEU—it wanted guarantees that the

Vienna Group would make its reciprocal move. "From the outset, Iran was ready to ship out the LEU, granted that a guarantee for delivery of the fuel pads was given," an Iranian negotiator said.[40]

The Iranians asked the Vienna Group to present a mechanism for guaranteeing delivery and also offered several ideas of their own. The U.S. had suggested that the LEU could be held in the custody of IAEA, which would guarantee that no country could confiscate it. The Iranians countered by saying that if IAEA custody was acceptable to the West, then the LEU could be put under IAEA custody while remaining on Iranian soil, perhaps on the island of Kish in the Persian Gulf. Moreover, instead of sending out the LEU in one shipment, the risk would be more evenly spread if it were divided into two or three shipments. For each shipment, Iran would simultaneously receive fuel pads. This way, neither side could benefit from violating the agreement. But these proposals were not acceptable to the U.S., Russia, and France. "The confidence-building value in our view was getting fuel out of Iran right away," one of the American negotiators explained. The political time and space the Obama administration sought from the deal could be achieved only if the Iranian LEU stockpile was drastically reduced at once. And just as the Iranians did not trust that IAEA custody of the LEU would prevent the West from confiscating the material if it chose to do so, the U.S. had little faith that the Iranians would not take back the LEU from the IAEA if it remained on Iranian soil. "If Iran wants to take it, it takes it. It takes the wire cutters and cuts the seals and that's that," the American negotiator said. Similarly, the American offer to guarantee the delivery of fuel pads by signing a contract with Iran or by committing to the deal publicly did not impress the Iranians. "For Iran, a written guarantee had no value—it already had that from the French regarding Eurodif—it was worth nothing," an Iranian negotiator complained bitterly.[41]

To break the deadlock and to provide Iran with more incentives, the U.S. approached ElBaradei and asked him to arrange a trilateral meeting between the U.S., Iran, and the IAEA. Poneman, Soltanieh, and ElBaradei held a separate meeting in which the U.S. offered to provide an upgrade to the safety of the Tehran reactor. This offer was also motivated by the Iranian complaint that the U.S. itself seemed to play no role in the swap; all components of the exchange were handled by Iran, Russia, France, and the IAEA. So what was the U.S.'s role in the swap, and why should Iran negotiate with a country that was not involved in the exchange? the Iranians complained. Though Poneman emphasized the humanitarian motivation behind the American offer, the Iranians were unimpressed.[42]

By the third day, it was becoming increasingly clear that the talks were heading toward collapse. The Iranians did offer a key concession—they agreed to ship out the LEU instead of conducting the swap on Iranian soil—but they still insisted on guarantees for delivery. But at the end of the day, neither side had moved significantly from its original position. Two proposals remained on the table at the end of the talks: the Iranian one and the Russian-American one as presented by ElBaradei, and neither had gone through any major revisions. The Iranian proposal specified that Tehran was ready to buy and pay for the fuel pads. It would also accept shipping out the LEU but only if Iran was simultaneously offered the fuel. The Russian-American proposal specified that the 1,200 kilograms of LEU would be transferred in one shipment but the fuel would be delivered to Iran at a later date. No important revisions had been made to that plan either. Instead, the U.S. and its partners sought to pressure Iran to accept the proposal. It was made abundantly clear to the Iranians that this was the best deal they could get and that failure to accept it would lead to a new round of UN Security Council sanctions. "At that point we were saying, 'Look, do you accept Mohammad ElBaradei's proposal or not?' " a senior State department official recalled.[43]

In a last-ditch effort to rescue the talks, ElBaradei offered the parties two choices: either he could tell the media that the talks had failed and that no agreement had been reached, or all parties could go back to their respective capitals and return with a final answer by October 23. The parties agreed by consensus to go with the second option. Thus, ElBaradei would tell the media that the talks had been constructive and that each country would consult with their capitals before providing a final answer. On top of that, a gentleman's agreement was reached that none of the parties would deviate from that message. Yet the two sides were deeply frustrated with each other, and each side concluded that the other one had come to the talks with instructions both not to make any compromises and not to agree to the proposal at all. "Iran had compromised, but unfortunately they did not compromise," Soltanieh complained, referring to the Iranian agreement to ship out the fuel. The Americans, in turn, complained about Soltanieh's instructions. "[Soltanieh] came there on the 19th of October, I think, instructed not to accept this," said one of the American negotiators.

In front of the cameras, ElBaradei tried to convey more optimism. He set a deadline of October 23 "to give, I hope, affirmative action" to the agreement, which he said was "a balanced agreement." He expressed hope that leaders in the West and in Tehran would "see the big picture" and approve the agreement. But according to the *New York Times,* his voice was tinged with doubt. For the Obama administration, this was a crucial moment. Time was running out for diplomacy, and, if Iran gave a negative response, Obama's outreach to Tehran might be deemed a failure. If, on the other hand, an agreement was reached, time and space for diplomacy would be gained—including the ability to push back against Israeli pressure for military action. "There's a part of this that's about getting our diplomacy with Iran started, and a part that's about convincing the Israelis that there's no reason to drop hints that they are going to reach for a military solution," a senior administration official said.[44]

On October 23, 2009, the United States, Russia, and France conveyed to the IAEA their positive response to the swap proposal as presented by ElBaradei. The Iranians, however, verbally informed ElBaradei "that it is considering the proposal in depth and in a favorable light, but it needs time until the middle of next week to provide a response." Washington was not pleased with Iran's request for more time, but it recognized that divisions in Tehran made the already slow decision-making process in Iran even slower. And, based on their public statements, Iranian decision makers were deeply divided. Several key officials who had earlier supported the swap in principle had now turned against the deal, ostensibly over its details and the Iranian view that it did not provide Tehran with sufficient guarantees for delivery.[45] "My guess is that the Americans have made a secret deal with certain countries to take 4.5 percent enriched uranium away from us under the pretext of providing nuclear fuel to us, and we hope Iranian officials will pay due attention to this issue. Giving away enriched uranium in return for nuclear fuel cannot be logically or legally justified," Larijani stated. Other prominent Iranian figures argued that, because of the history of mistrust, Iran should agree only to a swap in which its LEU is sent out in phases. This stood in contrast to Ahmadinejad's statements, which still sought to cast the agreement as a victory for Iran. The West had changed its policies from "confrontation to cooperation" as a result of Iran's "resistance," he said. "In the past they said that we had to halt our nuclear activities. But today they say, 'Come consult about finding solutions for world problems.' "[46]

On October 29, Iran conveyed another verbal message to the IAEA. Soltanieh informed the agency that Iran was ready for a second round of negotiations in order to reach an agreement on guarantees and assurances. Substantively, the Iranian response was not categorical, and since it was not a clear acceptance of additional negotiations, it was regarded as a rejection. Although the Iranians offered technical talks, the U.S. was open to additional meetings only on the political level. Further engagement at the technical level could trap the parties in endless wrangling over the technical details of the swap, Washington reasoned. And since time was of the essence, pressuring Iran to accept the deal was preferred over entering into a new round of technical talks. The message from Washington was clear: take it or leave it. "This is a pivotal moment for Iran. We urge Iran to accept the agreement as proposed and we will not alter it and we will not wait forever," Secretary of State Hillary Clinton told reporters in Washington.[47]

The End of Diplomacy

Ultimatums had not worked on Iran in the past, and there was little faith that one would do so now. The deal was hinging on a question of guarantees, according to ElBaradei. "The Iranians are distrustful that if their material will go out of Iran, they might not get it back in the form of fuel," he explained. Though Washington tried to remain hopeful, the initial optimism from the first meeting in October had turned into deep disappointment by the first week of November. Whether Iran was procrastinating and playing for time, or whether it had genuine apprehensions about the swap, its failure to accept the deal was a major blow to Obama's diplomacy. And the discontent was not limited to Washington. Moscow felt that dealing with the Iranian government had been "frustrating," and that Tehran's refusal to accept the deal suggested that Iran did not trust Russia. In Europe, there was "great disappointment," particularly among the member states that were betting on the continuation of diplomacy. The argument suggesting that continued talks could provide a breakthrough had few supporters. "We came to the conclusion that they missed an opportunity and that it would be wrong to make it even more attractive for them because we could not be sure that they would come around," Ambassador Wittig said. "For us there was never ever a very thorough soul-searching discussion whether we should modify it or not." More hawkish voices in Europe and Washington felt that their suspicions about Iranian intentions had been vindicated. "The only possible explanation is that their objective unfortunately is to have the bomb or in reality to have a very strong enrichment program," a senior EU official commented.[48]

The disappointment was particularly deep because the U.S. had been a full and active partner at the negotiating table for the first time. During the years in which the Europeans conducted the negotiations without any U.S. presence at the talks, it was widely believed that the absence of America explained the lack of progress—the Iranians were looking for a deal not with the EU but with Washington. As a result, it was believed, it would run against their interest to make any major concessions to the EU; important compromises would be offered only in a deal with the United States. But now this rationale seemed to have been proven wrong. The U.S. was at the table, and, in the words of ElBaradei, "Barack Obama is stretching backward, frankly, to engage Iran. And I have been saying to the Iranian leadership privately and publicly, 'Make use of that opportunity.'"[49]

While there was little appetite for any significant effort to revive the talks, tensions emerged between Washington and some of the EU capitals that preferred to move quickly toward sanctions. The hawkish camp argued that the Iranians had rejected the deal and that sanctions should be enacted promptly. But the Obama administration was split, with some preferring swift punitive actions and others arguing that more time should be given to the Iranians. After all, the deadline for diplomacy was the end of the year—several weeks remained that could be used for mediation.

The Obama administration made inquiries with other states to determine who could fabricate the fuel the fastest. The problem was that the Iranians would not release the LEU until they first got the fuel. "We were trying to accelerate the delivery of this fuel to narrow this gap," a senior State Department official explained. "But we came up against serious technical limitations." The administration also pushed for another P5+1 meeting with Tehran, but the Iranians would agree only to discuss issues of common concern, and these did not include the nuclear file. Washington was also open to efforts by some non-P5 states to intervene and possibly even mediate. Two countries in particular offered assistance to secure a diplomatic breakthrough—Japan and Turkey.[50]

For Japan, resolving the nuclear dispute could bring some direct benefits to Tokyo. U.S.-Iran tensions had led Washington to adopt an increasingly aggressive profile against states that traded with Tehran. Since the 1990s, Washington had repeatedly pressed Japan to downgrade its trade and investment ties with Iran. Since Japan had a more limited ability than its competitors—primarily China and Russia—to resist such pressures, heightened tensions increased the risk of Japan losing lucrative business deals to its rivals. Japan's top oil explorer, Inpex, originally held a 75 percent share in the massive Azadegan oil field in Iran. Due to sanctions, Inpex cut its share to 10 percent in 2008 and then abandoned the oil field altogether in 2010. A Chinese company picked up the strategic stake in the oil field. The combination of Japan's strategic interests in the Middle East, the desire to raise Japan's diplomatic profile, and the need for measures to strengthen U.S.-Japanese ties—to create "beautiful things" for the U.S. and Japan—prompted Tokyo to seize the opportunity to salvage the TRR deal. Prime Minister Yukio Hatoyama himself made the decision to embark on the mediation effort.[51]

The Japanese reached out to the Iranians and began some low-level negotiations in November. By December 2009, they intensified their efforts and invited Jalili to Tokyo, followed by a visit by Larijani in February 2010. The discussions centered on a proposal to place 1,000 kilograms of Iranian LEU in Japan. The nuclear material would be transferred to Japan in one shipment, and Tokyo would take responsibility for the stockpile and ensure delivery of the fuel pads to Iran. The Iranians insisted, according to the Japanese, that they did not want Russia or France to be involved in the swap. The Obama administration was regularly updated on the status of the talks, and by mid-January Tokyo felt that it was close to reaching a deal. The Japanese prime minister dispatched Foreign Minister Katsuya Okada to Washington to win the Obama administration's support for the deal. Because of unforeseen events, a meeting with National Security Advisor Jim Jones could not take place. Instead Okada and Jones spoke by phone. In spite of initially supporting the Japanese solution, Jones now "completely refused" to accept the idea, leaving Japan in a "touchy situation." A mediation effort that

Japan had initiated to strengthen ties with Washington had now instead become an irritant between the two states.

By February 2010, after Larijani's visit to Tokyo, Japan ceased its efforts to mediate between the U.S. and Iran, realizing that Washington's appreciation for Japan's efforts had come to an end. While Washington was seeking a deal on the TRR throughout 2009, by early 2010 the situation had "totally changed," according to a Japanese diplomat involved in the efforts. Between a leadership in Iran whose sincerity in diplomacy was uncertain—one former Iranian diplomat who continues to advise the Iranian foreign ministry said that Tehran "was only playing tactics with the Japanese"—and an administration in Washington that had lost interest in the deal, there was little Japan could do.[52]

While Japan was seeking to mastermind a breakthrough between the U.S. and Iran, Turkey was pursuing a similar effort. Only days after Obama's election in November 2008, Ankara had expressed its interest in helping to reconcile the differences between the U.S. and Iran. "We are ready to be the mediator," Turkey's Prime Minister Recep Tayyip Erdogan said in mid-November 2008. "I do believe we could be very useful." At the time, Iran cautiously welcomed Turkey's bid to mediate while pointing out that its differences with Washington were deep-rooted. Washington, in turn, publicly welcomed Turkey's initiative, with Clinton pointing out that "you [Turkey] know the Iranians better than we do" and that "we [the U.S.] are going to ask for your help in trying to influence Iranian behavior." By October 2009, Washington's enthusiasm for Turkish mediation had increased, despite a waning confidence in Turkey based on some of Erdogan's public statements. During a visit to Iran on October 20, 2009, Erdogan had dismissed allegations of Iran's intent to acquire nuclear weapons as "gossip." The statement had deeply irritated Washington, which felt that Turkey had inadvertently weakened the international consensus against Iran. The day after the statement was made, the U.S. ambassador to Turkey warned the

Turkish undersecretary of state, Feridun Sinirlioglu, that Washington was now wondering if it could any longer count on Turkey to assist with the Iranian nuclear challenge.[53]

By November 2009, despite its reservations, and partly due to ElBaradei's efforts to involve the Turks, Washington enlisted Ankara to convince Tehran to accept some variation of the TRR proposal. Jones suggested to Turkish foreign minister Ahmet Davutoglu during a call on November 11, 2009, that he should suggest to the Iranians that they simultaneously transfer 600 kilograms of the LEU to an Iranian island in the Persian Gulf and 600 kilograms to Turkey. The idea of putting some of the LEU in Turkey had already been raised by ElBaradei during the Vienna talks as a way to provide Tehran with the necessary guarantees for delivery. The IAEA director had held two long, "harsh" sessions with the Iranians on November 8, 2009, discussing the idea further. The Iranians had expressed a willingness to meet with the EU's Solana and the Americans again to discuss the details of the TRR deal, but they wished to avoid the British because they had "more trust" in the United States. And as with the Japanese, the Iranians had told ElBaradei that they preferred to get the fuel from the Americans rather than the Russians. But like the Japanese effort, the Turkish mediation never yielded any results, nor did efforts by Russia, China, or the EU commission. At one point, so many different entities were seeking to resolve the conflict that managing their efforts was like "herding cats," according to a senior Obama administration official.[54]

Washington itself did not engage in any additional diplomacy with Iran, though it did seek to meet with Tehran through the P5+1. Aside from the Turkish and Japanese efforts, there was little diplomatic engagement with Iran after November. In the words of ElBaradei, the ball was in Iran's court, leaving the U.S. and its allies in waiting mode. "Sometimes there are situations where you have to wait for the Iranians or for your counterpart to move forward," Wittig explained. "I think this was very much one of those phases. I mean, what could we do?"[55]

Paralysis in Tehran

The Obama administration took a calculated risk when it chose to engage the Iranian government so soon after the election scandal. Success could open up significant space for additional diplomacy, but failure—particularly if caused by repercussions of the election dispute—could risk giving the impression that diplomacy as a whole had been exhausted. At the end of the day, it was a risk that did not pay off for the president's desire to resolve tensions with Iran through diplomacy.

While Iran's many objections to the deal—which centered on shipping out the LEU without receiving adequate guarantees for delivery of the fuel pads—were genuine and rooted in mutual distrust between Iran and the West, the political chaos and infighting in the aftermath of the election dispute rendered these objections all the more insurmountable. The intense level of political infighting caused by the elections dispute and the ensuing human rights abuses indicated that the Islamic Republic was facing an existential crisis. Iran's decision-making process, which was already taxing and slow, reached a state of near paralysis since "self-preservation took precedence over all other issues." Even if Iranian officials wanted to engage, they had been hamstrung because of the protests. "It is the internal crisis that really worries our leaders. They can't speak with one voice in the international community at this point," said reformist politician Mashallah Shamsolvaezin.[56]

After first having praised the swap concept, several high-profile political opponents of Ahmadinejad came out against the deal after the Vienna meeting. This created an awkward political situation for the Obama administration in which Ahmadinejad was more favorable toward the deal than his political opponents with whom Washington preferred to deal. The Turkish foreign minister told Obama administration officials that, in Turkey's assessment, Ahmadinejad was "more flexible" than other Iranian government officials and that he was not opposed to the deal but needed to find a way to manage the public perception. Almost all political factions—among whom a consensus emerged that a deal without additional guarantees was not acceptable—criticized the deal and deliberately increased the political cost for Ahmadinejad to pursue it. The political nature of the criticism was oftentimes evident. Mousavi, for instance, gave a scathing critique of the deal and of Ahmadinejad's diplomacy, which the Green leader argued had put Iran in an impossible situation.[57] He said,

> Today it seems like we have to surrender a major portion of the product of our country's nuclear program, which has caused so much uproar and has brought upon our people so many sanctions, to another country in hopes that they may out of kindness provide us with this [TRR fuel] basic need sometime in the future. . . . Is this a victory? Or a lie portraying surrender as victory? Not only have the officials been unable to solve global problems, but they are not even safeguarding the undeniable rights of our people and have generously given these rights up. This shows that the officials are extremists even when it comes to surrendering and bowing down [to foreigners].[58]

Mousavi then cleverly positioned Ahmadinejad in a no-win situation by declaring, "If [the swap is] put in place, all the efforts of thousands of scientists will go to the wind. If [it is] not put in place, the foundations will be laid for wide-ranging sanctions against Iran, and this is the result of a confrontational stance in foreign policy and the neglect of national interests and principles." The Greens feared that the U.S. preferred to negotiate with a weak Ahmadinejad. Yet, they were not unhappy that negotiations took place. Rather, they were concerned about the nuclear-centric agenda that ignored the domestic situation in Iran. "This is really a nonissue in Iran. Iranians are all united on Iranian nuclear rights and they think that this is actually picking the wrong fight," said Lake Forest University professor Ahmad Sadri. "The more the West, the EU governments, and

U.S. with the prodding of Israel foreground the nuclear issue in Iran, the more they distract from the real issue."[59]

The combination of pressure from conservatives and reformists alike prompted Supreme Leader Khamenei to withdraw his initial support for the proposal, according to a former Iranian diplomat. The argument that Iran was unjustifiably putting its trust in the hands of the West was powerful; no Iranian politician wanted to come across as soft or naïve when dealing with the West. Accordingly, even the proponents of the deal refrained from defending it in public. "Whether you can win over the various segments of the Iranian political establishment and public opinion, you have to make an effort to sell it," Wittig said. "And this effort apparently was not really made." But while Ahmadinejad's opponents blasted the deal on its merits, it is not clear whether their intent was to scuttle it or simply to make its acceptance as costly as possible for Ahmadinejad. Mindful of the ongoing internal political fights and the brutality with which Ahmadinejad had responded to his many domestic opponents, it was natural that Ahmadinejad's rivals were not going to permit him to score any victories that could boost his political standing in Iran. "No one wanted Ahmadinejad to get credit, particularly if this was a good deal for Iran," a senior State Department official said. Emotions were running high. After all, Iran's political elite was literally at war with itself. "They were so angry. They were so mad," one of Mousavi's advisers said of Ahmadinejad's rivals. "I mean, their kids were in jail, their brothers were in jail." Furthermore, in light of Ahmadinejad's past hard-line stance and criticism against previous nuclear agreements between the West and Iran, his support for the swap provided his opponents with an opportunity to hurt him and his own hard-line base. "Everybody is getting into a payback situation," ElBaradei said of the internal dynamics around the TRR deal. "Everybody is trying to outbid the other by turning that issue into a national pride issue."[60]

The infighting in Iran had led to "massive political irresponsibility" in which all factions were "playing politics with issues of [Iran's] national interest," according to Sadri, who maintains close ties with several figures within the Green movement. Iran was simply not ready to negotiate under these circumstances, admitted a former Iranian diplomat. Under other circumstances, Iran might have accepted the fuel swap proposal. This point was not lost on the White House, which recognized that Tehran "was not in a position to accept" the deal since it had become "a victim of internal politics." According to David Miliband, then–foreign secretary of the United Kingdom, "The bilateral outreach the Americans made fell victim to internal Iranian politics." The entire episode left all parties involved with a bitter taste. And because of the actions—or inactions—of both sides, a deal that was supposed to build confidence between Iran and the international community ended up doing the opposite. "I think it turned out to be a confidence-eroding measure," one of the key architects of the swap at the State Department complained.[61]

Nine

The Second Track

A train can't run on two tracks.

—Former senior Obama administration official, October 2010

After two disappointing face-to-face meetings with the Iranians, the Obama administration was ready to forgo diplomacy and activate the pressure track. Diplomacy had run into its first hurdle—the swamplands of internal Iranian politics and the web of mistrust entangling U.S.-Iran relations. Already on October 7, 2009, before the Vienna meeting, Obama had gathered like-minded states for a meeting in Washington to prepare the ground for sanctions. Some senior officials at the State Department and the White House had spent most of 2009 developing various sanctions strategies in anticipation of the collapse of diplomacy. By late November 2009, weeks before his official deadline for progress on diplomacy, President Obama gave a green light to the sanctions track. It was not a sudden shift, but rather a gradual realization that the initial attempt at dialogue had not yielded results. "What is the value of us investing that energy both internally and with our allies—the president's political capital—if the sense is that the Iranians, to be glib about it, don't have their act together?" asked Michael Ratney of the State Department. Diplomacy was not dead, but it was abandoned.[1]

It was not an easy decision, nor did it lack critics within the administration itself. Some were concerned that diplomacy had been abandoned too quickly, and that, if the problem lay in the inability of the Iranians to break out of their political paralysis, then sanctions would be of no value anyway. "We knew [diplomacy] is going to be hard, but it is in our interest to do it because thirty years of the other stuff has not gotten us anywhere," a skeptic of the sanctions track at the State Department said. Instead, sanctions would only undo the administration's groundwork for diplomacy. Moreover, there was opposition to the very concept of a dual-track approach—the idea that diplomacy must be coupled with sanctions to succeed. In a dysfunctional relationship, where the biggest obstacle to progress was mistrust, rather than limiting one side's ability to hurt the other, exercising pressure could undermine the effort to bridge the trust gap. Balancing these two tracks was not only conceptually difficult; it also created practical challenges. "A train can't run on two tracks," the State Department official quipped. "The conversation almost became metaphysical because, are we on track one? Are we moving from the engagement track to the pressure track, or are we on both tracks simultaneously? Or, you know, just what are we doing?"[2]

For the Obama administration, however, the duality of the policy was central. Just as diplomacy could not work without pressure, sanctions could not work unless coupled with diplomacy. Obama emphasized this when accepting the Nobel Peace Prize in Oslo, Norway, on December 9, 2009:

> Let me also say this: the promotion of human rights cannot be about exhortation alone. At times, it must be coupled with painstaking diplomacy. I know that engagement with repressive regimes lacks the satisfying purity of indignation. But I also know that sanctions without outreach—and condemnation without discussion—can carry forward a crippling status quo. No repressive regime can move down a new path unless it has the choice of an open door.[3]

Nevertheless, once the sanctions track was activated, it became the only track. In his 2010 State of the Union Address, only weeks after accepting the Nobel Peace Prize, Obama made no mention of engaging Iran. He instead focused on isolating and punishing the Islamic Republic. According to a European diplomat, more than 90 percent of the West's focus was on marshaling sanctions once the Obama administration moved to the pressure track. "Basically the sanctions sucked all the air out of the room," a senior State Department official said. Preparing sanctions took much more resources than diplomacy did. Though it was familiar territory—Washington had already imposed several sets of sanctions on Iran—it was a battle fought on different fronts, with numerous variables that were partly out of U.S. control. "Diplomacy takes a lot less resources than trying to marshal international resources, international political capital towards sanctions enforcement," Ratney explained. In the case of sanctions on Iran, it was a multifront battle between the White House, Congress, pro-Israeli pressure groups, and the Israeli government on the one hand, and Russia, China, and EU states skeptical of sanctions on the other. It was also a struggle about the scope of sanctions—broad or targeted—and their international support base—multilateral sanctions through the UN or unilateral sanctions imposed by a coalition of like-minded states.[4]

The White House's preference was to first impose sanctions through the UN Security Council, targeting Iran's nuclear program and possible arms sales. The Security Council resolution would then provide a legal basis for the EU and other allied countries to work together with the U.S. to impose additional financial sanctions on Iran. The Obama administration had already continued and intensified the financial sanctions imposed by the George W. Bush administration. Targeted sanctions that hit the Iranian leadership were preferred over broad sanctions that hit the Iranian people and the entire economy. "We have never been attracted to the idea of trying to get the whole world to cordon off their economy," said a senior U.S. official. "We have to be deft at this, because it matters how the Iranian people interpret their isolation—whether they fault the regime or are fooled into thinking we are to blame." But securing greater international buy-in for this sanctions regime—by securing multilateral sanctions first—was a major challenge. The Israelis and the U.S. Congress were far more impatient, wanting to impose unilateral sanctions targeting Iran's gasoline imports right away. The White House feared that such a move would undermine the consensus it was building at the UN for a new sanctions resolution, and that it carried the risk of alienating the Iranian people because the gasoline sanctions would likely hurt them more than they would the Iranian government.[5]

The Israelis, who had told the Obama administration that they could accept diplomacy as long as Washington expected it would fail, pushed the U.S. to quickly impose "crippling sanctions." Israeli prime minister Benjamin Netanyahu did not believe that going through the UN was necessary. Instead, he advocated for a coalition of the willing, together with the Europeans, to sanction Iran's gasoline sector. If the world "is serious about stopping Iran, then what it needs to do is not watered-down sanctions, moderate sanctions . . . but effective, biting sanctions that curtail the import and export of oil into Iran," Netanyahu argued. "And if this cannot pass in the Security Council, then it should be done outside the Security Council, but immediately." The Israelis argued that Iran's Achilles' heel was its importation of foreign-refined gasoline. In spite of its oil wealth, Iran's refining capacity stood at 1.6 million barrels a day, well short of Iran's domestic fuel demand. As a result, Iran imported roughly 30 percent of its domestic gasoline needs. In the midst of major domestic political upheaval and a global economic crisis, the Israelis argued that the use of sanctions would limit Iran's access to gasoline markets, drive up the price Iran would pay for gas imports, and undermine Ahmadinejad's ability to maintain the country's economic stability.[6]

The Europeans by and large supported the move toward sanctions. Among the EU states, France was the key advocate for punitive measures. The Europeans wanted to keep the door for diplomacy open, though they recognized that the Iranian government might not be capable of negotiating due to infighting. Yet, in their view, the internal paralysis did not mean that the West should let up on pressure. While there was not much enthusiasm for sanctions, with the possible exception of the French, most EU states felt that Iran's refusal to accept the U.S.-Russian proposal "must carry a price." "People had become sick of what was perceived as Iranian bad faith . . . we thought there was a lot of game-playing going on over there," then-foreign secretary of the United Kingdom David Miliband said. Many in the EU bureaucracy, as well as the top leadership in Europe, had severe doubts about the utility of sanctions but felt they had become a political inevitability. Still, the actual dimension and form of the sanctions were debatable. Most EU states believed that a UN framework, including a new Security Council Resolution, was necessary. Some favored adopting any future UN Security Council resolution into EU law, but the French favored using the UN resolution as a platform for more expansive EU sanctions than were likely to be adopted by the UN. Other states, including Germany, emphasized the need to design the sanctions so that they would target the leadership of the Islamic Republic and not the general population. Mohamed ElBaradei, director general of the International Atomic Energy Agency (IAEA), also favored this approach. "I am not a great fan of sanctions, but if you have sanctions, you have to apply it to the regime," he said on *Charlie Rose*. "We've seen it in the case of Saddam Hussein, who was a horrible dictator, he made use of the sanctions . . . and it was really the innocent Iraqis who died in the process." There was also an awareness that gasoline sanctions were risky because they could prompt Tehran to cut its gasoline subsidies, which would put the burden on the general population and actually help save the Ahmadinejad government money. But the election fraud of June 2009, and the failure of the talks in Vienna, eliminated much of the resistance in Europe against sanctions.[7]

Russia and China were two of the principal skeptics of sanctions. The Chinese had both economic and political motivations for their resistance against the sanctions push. First and foremost, Iran is China's second-biggest supplier of oil—the Iranians sell 540,000 barrels a day to the Chinese. Any disruption to Beijing's energy access could harm China's economic growth and the Chinese government's efforts to bring millions of its people out of poverty. After all, China's rapid economic growth is the ruling Communist Party's single most important claim to legitimacy. Moreover, China has been a major beneficiary of existing sanctions that pushed Western companies out of Iran while doing relatively little to limit Beijing's expanding presence. As Iran's top economic partner since the mid-2000s, China has invested heavily in the energy sector and filled the gaps left by Western firms forced out by U.S. sanctions. China's state-run oil behemoths have committed so much money to Iran—an estimated $120 billion over the past five years—that questions have arisen as to whether China's engineering firms will be able to handle all the work. "While we in the West are going through economic hara-kiri, the Chinese are out there taking all of the oil and gas deals," said Michael Economides, professor of chemical engineering at the University of Houston. "The Chinese don't look at Iran as the country of the mullahs that everybody is afraid of; they look at it as a country with lots of oil and gas. Every time I go to China, they ask me, 'Why are you in the West letting us have it so easy?' "[8]

On the political side, the Chinese viewed sanctions as both ineffective and interference in the affairs of another state—a principle Beijing holds dear as a protection against Western criticism of, or interference in, its own internal matters. The Chinese themselves developed their nuclear program in the face of Western sanctions, which fueled their skepticism and suspicion of U.S.-sponsored sanctions efforts. Like many other states, Beijing feared that sanctions eventually would lead to a U.S. request for the use of force at the Security Council—as it did in the case of Iraq. Strongly opposed to a military confrontation with Iran, the Chinese viewed resistance to sanctions as resistance to war. "They are anticipating that the more they put the brakes on sanctions now, the more they are delaying really troubling decisions to authorize force down the line," former National Security Council director Michael Green said. The fear that sanctions would deteriorate into a military confrontation was also exacerbated by Beijing's belief that the Obama administration played a role in the 2009 antigovernment demonstrations in Iran. Moreover, if China supported sanctions, in contradiction to its principle of noninterference in the internal affairs of other states, Tehran could retaliate by fueling tensions in China's Muslim-dominated Xinjiang region. During the summer of 2009, riots broke out in Xinjiang. In a stern warning to the Chinese, two senior Iranian ayatollahs publicly criticized China for the treatment of its Muslim minority. Similarly, Russia had both economic and political ties to Iran that it believed would come under threat if sanctions were imposed. But Obama's policy of "reset" with Russia, and the effort to deeply involve Moscow in all diplomacy with Iran, had created an opening to reduce Russia's resistance.[9]

Congress Versus the White House

The first battle line, however, was drawn between the White House and Congress. As it became clear that the White House was abandoning diplomacy and focusing on sanctions, pressure was quickly amassed on Capitol Hill to pass broad energy sanctions. The push from Congress to act unilaterally became a major—if not the most important—driving force of the pressure track. "The whole pressure track and the whole sanctions effort at the UN was driven in large part by Congress," a senior Senate staffer told me. "If you had taken that away, I'm not sure that we would have gone down this track at all." Under pressure from Congress, the administration scheduled a meeting with the permanent members of the UN Security Council and Germany (P5+1) on December 25, 2009, to discuss sanctions. But Congress was not in the mood to wait for the result of the meeting. Instead, on December 15, 2009, the House of Representatives passed legislation sanctioning Iran's gasoline imports. Unlike the Chinese, who viewed sanctions as a pathway to war, the sponsor of the sanctions bill, House Foreign Affairs Committee Chairman Howard Berman (D-CA), viewed sanctions as the only way to prevent war. The move came after intense lobbying by pro-Israel groups, including the American Israel Public Affairs Committee (AIPAC) and the Israel Project. "Since Iran imports up to 40 percent of its refined petroleum, curtailing its ability to purchase gas and diesel fuel could have a severe impact on the Iranian economy, forcing the regime to confront a real choice: continue its illicit nuclear program and risk economic ruin or suspend their nuclear program and open the door to relief from sanctions," said Josh Block, a spokesperson for AIPAC. Israeli ambassador to the U.S. Michael Oren also praised the House vote. More notably, the more dovish pro-Israel group J Street also threw its support behind the sanctions, after having opposed the measure earlier in the year.[10]

Though the White House did not publicly comment on the House move, there were some indications that the Obama administration was not pleased with the pressure from Congress. Deputy Secretary of State James Steinberg wrote Senator John Kerry (D-MA), chair of the Senate Foreign Relations Committee, only days earlier to express the State Department's reservations about gasoline sanctions. "We are entering a critical period of intense diplomacy to impose significant international pressure on Iran. This requires that we keep the focus on Iran. . . . At this juncture, I am concerned that this legislation, in its current form, might weaken rather than strengthen international unity and support for our efforts," the letter said. Steinberg went on to caution the Senate about the State Department's "serious substantive concerns" with the sanctions act and "unintended foreign policy consequences" it could cause. But the letter was too little, too late. And the White House knew this, which was why the letter was signed by Steinberg, and not Secretary of State Hillary Clinton, and why it was sent to Kerry—whose committee did not handle the legislation—rather than to Senator Chris Dodd (D-CT), chair of the Senate Banking Committee, which oversaw the Senate version of the gasoline sanctions bill. Instead, the intent of the White House's admittedly limited maneuver was to delay the process in order to avoid infuriating Washington's partners in the Security Council and stifling UN process.[11]

The opposition in Congress against sanctions centered on the issue of timing; the inefficiency of sanctions; the likelihood that sanctions would derail the international consensus against Iran; and whether the approach would be counterproductive by adding pressure on the Iranian people rather than on the Iranian government. "I find it predictably ironic that less than a year after the Obama administration began its efforts to engage the Iranians in a comprehensive diplomatic dialogue, the discourse in Washington and around the world has already shifted toward an enthusiastic embrace of punitive measures," said Suzanne Maloney, a senior fellow at the Brookings Institution. "The notion that Iranians would welcome American efforts to cut off supplies of heating and gasoline to me sounds like the same kind of logic that suggested Iraqis would greet us as liberators after we violently removed their regime." The skepticism was shared by a small number of lawmakers who pointed out that previous crippling sanctions imposed by the U.S. on Iraq and Cuba ended up hurting their populations rather than their governments. The punitive nature of the legislation could rally the populace to support the sitting government, veteran American journalist Robin Wright warned. "Persian nationalism is among the strongest forces in the world," she said. "If you know a Texan, add 5,000 years and you've got Persian nationalism."[12]

Generally, the critics of sanctions had key figures in the Iranian opposition on their side. Nobel laureate and human rights defender Shirin Ebadi told the BBC, "We oppose military attack on Iran or economic sanctions because that's to the detriment of the people." Another key figure, Mohsen Kadivar, a dissident cleric who served an eighteen-month prison term in Iran for having criticized Ayatollah Ruhollah Khomeini's theory of Islamic government, told the German magazine *Der Spiegel,* "The tightening of sanctions is not the right path ahead. They affect the people more than the government."

Among the opposition, there was widespread frustration with the swiftness with which Western governments had tended to write them off. This frustration was particularly visible around the time the pressure track was activated, as it coincided with the death of Ayatollah Hossein-Ali Montazeri on December 19, 2009. Montazeri, a prominent Iranian scholar and Islamic theologian, was once the designated successor to Ayatollah Khomeini. But before Khomeini's death, the two had a falling-out and Montazeri spent the rest of his life as one of the Islamic Republic's main internal critics. He was a staunch supporter of the Green movement, and his death and the commemorations seven days later on Ashura, the holiest day of the Shiite calendar, caused some of the biggest clashes between protestors and the security forces of the Islamic Republic. Dozens of people were killed, including the nephew of Mir-Hossein Mousavi. These events indicated that the Green movement was still a force to be reckoned with, and that the Ahmadinejad government had failed to root out the opposition.[13]

But the courage of the Iranian protesters failed to impress lawmakers in Washington. In spite of the efforts of Iran's youth, many in Washington agreed with Berman's assessment that the democracy clock was not moving as fast as the nuclear clock. By late January, efforts to delay voting on the Senate version of the sanctions bill ran out of steam. The political upside of opposing sanctions on Iran was simply nonexistent. In fact, the White House's Republican opponents welcomed an opportunity to debate the issue publicly. "We're only too happy to have a floor fight about that," said one senior GOP Senate aide. Even if the White House wanted to fight the legislation head-on, there was little to suggest that it possessed the necessary political capital to do so. The health care reform bill topped the president's legislative agenda, and his legislative bandwidth was limited, to say the least. Between health care and sanctions on Iran, the choice was easy from a political standpoint, because health care "was potentially an existential issue for the White House," a senior Senate staffer explained. On January 29, 2010, the Senate passed gasoline sanctions on Iran after seven senators had written Obama to say that they had had enough of waiting for the pressure-track activities to begin, arguing that Obama's December deadline for diplomacy had long passed. "Now that this deadline has passed, we believe that it is imperative to put into action your pledge of increased, meaningful pressure against the Iranian regime—what Clinton called 'crippling sanctions,'" the letter said.[14]

Congress had raised the stakes. Both chambers had now passed draconian sanctions legislation on Iran, and once the differences in the two bills were reconciled the legislation would be sent to the president for his signature. It was therefore only a matter of time before the bill reached Obama's desk. If it did so before the administration could manage to secure a Security Council resolution, it could unravel the White House's diplomatic efforts at the UN. At the same time, the existence of a ready piece of legislation awaiting the president's signature also served to pressure the Security Council to move sooner rather than later on sanctions. And the White House was not shy to use the threat of congressional sanctions to pressure other governments. "There was some good-cop-bad-cop play between White House and Congress," a senior Senate staffer explained.[15]

Susan Rice Steps In

Once the Obama administration fully embarked on the sanctions track at the UN, the show moved from Washington to New York. There, Obama's trusted confidante, U.S. Ambassador to the UN Susan Rice, took charge and began negotiating the UN sanctions resolution with her counterparts on the Security Council. Obama fully empowered her to negotiate the text of the resolution, which meant that most of the haggling over the resolution occurred in New York rather than directly between the political directors in the capitals of Security Council member states, which had been the case with the previous three UN Security Council sanctions on Iran.

Rice is a tough negotiator who is not afraid of ruffling feathers—

be they the feathers of her colleagues in the Obama administration or those of America's partners at the UN. And she made it abundantly clear to the other Security Council states that she was the authority on this matter, in order to prevent Security Council members from trying to sidestep her and turn to Washington directly. Rice also made sure that nearly all major papers and decisions on Iran within the State Department would have to be signed off by her office at the UN—a measure that gave her greater control but that also significantly slowed the decision-making process at Foggy Bottom. At one point in the UN negotiations, a disagreement emerged between her and one of the EU ambassadors. The ambassador, himself not a pushover, sought to checkmate Rice by declaring that his government had received the Obama administration's agreement for a request from National Security Advisor Jim Jones himself. "I'm really sorry, Susan, but here we have an agreement by General Jones," the ambassador said. Without blinking, Rice countered, "I am really sorry, Ambassador," she said, "but I outrank Jones." That sentence immediately made it back to the capitals of other EU states, which took note of who in the Obama administration was the authority on UN sanctions issues.[16]

From the outset of the talks, it was clear that the biggest hurdle to an agreement among the P5+1 would be the Chinese. Even the Russians, who traditionally were skeptical of sanctions, did not take as hard a stance as the Chinese did. Already in November 2009, Russian foreign minister Ivan Lavrov had told his British counterpart that Russia was ready to consider sanctions, though Moscow believed it was still too early to embark on that path. But with the Chinese there was no indication of an opening on the sanctions issue. To make clear their disapproval of the sanctions approach and its timing, Beijing decided to send a lower-level official to the mid-January talks among the major powers in New York. This was the second month in a row that Beijing declined to send a senior Chinese official to attend a P5+1 meeting to discuss new sanctions against Iran. The other P5+1 states were represented by the political directors of their foreign ministries.[17]

The previous week, the Obama administration had circulated among the P5+1 a rough draft of possible sanctions categories. But the Chinese, who were furious about the $6.4-billion U.S.-Taiwan arms deal that had just been concluded that same month, showed no interest and refused to "engage substantively" on the issue of sanctions. In the early phases of what ended up being very tense negotiations within the P5+1, the realistic expectation among the Europeans and the U.S. was that China would, in a best-case scenario, abstain rather than vote in favor of a sanctions resolution. "The Chinese and the Russians are in a sense not *demandeurs* of the sanctions," France's UN ambassador explained. "So they lean back and relax . . . they have absolutely no reason to rush."[18]

The push for sanctions received a boost on February 7, as the Iranian government informed the IAEA that, because of the failure of the Vienna Group to respond positively to Iran's proposal for a fuel swap, Iran had no choice but to begin indigenously enriching uranium at the 19.75 percent level in order to produce the fuel pads for its research reactor. "Until now, we have not received any response to our positive logical and technical proposal," Ambassador Ali Asghar Soltanieh told the Associated Press. "We cannot leave hospitals and patients desperately waiting for radioisotopes" being produced at the Tehran reactor for use in cancer treatment, he added. The U.S. and its EU allies viewed the Iranian move as a provocation and escalation. Their efforts had been aimed at reducing the Iranian LEU stockpile and preventing Iran from increasing its enrichment levels. Now, instead, the LEU stockpile continued to grow and the Iranians also expanded their level of enrichment activities. Though Iran was unable to produce the needed nuclear fuel in time to ensure the uninterrupted production of medical isotopes by its research reactor, its refusal to purchase the radioisotopes from the international market fueled suspicions that Tehran indeed sought to build nuclear weapons. In a letter to the IAEA dated February 12, France, Russia, and the U.S. argued that the Iranian move was "wholly unjustified, contrary to the UN Security Council resolutions, and represents a further step toward a capability to produce highly enriched uranium." In a moment of frustration, two days after the Iranian announcement, Obama told reporters that he had "bent over backwards to say to the Islamic Republic of Iran that we are willing to have a constructive conversation" about issues between the two countries. "They have made their choice so far."[19]

To get the Chinese and Russians to come around on sanctions, the Obama administration turned to Saudi Arabia and Israel. To the Chinese, the Saudis emphasized the importance of forsaking diplomacy and moving toward sanctions. They had also offered to alleviate Beijing's primary concern—that sanctions would impede China's access to oil—by offering to guarantee Beijing's demand for energy on the condition that China would support sanctions. The Saudis justified the sanctions move by arguing that it offered an alternative to military action, and because it illustrated "a unified international stand against nuclear proliferation in the [Persian] Gulf region, therefore disabling Iran from relying on international contradictions among major international powers." By March, both Saudi Arabia and the United Arab Emirates had boosted their exports to China as part of this pressure campaign. Shipments increased from about 50,000 barrels per day in 2009 to 120,000, with a goal of up to 200,000 barrels per day by the end of 2010.[20]

The Israelis, on the other hand, used their leverage with Russia to convince Moscow to support sanctions. In early January, the Israelis had enthusiastically set high expectations for the Security Council, declaring that a sanctions resolution would be implemented within a month. "The world is uniting against Iran's nuclear program, and within a month we will see UN Security Council sanctions," Deputy Foreign Minister Danny Ayalon said. "There is agreement in Washington, Moscow and Beijing that a nuclear Iran would destroy the current world order." While Ayalon's statement turned out to be overly optimistic, the Israelis were hearing encouraging language from Moscow during private meetings. Israeli diplomats attributed Russia's shift to the failure of the talks in Vienna and to the Iranian decision to enrich uranium to 19.75 percent.[21]

Israel Versus Obama—Round Two

Although Israel was pressuring Russia, it was putting even greater pressure on the U.S. The White House viewed Israel as the greatest wildcard in its Iran policy fiasco and feared that the Jewish state would take unilateral military action against Iran—especially as it became clear that the sanctions process would not be expeditious. Originally the Obama administration had promised to secure a resolution by the end of February, when the French held the rotating presidency at the UN. That was later changed to March, and then it was postponed to April. The sanctions process moved forward much slower than the U.S. had anticipated—much to Israeli discomfort. All in all, the situation created great uncertainty between the U.S. and Israel. "Currently, the feeling in the U.S. is that you can no longer count on Israel to see the broader picture and you can no longer take Israel's cooperation for granted," said Yoram Peri, director of the Joseph and Alma Gildenhorn Institute for Israel Studies at the University of Maryland. "Israel's politics became more extreme, and its sense of besiegement is stronger, and that gave power to more extreme voices in the country's leadership." Besieged or not, the White House could not afford any Israeli adventurism with Iran. To drive the point home, the Obama administration sent an army of high-level officials to Israel with the aim of pressing the Israelis to give Obama the time he needed to get a strong UN Security Council resolution. In the span of a few weeks between January and March, Deputy Secretary of State Jim Steinberg, Undersecretary of Defense Michèle Flournoy, Defense Secretary Robert Gates, CIA director Leon Panetta, National Security Advisor Jones, Chairman of the Joint Chiefs of Staff Admiral Mike Mullen, Deputy Secretary of State

for Management and Resources Jack Lew, and Vice President Joseph
Biden were all dispatched to Israel. While most of these visits maintained a low profile, Mullen took the unusual step of convening a
press conference to send a clear message to the Israeli public: an
Israeli strike against Iran would "be a big, big, big problem for all of
us, and I worry a great deal about the unintended consequences of a
strike," he said.[22]

The pressure from Israel came both directly and through the
U.S. Congress, where many lawmakers sided with the Israelis. On
March 11, the Senate appointed its conferees to reconcile the Senate
and House bills and send a final version to Obama to sign. Once the
conference process began, the administration became more active
and sought to affect the sanctions push with three specific objectives:
delay its progress so that it would not affect the UN process; make
certain that the sanctions provided the president with sufficient
waiver opportunities; and ensure that the sanctions permit exemptions for companies from countries that are working in "close cooperation" with the United States to develop international sanctions.
Defining the criteria for determining what "close cooperation"
meant and the issue of timing were two of the main points of contention between Congress and the White House in the protracted conference talks, with AIPAC pressing both to "enact—without delay—
the Iran sanctions legislation currently before Congress."[23]

The day after the Senate appointed its conferees, a major crisis
erupted between Israel and the U.S. over a different issue. Frustrated
with the stalemate in talks between Israel and the Palestinians over
the expansion of illegal Israeli settlements in Palestinian territory,
Biden traveled to Israel to resume negotiations. But on the day that
the vice president arrived, the Netanyahu government announced
that another 1,600 apartments would be built in a settlement in Arab
East Jerusalem. The Israeli move infuriated the Obama administration, which viewed it as a provocation and an insult. Such a blatant
show of defiance by Israel against the U.S. served only to further
weaken Washington's position in the region, the administration be-

lieved. Senior Obama aide David Axelrod told the U.S. press that the move was "very destructive" and a blow to the peace process. "This was an affront, it was an insult but most importantly it undermined this very fragile effort to bring peace to that region," he said. Biden himself was infuriated and had an angry exchange with Netanyahu, according to the Israeli daily *Yedioth Ahronoth*. "This is starting to get dangerous for us," Biden reportedly told Netanyahu. "What you're doing here undermines the security of our troops who are fighting in Iraq, Afghanistan, and Pakistan. That endangers us and it endangers regional peace," he said, linking negative sentiments in the region against the U.S. to Israeli actions in the Palestinian territories. These comments enraged the Israelis, who categorically rejected any suggestion that the Israeli-Palestinian conflict could fuel anti-American terrorism. Netanyahu's brother-in-law Hagai Ben-Artzi even went so far as to accuse Obama on Israeli radio of being an anti-Semite. "When there is an anti-Semitic president in the United States, it is a test for us and we have to say: we will not concede," he said. "We are a nation dating back 4,000 years, and you in a year or two will be long forgotten. Who will remember you? But Jerusalem will dwell on forever."[24]

The dispute shed further light on the split within the Jewish-American community, with AIPAC openly siding with the Netanyahu government, and the progressive outfit J Street standing behind Obama. AIPAC said in a statement that the Obama administration "should make a conscious effort to move away from public demands and unilateral deadlines directed at Israel," while "strongly urg[ing]" the White House to "work closely and privately with our partner Israel, in a manner befitting strategic allies." J Street, in turn, called the Obama administration's reaction to the Israeli move "understandable and appropriate." The combination of tensions between the U.S. and Israel over Iran, the Israeli-Palestinian issue, and broader regional issues led to what Israel's ambassador to the U.S. called "their worst crisis in 35 years."[25]

The U.S.-Israel drama escalated further a week later during

Netanyahu's visit to Washington. The visit coincided with AIPAC's annual policy conference, which provided AIPAC and Israel an opportunity to display their ability to mobilize opposition to Obama and his policies. In just three days AIPAC coordinated a letter that was signed by a whopping 326 members of Congress and sent to Secretary Clinton, asserting that "it is in U.S. national security interests to assure that Israel's security as an independent Jewish state is maintained." And a bipartisan chorus of lawmakers spoke aggressively against the administration and in favor of the Israeli position at the conference itself. Senator Lindsey Graham (R-SC) told the cheering crowd that "all options must be on the table" and "you know exactly what I'm talking about," indicating his support for military action against Iran. "Sometimes it is better to go to war than to allow the Holocaust to develop a second time," he concluded somberly. And the attack should not be limited to the country's nuclear program, he added. "If military force is ever employed, it should be done in a decisive fashion. The Iranian government's ability to wage conventional war against its neighbors and our troops in the region should not exist. They should not have one plane that can fly or one ship that can float." Senator Charles Schumer (D-NY), a close Obama ally, added to the anti-Obama chorus at the conference. "Diplomatic efforts have failed. We are too close [to a nuclear Iran] to simply continue those efforts," said Schumer. "The U.S. must hit Iran first, on our own, with unilateral sanctions, no matter what the other nations of the world do. And we cannot wait, we must push those sanctions now."[26]

At the same time, only a few blocks away at the White House, Obama and Netanyahu were staring each other down. Obama had presented Netanyahu with a list of thirteen demands designed both to end the feud with his administration and to kick-start peace talks. The most important demand was to halt all new settlement construction in East Jerusalem. But Netanyahu would not yield, prompting Obama to abruptly rise from his seat and declare: "I'm going to the residential wing to have dinner with Michelle and the girls."

Obama did leave the Israeli leader with an opening, though, telling him that he would still be available if Netanyahu were to change his mind. Netanyahu and his aides stayed in the Roosevelt Room in the White House for about an hour to prepare a response to Obama's demands. But no resolution was found. The tensions with Israel and the debate inside the White House got so heated that leaks suggesting dual loyalty among some senior Obama administration officials emerged. Laura Rozen of the news website Politico reported that some White House officials blamed Middle East envoy Dennis Ross for the dispute with Israel due to his alleged inclination to side with the Israelis more than with the U.S. "He [Ross] seems to be far more sensitive to Netanyahu's coalition politics than to U.S. interests," one U.S. official said. "And he doesn't seem to understand that this has become bigger than Jerusalem but is rather about the credibility of this administration."[27]

As U.S.-Israel relations plummeted, so did Israel's and Congress's patience with the Obama administration's sanctions progress. It was now April, and sanctions were two months overdue. Questions began to arise over whether the sanctions could be passed at all; the Russian and Chinese resistance was surprisingly firm. Rather than wait for the sanctions process to result in failure, the U.S. should circumvent the UN and impose "crippling sanctions" right away, Netanyahu demanded publicly with increased frequency. "If you stop . . . Iran from importing . . . petrolcum, that's a fancy word for gasoline, then Iran simply doesn't have refining capacity and this regime comes to a halt. I think that's crippling sanctions," he said.[28]

The Breakthrough

While the Obama administration and the Netanyahu government were clashing in Washington, China and Russia had embarked on a diplomatic mission to Iran with the aim of convincing the Iranians to show greater flexibility. "Russia and China had a demarche in Tehran to try and get them to shift their position on the nuclear issue, particularly with regard to the Tehran Research Reactor," a European diplomat said. "The Russians and Chinese were saying that their position [on a new sanctions resolution] would depend on Iran's response to the demarches." But after a few meetings, including a trip by Iran's lead nuclear negotiator, Saeed Jalili, to Beijing, Russia and China both left empty-handed. Russia's UN ambassador, Vitaly Churkin, voiced his country's frustration with Iran. "I don't think any of us wants to impose sanctions; what we want is to have a diplomatic solution," he said. But "if Iran wants to negotiate, it should start negotiating." Shortly thereafter, on March 30, the Chinese finally agreed to engage substantively in sanctions negotiations.[29]

Initially, Chinese involvement centered on objecting to various measures suggested by the United States. Most of the negotiating was between the U.S. and China and, to a lesser extent, the U.S. and Russia. Chinese objections were largely economic in nature—ensuring that sanctions do not punish the Iranian people; avoiding measures that could destabilize the Persian Gulf and the flow of oil; ensuring that "legitimate trade relations" were not harmed; and ensuring that sanctions would not undermine the recovery of the world economy. The Russians focused on ensuring that sanctions would be targeted and hit the nuclear program rather than the entire Iranian economy, and also be aimed at changing Iranian behavior rather than achieving regime change or paving the way for a military confrontation. "A total embargo on deliveries on refined oil products to Iran would mean a slap, a blow, a huge shock for the whole society and the whole population," said Sergei Ryabkov, Russia's deputy foreign minister. "These types of things that shock the fundaments of a society or country are something that we definitely are not prepared to consider." In addition, the chief of staff for Russian general Nikolai Makarov went so far as to declare that any air strike against Iran by the United States or Israel would be "unacceptable." In spite of these limitations, the fact that China and Russia were now onboard to discuss sanctions—meaning that they no longer opposed the principle—was a major breakthrough.[30]

After Jalili's unsuccessful trip to Beijing, the Iranians understood that a consensus was building against them among the P5, and that sanctions were inching closer. But Ahmadinejad's response was defiant. Speaking on Iranian TV, he argued that Iran was Obama's "only chance" to succeed after the crises Washington faced in neighboring Iraq and Afghanistan. "Mr. Obama has only one chance and that is Iran. This is not emotional talk but scientific. He has but one place to say that 'I made a change and I turned over the world equation' and that is Iran. . . . He has but one chance to stay as head of the state and succeed. Obama cannot do anything in Palestine. He has no chance. What can he do in Iraq? Nothing. And Afghanistan is too complicated. . . . The best way for him is to accept and respect Iran and enter into cooperation. Many new opportunities will be created for him," Ahmadinejad said.[31]

Ahmadinejad's speech may have been wishful thinking. But on the eve of Obama's success, it was not the activities of Iran, but those of two U.S. allies—Turkey and Brazil—that turned victory bitter.

Ten

The Art of Taking Yes for an Answer

We could not take yes for an answer.

—Senior Obama administration official, September 2010

After months of diplomatic wrangling with hostile and friendly elements and states alike, the Obama administration was finally on the verge of passing a UN Security Council resolution sanctioning Iran's nuclear activities. Concessions had been given to the Russians and Chinese; pressure from Israel, Saudi Arabia, and Congress had been heeded; Iranian maneuvers to influence the vote had been countered; and a plan of action with the EU had been agreed upon. All that remained were the formalities.

But in that last moment, Washington miscalculated the diplomatic skills of two up-and-coming states—Brazil and Turkey—and their desire to demonstrate the ability to take on diplomatic challenges usually reserved for the great powers. Both had followed the Iranian nuclear file for some time and both elevated their efforts to assist in finding a solution once the nuclear swap deal failed to gain traction in the fall of 2009. At first they were encouraged to help. But by the time the pressure of the sanctions track overshadowed the diplomacy track, their involvement and mediation efforts became increasingly problematic for the Obama administration, which feared that the Iranians would only use Brazil and Turkey to split the Security Council, breaking the consensus on sanctions that Obama had spent a considerable amount of political capital to achieve. On May 15, 2010, Brazilian president Luiz Inácio Lula da Silva traveled to Iran with an entourage of some three hundred Brazilian business-men. It was his first visit there, and he would seek Iran's agreement over the nuclear fuel swap in what the Obama administration and French president Nicolas Sarkozy described as the "last big shot at engagement." Soon thereafter, Turkish prime minister Recep Tayyip Erdogan and his energetic foreign minister, Ahmet Davutoglu, joined Lula in an effort to convince Iran to ship out its low-enriched uranium (LEU). Two days later, Lula and Erdogan stunned the U.S. and the world—they had a deal.[1]

Contrary to expectations, and arguably to the hopes of some, they succeeded in convincing the Iranian government to agree to a deal based on the American benchmarks—that 1,200 kilograms of Iranian LEU would be sent out in one shipment, and Iran would receive fuel pads for its Tehran Research Reactor roughly twelve months later. For a moment, it looked as if diplomacy had succeeded after all. But what could have been viewed as a diplomatic break-through—with Iran blinking first and succumbing to American de-mands—was instead treated as an effort to sabotage the new and higher objective of imposing sanctions. The twisted dance of hos-tility and missed opportunities between the U.S. and Iran that Obama hoped to end had just come full circle—and all within the first sixteen months of his presidency.

The "New" Kids on the Block

Unlike other actors involved in the Iranian nuclear file, Brazil and Turkey were two of the few states that pressed the Obama admin-istration to pursue more robust diplomacy rather than sanctions. Both are rising regional powers whose new and assertive foreign policy profiles have fueled the inevitable frictions that emerge be-tween great and middle powers as the latter seek opportunities to enhance their role in international affairs. In the case of Brazil, tensions had been brewing for a few years between Washington and Brasilia not only over President Lula's posture in Latin America, but increasingly over the Middle East in general and Iran in particular. During the Bush administration, Washington witnessed how relations between Brazil and Iran warmed while the Brazilians became more vocal in their criticism of U.S. policies in the Middle East. The U.S. embassy in Brasilia regularly sent cables back to Washington warning of the left-wing Brazilian government's flirtation with Tehran's anti-imperialist messages. Washington viewed Brazil as uninformed about the realities of the Middle East, and its many efforts to sensitize Brasilia had been rebuffed. The Brazilian foreign ministry felt no need to "ask permission of the United States in carrying out foreign policy initiatives" and warned that "the United States should expect more Brazilian statements on Middle East issues."[2]

Brazil's position on the nuclear issue had given U.S. policy makers a headache for some time. For several years Brasilia opposed Washington's efforts to get the IAEA to refer Iran to the Security Council until the vote within the agency had become a foregone conclusion by 2006, and it did not support a UN Security Council vote to condemn Iranian nuclear activities until Iran missed the UN-mandated deadline for allowing international inspectors to visit suspected nuclear facilities. In retrospect, Brazil's foreign minister, Celso Amorim, even expressed regret over that vote. "Today, I doubt if we did the right thing," he told me, as he contemplated how that decision paved the way for the current stalemate. In spite of that vote, Lula publicly defended Iran's record of compliance with the IAEA and its right to enrichment on numerous occasions. "Iran has the right to conduct its own experiments provided they are for peaceful purposes . . . so far Iran has not committed any crime against the direction of the United Nations in relation to nuclear weapons."[3]

At the heart of the matter was Brazil's own nuclear program, which was more advanced than the Iranian program and did not receive as much attention from IAEA inspectors. Moreover, the Brazilians feared that UN action on the Iranian nuclear file would set a precedent that defined enrichment of uranium as a military activity. The Brazilians enjoyed credibility on this issue since they had voluntarily dismantled their established nuclear weapons program, and even added a ban on such weapons to their constitution. But giving up nuclear weapons was different from giving up the production of civilian nuclear energy and the required enrichment. "I want for Iran the same thing that I want for Brazil, to use the development of nuclear energy for peaceful purposes," Lula said. "If Iran is in agreement with this, then Iran will have the support of Brazil."[4]

Of the many factors that colored the Brazilian view of Iran, the experience with both sanctions and war in Iraq played a central role. Amorim had served as Brazil's UN ambassador in the Security Council in the late 1990s. He chaired three panels at the council handling the Iraqi sanctions and witnessed firsthand their devastating effect on the civilian population. "Most of the times, sanctions affect the most vulnerable people. They have no effect whatsoever on the leadership," he said. Moreover, after sanctions devastated Iraq and, according to a UN official, contributed to the death of 500,000 Iraqi children in the period 1990–2000, the United States proceeded to invade the country in a war that has yet to come to a full conclusion. Amorim "warned that the last time the Security Council voted on the basis of inconclusive evidence, the world ended up with a major illegitimate intervention in Iraq that undermined the principle of collective security." Similarly, the view in Brasilia was that sanctions would not resolve the nuclear problem but rather harden the positions of all sides, devastate the Iranian economy, and—as in Iraq—pave the way for war. Brazilian diplomats feared that the mere passage of a UN Security Council sanctions resolution could be interpreted by Israel as a green light for a military attack (Brazil repeatedly sought assurances from the U.S. that it would rein in Israel's bellicose posturing). Moreover, a confrontational approach would increase Iran's incentives to seek a nuclear deterrent, Brazilian decision makers believed. This reasoning was based on its own experience. Brazil's civilian nuclear program faced strong American opposition in the 1970s, causing the Brazilians to pursue secret nuclear capability as a result. From Brazil's perspective, the similarities with the Iranian situation were striking. "When Brazil looks at Iran it doesn't only see Iran, it sees Brazil too," a high-ranking official in Brasilia said.[5]

Beyond fear of war and skepticism of sanctions, Brazil made itself a player in the Iran conundrum because it saw two opportunities. First, it could prove its ability to resolve international problems and, in doing so, boost its chances for a permanent seat at the Security Council. Second, this was an opportunity to challenge what it perceived to be an unjust and outdated world order. Brasilia's involvement in this issue was questioned both at home and on the international scene, particularly in Washington. What interest did Brazil, a South American country thousands of miles away from the Middle East, have in the Iranian challenge, critics of the Lula government asked. But for the Brazilian government, it could not couple its demand for a permanent seat at the Security Council with continued indifference to matters of world peace. "It's a global issue," a senior adviser to Lula told me. "Not just because we have 12 million Arabs and 500,000 Jews. It's because it's in the interest of global peace. . . . What do we want to become a member on the Security Council for if we don't have anything to say about the Middle East?" Brazil's growing power over the course of the past decade simply did "not allow us to stay indifferent to these questions," Amorim said in a speech to the Brazilian diplomatic corps two days after signing the accord between Brazil, Turkey, and Iran known as the Tehran Declaration.[6]

For a country that had long felt uncomfortable with the international order and had argued for greater equality between nations and a "democratic international system," there were few opportunities to change "the rules of the game" of global governance and how the Security Council worked. Even though it was one of the most difficult opportunities Brazil could have chosen to pursue, the Iranian file became the litmus test of the Brazilian proposition for a more representative Security Council and world order. "For Lula, the Iran [question] is not important as such," said Professor Oliver Stuenkel of the University of São Paulo in Brazil. "He is making a broader argument that current structures of global governance are unjust and that emerging powers should have a greater say." These structures were particularly problematic in the case of the nonproliferation regime because, according to Brazil, the regime had become a "politically driven tool in the hands of the United States to selectively 'lay down the law' on weaker states." There were so many contradictions within the regime: Iran was facing major sanctions for pursuing enrichment while little was said about Israel's nuclear arsenal; India (a country which, like Israel, is not a party to the Non-Proliferation Treaty) was rewarded by Washington with a major nuclear deal, while states with nuclear weapons avoided commitments to fully disarm. These double standards could precipitate the collapse of international nonproliferation efforts. And while Brazil's position could superficially be interpreted as a challenge to America's leadership, Brazilian decision makers viewed it as the effort of "an emerging country with a long history of frailty and dependence" to seek protection and hedge "against great-power use of international norms to impose their will on weaker nations." For Lula, gaining a greater voice and recognition as a major player on the international scene was not enough. With that role came the responsibility to change the status quo for the better. "We should reform the international system," a Brazilian diplomat told me. "There is a major deficit of governance in this international order. We cannot continue like this." For Brazil, Iran became the vehicle to achieve this larger goal.[7]

Brazil's deeper involvement in resolving the Iranian nuclear standoff began in July 2009. During a brief discussion on Iran between Lula and Obama at the G8 Summit in Italy, the Brazilian president mentioned that he wanted to meet with the Iranians. Obama took note of this and said he would appreciate anything Lula could do to be helpful. Lula interpreted this to mean that the Obama administration tacitly supported Brazil's efforts to engage the Iranians. Months earlier, Amorim had paid his first visit to Iran. Both

Brazilian diplomats in Tehran and Iranian officials had pushed for a visit for some time, but Amorim had been reluctant to go and always found an excuse to avoid the issue. Unlike Lula, Amorim originally viewed the Iranian issue as poisonous, according to a Brazilian diplomat. But upon visiting Iran, his views changed. The Brazilian foreign minister was surprised by what he saw and the treatment he received, and he began echoing Lula's enthusiasm about engaging Tehran. "I think that was a major landmark, a milestone," a Brazilian diplomat involved in the visit explained.[8]

Fall of 2009 saw a lot of diplomatic activity between Brazil and Iran. In spite of the election crisis, the Brazilians tended to view Iran as a "compromised democracy" whose robust civil society would ultimately ensure openness to negotiation. Though the Brazilian embassy in Tehran reported that the election had been fraudulent, higher-level Brazilian officials still concluded that Ahmadinejad had won. All in all, Brasilia believed that the nuclear issue needed to be resolved regardless of what had happened in the election. In conversations with U.S. diplomats, the Brazilians praised the Obama administration's "excellent" opening to Iran and repeated their offer to help, although "not just to pressure" Iran. They did, however, emphasize that Brazil would vote in favor of sanctions if diplomacy fell through. Amorim also reiterated Brazil's opposition to any effort to prevent Iran from pursuing enrichment for peaceful purposes.[9]

Lula then met with Ahmadinejad for a full hour at the annual UN General Assembly opening on September 23. The Brazilian president pressed Ahmadinejad on the importance of opening up Iran's nuclear program for more IAEA inspections and took the opportunity to challenge his statements denying the Holocaust. Lula was upbeat after the meeting and felt that an opening on the issue could be achieved. The two leaders met again two months later in Brasilia, during Ahmadinejad's state visit to Brazil on November 23. Lula welcomed Ahmadinejad—his "good friend"—and expressed support for Iran's right to a nuclear program for civilian use, but made no public comments on the Russian-American swap proposal or the state of human rights in Iran. Privately, however, Lula pressed the Iranian president to accept the nuclear swap offer. Though Ahmadinejad's visit was controversial (many in Brazil were appalled by it on human rights grounds), it did help Brazil achieve one of its diplomatic objectives—to "get in the game" of high politics with the big powers.[10]

Only ten days later, Amorim paid another visit to Iran, this time to the ancient city of Isfahan, where he met with Ahmadinejad and Iran's foreign minister, Manouchehr Mottaki. Part of Amorim's mission was to help get Iran and France back on speaking terms, per the direct request of French president Nicolas Sarkozy. The Iranians had arrested Clotilde Reiss, a young Frenchwoman studying in Iran, and charged her with espionage. Sarkozy had requested help from Brazil to negotiate for her release. During the most sensitive parts of the discussions, Amorim's entire staff was ordered to leave the room, including his chief of staff. The only people remaining in the room were Ahmadinejad, Mottaki, Antonio Luis Espinola Salgado (Brazilian ambassador to Iran), and Amorim himself. In addition to Reiss's case, Amorim also addressed Iran's enrichment of uranium to 19.75 percent. He succeeded in convincing Ahmadinejad to postpone any enrichment at that level for two months. Ahmadinejad agreed but explained that he could not present the agreement publicly as a concession due to political factors in Iran. Amorim was surprised to hear Ahmadinejad admit that he was facing domestic problems. When Amorim later briefed the U.S. and its allies on his conversation with Ahmadinejad, few were impressed by Ahmadinejad's offer.[11]

Turkey had a more complicated history with Iran but shared Brazil's perspective on how to deal with its neighbor to the east. Turkish prime minister Erdogan offered to mediate between the U.S. and Iran immediately after Obama's presidential win in 2008. Under the rule of Erdogan's AK Party, Ankara's relations with Iran, as well as with the rest of the Middle East, had flourished. Only a decade earlier, Turkey was in conflict with almost all of its neighbors and its foreign policy relied heavily on military means. Now not only was it on good terms with its neighbors, the country even mediated regional and intrastate conflicts. Its economy was booming, and its trade ties with historical rivals such as Iran were on the rise. Already the seventh-largest economy in the EU, Turkey aspired to become one of the ten largest economies of the world by 2023, the one hundredth anniversary of the modern Turkish republic. To continue its growth, Turkey needed stability in the region and access to energy for its booming economy. Both would come under threat if the standoff over Iran's nuclear program escalated into open conflict.[12]

From Ankara's perspective, U.S. policies in the region had cost Turkey dearly by increasing instability and undermining the business environment. The UN sanctions on Iraq in the 1990s had cut off Turkey from one of its key trading partners and laid the ground for the establishment of an autonomous Kurdish state adjacent to Turkey's border. The U.S. invasion of Iraq in 2003 had spread instability and fanaticism in the region while strengthening both the Kurds and Turkey's historical rival, Iran. Another war in the region, or a continuation of policies centered on isolating Iran, could derail the projected growth of Turkey's economy while further destabilizing the region. Like Brazil, Turkey feared that the absence of diplomacy would lead to war. Erdogan did not mince words when expressing his country's opposition to war with Iran, calling it "crazy." In the view of the Turkish government, war would be the worst outcome—even worse than Iran going nuclear. The Turkish public supported this view. According to polls, one-third of the population did not even view a nuclear Iran as a threat—a very low number compared with public opinion in other Western states.[13]

Like Brazil, Turkey's rise in power was coupled with a desire for a greater leadership role. But in Turkey's case, the staking out of a regional leadership position that put Turkey "at the fulcrum" and made it an indispensable partner with the West was also driven by the vacuum that emerged with the decline of America's power following its occupation of Iraq, and Iraq's own weakened position as the regional Arab counterweight to Iran. Because of Washington's discomfort with one aspect of Turkey's efforts to be recognized as a regional leader—its policy of "zero problems" with its neighbors, which in Washington's view made Ankara far too friendly toward Tehran—it tended to overlook the fact that much of Turkey's maneuvering was aimed at checking Iran's attempts to fill that same vacuum. Since 2003, much to Iran's irritation, "wherever Iran went, Turkey was there as well," to check Iran's growing influence, a senior Turkish diplomat explained. "No other regional state has the military and economic power to serve as an effective counterweight to Iran," Turkish leaders told the Obama administration. In this struggle for regional leadership, Turkey had provided a "third option" in addition to Iran and the Saudis, which, according to Davutoglu, helped "limit Iranian influence in the region." In the new fault lines of the Middle East, the age-old rivalry between Turkey and Iran was once again rising in prominence. The difference, however, was that Turkey and Iran were each seeking to engage the other in a sophisticated game of competition and cooperation, in order to reduce the risk of the rivalry turning hostile. For instance, Turkey sought to bring Iran into regional organizations and, by doing so, secure Iran's commitment to a shift in behavior toward greater cooperation—that is, check Iran's influence and change its foreign policy by integrating Iran into the region through diplomacy and trade. If this approach was not pursued, not only did the nuclear standoff risk sparking a war, but Turkey's ability to avoid a confrontation with Iran down the road would also decrease.[14]

The idea of Turkish mediation was welcomed early on. In March 2009 Secretary of State Clinton told Turkey's Kanal D television that the Obama administration welcomed any Turkish efforts to help sway the Islamic Republic. But the U.S. felt increasingly uncomfortable with the Erdogan government's efforts to gain Tehran's trust. Turkey's emphasis on diplomacy and its rejection of war and sanctions, combined with statements dismissing the threat from the Iranian nuclear program and Tehran's problematic record with the IAEA, made Washington hesitant about the idea of Turkey as a mediator. Washington pushed Ankara to adopt a sterner public posture, but the Turks pushed back, arguing that Turkey's foreign policy is giving a "sense of justice" and a "sense of vision" to the region. It did not help that tensions between Israel and Turkey were on the rise, which many unreflectively attributed to the AK Party's Islamic nature. U.S. diplomats stationed in Turkey shared this view and reported back to Foggy Bottom that "Erdogan simply hates Israel." Ankara's affable attitude toward Tehran also won it the anger of some members of the Green movement, who viewed Turkey as fully committed to the Iranian regime's survival in the name of regional stability and at the expense of the Iranian people's democratic aspirations. Still, Washington welcomed Turkey's efforts to persuade Iran to accept the Russian-American proposal for a fuel swap. But after several meetings and weeks of intense, personal diplomacy by Davutoglu, supported by interventions from President Abdullah Gul and Prime Minister Erdogan, Turkey could not manage to convince Tehran to agree to the fuel swap. This further fed Washington's skepticism about the utility of the Turkish approach, as well as Turkey's capabilities as a mediator.[15]

The Turks and Brazilians did not initially coordinate their mediation efforts. By early 2010, however, there was both greater awareness of each other's activities and a greater sense of commonality between them, as they were both frustrated with what they viewed as prematurely aborted diplomacy. Further, in 2010 they both served on the Security Council as nonpermanent members. In January 2010 Amorim was invited to Turkey to address the annual meeting of all ambassadors of the Turkish foreign ministry. There, Amorim and Davutoglu exchanged notes on their activities on Iran and decided to coordinate their efforts. This quickly led to a very intense dialogue between the two rising middle powers. For the Turks, Brazil's involvement was heaven-sent. As a Catholic Western power, Brazil gave Turkey—and the Islamist AK Party—excellent political cover. It would be much more difficult to cast Turkey's position as a mere whim of religious solidarity between the fundamentalists in Tehran and Turkey's Islamists.[16]

The Race Against Diplomacy

While Washington was working on getting the permanent members of the Security Council to sign on to a new sanctions resolution, Brazil and Turkey were pursuing the revival of diplomacy. For them, the fight for diplomacy was a race against sanctions. U.S. diplomats did not discourage Brazil and Turkey's diplomatic efforts, but the Americans and the French were growing increasingly worried that they might vote against the resolution. Though their votes were not crucial for passage of the resolution, a unified council would send a powerful signal to Tehran. The U.S. strategy essentially came down to giving Turkey and Brazil a double message: efforts to convince Tehran to agree to the fuel swap were encouraged, but it was also important to impose new sanctions on Iran. And, according to the Obama administration, sanctions would actually help get the Iranians to agree to the fuel swap. While the Brazilians contended that sanctions could "close the door to further diplomatic efforts," the U.S. argued that sanctions would keep "the diplomatic option alive" and reduce the risk of a military conflict. "Personally speaking, I think it's only after we pass sanctions in the Security Council that Iran will negotiate in good faith," Clinton said.[17]

But the argument did not resonate. In early March Clinton traveled to Brazil to win Brasilia's support for sanctions. Even though she offered full U.S. backing of Brazil's bid to gain a permanent seat on the Council, the Brazilians would not bend. Lula and Amorim politely but clearly rebuffed Clinton. "We got nothing," a U.S. diplomat told me after the trip. "The Brazilians made it clear that they would get the permanent seat anyways." Ankara showed similar resilience, publicly rebuffing the sanctions path and arguing for more diplomacy. "There is still an opportunity ahead of us and we believe that this opportunity should be used effectively. Not less, but more diplomacy [is needed]," Turkey's foreign ministry spokesman, Burak Ozugergin, said at a news conference in late March 2010.[18]

On April 12 and 13, world leaders gathered in Washington for a nuclear summit led by Obama. During the gathering, a three-way meeting was held between Lula, Erdogan, and Obama. Clinton, Amorim, Davutoglu, and a few advisers also joined the conversation. The meeting, which lasted no more than fifteen minutes, was tense and testy. Obama was dismissive of the prospects of diplomacy and signaled that Iran no longer preoccupied much of his time. There was nothing wrong with diplomacy, but the Iranians simply could not be relied upon, Obama indicated. But Erdogan and Lula insisted that they could convince Tehran to agree to the fuel swap. At the end of the meeting, neither side was satisfied. And the mixed messages from Washington continued; Obama was skeptical of diplomacy, yet softly encouraged Turkey and Brazil's efforts.[19]

After the summit, both the French and the Americans framed Lula's upcoming state visit to Iran as the last chance for diplomacy. "I'm not criticizing President Lula, but we've agreed with President Lula that this is the last chance, last-resort and last-chance initiative, and it has to happen very swiftly," Sarkozy told reporters. "It has to fit in with the timetable I presented to Iran, in other words, April or May." Davutoglu immediately shot back with a rejection of the constraints Sarkozy was seeking to put on diplomacy. "One of the most dangerous things in a process like this is to give a deadline. It is not the right course of action," Davutoglu said. "If one wants to manage the psychology of the process, one must avoid deadlines. Therefore, we do not say that this should happen at this time, and that should happen at that time." On this point, Turkey's position on diplomacy was now almost identical to that of Obama prior to the Vienna talks.[20]

A frenzy of diplomatic activities followed in the wake of Obama's nuclear summit. The Brazilians and Turks paid several visits to Iran:

Davutoglu met with Mottaki in Tehran on April 21; Amorim did the same five days later and also met with Iran's nuclear negotiator, Saeed Jalili, and the Speaker of the Iranian parliament, Ali Larijani; and Iran's foreign minister stopped in Istanbul on his way back from New York on May 7. Meanwhile, Iran embarked on its own diplomatic offensive to defeat the sanctions resolution. A week after Obama's nuclear summit, Iran held its own, titled "Nuclear Energy for All, Nuclear Weapons for No One." Tehran sought to bring attention to the lack of disarmament among the nuclear weapons states to counter their focus on Iran's enrichment program. Nearly sixty countries were represented at the meeting, suggesting that support for sanctions might not have been as widespread as the U.S. had hoped. Immediately afterward, Iranian diplomats traveled to almost all of the member states of the UN Security Council to present Iran's perspective on the nuclear issue. The Iranians also presented another counteroffer to the swap proposal from the fall, without introducing any new elements from those discussed in 2009. Finally, the Iranians held a most unusual dinner for all the UN ambassadors in the Security Council at the Iranian mission's Fifth Avenue townhouse in New York, hosted by Mottaki himself. All members of the Security Council were represented at the dinner, including Ambassador Alejandro D. Wolff, the second-ranking diplomat at the U.S. mission to the United Nations.[21]

As the time of Lula's state visit to Iran on May 16–17 inched closer, the public exchanges grew testier (it did not help that the Iranian media lauded Turkey and Brazil's intervention and branded it as taking Iran's side "in combating America's power"). Gary Samore, special assistant to the president on nonproliferation, expressed confidence that sanctions would be imposed "unless Iran does something significant," which he found unlikely because Iran, in his view, had no serious interest in a nuclear deal. Consequently, Brazilian and Turkish mediation was bound to fail, he maintained. Samore did, however, make clear that the 2009 swap offer was still on the table if the Iranians were willing to accept it. "The Iranians have frankly not been prepared to accept that offer, it's pretty clear to anybody," Samore said. "And Turkey will soon satisfy themselves of that."

The Obama administration emphasized publicly that sanctions were not inevitable; Iran could choose to accept Washington's offer. "Iran continues to have a choice," said Susan Rice, America's top diplomat at the UN. If Lula's efforts failed and Iran continued to refuse the offer, however, sanctions should follow. "Assuming it continues to make the wrong choices, that pressure will intensify," she declared. On the eve of Lula's visit, Clinton repeated her argument that sanctions would enhance rather than undermine diplomacy, while warning that Iran could use Lula's visit to stall for time. "We will not get any serious response out of the Iranians until after the Security Council acts," she said. The French went a step further, stating that Lula's mediation was simply misguided. French foreign minister Bernard Kouchner said Lula was "on the wrong track" and risked being "ensnared" by Iran's deception, contradicting earlier French statements, which cast Lula's trip to Iran as the last chance for diplomacy. Lula responded in kind, publicly censuring the Western powers for not being serious about diplomacy. "Why doesn't Obama call Ahmadinejad? Or Sarkozy, or Angela Merkel, or Gordon Brown?" he said of the leaders of the Western states. "People aren't talking," the Brazilian president added. "I'm going there to talk." (The Russians and Chinese had been slightly more supportive of Lula's mediation and expressed readiness to give the Brazilians and Turks the time they needed to broker a deal. Russian president Dmitry Medvedev had publicly given Lula a 30 percent chance of success.)[22]

The Tehran Declaration

Lula and Erdogan's frustration with public statements emanating from Washington and Paris stemmed from the contradiction between those statements and their private conversations with American and

European decision makers. In addition, Lula and Erdogan had in their hands a letter from Obama that spelled out the benchmarks of a deal the U.S. believed would be helpful. The letter was dated April 20, exactly a week after Lula and Erdogan's conversation with Obama at the nuclear summit in Washington. Obama clarified that the purpose of the swap was "for both sides to gain trust and confidence." He spelled out the important markers that any agreement would have to meet to be acceptable to the United States. "For us, Iran's agreement to transfer 1,200kg of Iran's low enriched uranium (LEU) out of the country would build confidence and reduce regional tensions by substantially reducing Iran's LEU stockpile. I want to underscore that this element is of fundamental importance for the United States," the letter said. Obama also presented a compromise mechanism that the U.S. had floated back in November 2009—the idea that the Iranian LEU could be held in Turkey in "escrow" until the fuel was delivered to Iran:

> Last November, the IAEA conveyed to Iran our offer to allow Iran to ship its 1,200 kg of LEU to a third country—specifically Turkey—at the outset of the process to be held "in escrow" as a guarantee during the fuel production process that Iran would get back its uranium if we failed to deliver the fuel. Iran has never pursued the "escrow" compromise and has provided no credible explanation for its rejection. . . . I would urge Brazil to impress upon Iran the opportunity presented by this offer to "escrow" its uranium in Turkey while the nuclear fuel is being produced.[23]

The letter spelled out three substantive points related to the questions of quantity (1,200 kilograms), timing (shipped out immediately, with the fuel rods delivered a year later), and place (an escrow in Turkey). The letter also included a formal point that Iran should send its reply to the IAEA in writing within seven days rather than to any individual state.[24]

With the letter in hand, Lula headed to Tehran. Two weeks before the meeting, the Turks had placed a senior intelligence officer in Iran to prepare the grounds for the negotiations. Davutoglu joined them shortly thereafter. Erdogan was ready to join Lula in Tehran but wanted Iran first to express publicly its determination to work with Turkey cooperatively to resolve the nuclear issue. The talks started without him. Foreign Minister Manouchehr Mottaki and the head of the Iranian Atomic Energy Organization, Ali Akbar Salehi, led Iran's negotiation team, with National Security Council head Jalili as the principal. Davutoglu headed the Turkish delegation and had with him five aides. On the Brazilian side were Amorim and his two advisers.[25]

The discussions were difficult, and privately neither the Turks nor the Brazilians had high hopes for a breakthrough. But there was one opening that gave Brazil and Turkey confidence: Washington's willingness to tacitly accept Iranian enrichment. Ankara and Brasilia had long believed that any deal that deprived Iran of enrichment was a nonstarter. The Iranians had no incentives to give up enrichment entirely, and the international community had no instruments to force it to do so. "I always thought it would be impossible to reach an agreement with Iran unless [the Western states] recognize their right [to enrich uranium]," Amorim told a closed session at the Brazilian foreign ministry after the negotiations. "If there was doubt, the doubt should be clarified. If there was need for more inspections, there should be more inspections. But the absence of entitlement made any solution to the problem, in my view, impossible." In an interview with me, Amorim was even more categorical. "Iran would never agree to anything, any kind of arrangement that would in theory or in practice deprive them of the right to enrich uranium." But the swap proposal from the fall of 2009 changed the picture. For the first time, there was a proposal that at least implicitly recognized Iran's enrichment program. Compared with all previous proposals, which at least in Brazil's view were all nonstarters, this one had promise. Washington's willingness to accept limited Iranian enrichment was even emphasized by the

Obama administration in its discussions with Brazil—not necessarily as recognition of Iran's right, but at least as acknowledgment of Iranian enrichment as fact. In the negotiations in Tehran, Amorim emphasized to Mottaki that this provided Iran with an opportunity. The Iranian foreign minister recognized this but pointed out that the swap would then also require Iran to give up its right to enrichment to 19.75 percent. Therein lay the essence of the deal: a quid pro quo that paved the way for limiting Iranian enrichment at the expense of recognizing Iran's rights.[26]

Iran made a concession toward the end of the first day of talks: it expressed a willingness to escrow its LEU in Turkey. Once this point had been confirmed, Erdogan decided to join the talks and flew in from Ankara around midnight on May 15. The discussions were exasperating. Between the Iranian mistrust of the West ("We would be very naïve to trust the West. Why do they insist on moving the uranium abroad? This is proof of their diabolical intent," said Ali Akbar Velayati, Supreme Leader Khamenei's senior adviser on international affairs), Ahmadinejad's fear of coming across as weak if he compromised, and the technical limitations of fuel production, the room for maneuvering was narrow. But as the parties were ready to break for the day, another hopeful sign emerged: the Iranians wanted to resume the discussions at 7:00 a.m. the next day. For Amorim, this was "the first time I felt there was a good prospect" because "only someone who is serious schedules a meeting for seven o'clock in the morning." The talks continued for several hours during the second day, totaling eighteen intense and exhausting hours of negotiations. The issue of trust was a constantly recurring one—not only as it related to Iran's mistrust of the U.S. or its fear that Turkey could be susceptible to pressure from Washington to violate the terms of its escrow, but also the fear that Turkey and Brazil would fail in securing American acceptance of the deal. Iran was very frustrated by its negotiations with Europe during the Bush administration. Tehran had at that time wrongly assumed that Europe would be able to deliver the U.S., that is, use its influence to win American support for any deal. It did not want to repeat that mistake with Turkey and Brazil. To reassure the Iranians, the Turks showed them Obama's letter to Erdogan (which was identical to his letter to Lula) and made the case that they had Washington's interest in the deal in writing. This proved decisive in convincing the Iranians to agree to the American parameters of the swap deal.[27]

By the end of the second day of talks, an agreement was within reach. The Turks and Brazilians had succeeded in convincing Iran to hand over 1,200 kilograms of LEU in one shipment in order to receive fuel pads for its research reactor within the next twelve months—the same parameters Tehran had rejected eight months earlier in Vienna. The LEU, however, would not go to Russia or France. Instead, it would be put in Turkey under IAEA seal, and, if the West violated the terms of the agreement, Iran could take its LEU back. This arrangement, Turkey and Brazil reasoned, would alleviate Iran's fear of undue exposure while putting the bulk of its trust in its neighbor Turkey rather than its adversary Washington. Before the deal was sealed, Lula also met with Khamenei. Though the nuclear issue was not raised in their discussions, it was clear from Khamenei's questions and body language that he endorsed the agreement. Amorim also had a session with Larijani, the head of the Iranian parliament and a sworn political enemy of Ahmadinejad. But at the last minute, the Iranians sought to include one more element in the agreement. They wanted the declaration to explicitly state that the acceptance of the agreement would be contingent upon new sanctions not being imposed on Iran. This language could strengthen the appearance that the negotiations were aimed more at staving off sanctions than at minimizing the risk of nuclear proliferation. Both Turkey and Brazil objected. The value of the agreement would be taken away if that language were to be included, they argued. Eventually, the Iranians withdrew their proposal and the agreement was saved. Against all odds, Turkey and Brazil had achieved in a few months, through intensive diplomacy, what the Western powers had failed to do in several years.[28]

The trilateral agreement between Brazil, Turkey, and Iran, later known as the Tehran Declaration, was no more than a page and a half long and contained only ten points. The first clause reiterated that all states have the right, according to the nonproliferation treaty (NPT), to develop the research, production, and use of nuclear energy for peaceful purposes without discrimination. The clause also made explicit that enrichment activities are included in that right—something the NPT did not do. The fourth clause clarified that the agreement "is a starting point to begin cooperation." The details of the agreement were spelled out in the following paragraphs:

5. Based on the above, in order to facilitate the nuclear cooperation mentioned above, the Islamic Republic of Iran agrees to deposit 1200 kilograms of LEU in Turkey. While in Turkey this LEU will continue to be the property of Iran. Iran and the IAEA may station observers to monitor the safekeeping of the LEU in Turkey.

6. Iran will notify the IAEA in writing through official channels of its agreement with the above within seven days following the date of this declaration. Upon the positive response of the Vienna Group (U.S., Russia, France and the IAEA) further details of the exchange will be elaborated through a written agreement and proper arrangement between Iran and the Vienna Group that specifically committed themselves to deliver 120 kilograms of fuel needed for the Tehran Research Reactor (TRR).

7. When the Vienna Group declares its commitment to this provision, then both parties would commit themselves to the implementation of the agreement mentioned in item 6. The Islamic Republic of Iran expressed its readiness to deposit its LEU (1200 kilograms) within one month. On the basis of the same agreement the Vienna Group should deliver 120 kilograms fuel required for TRR in no later than one year.

8. In case the provisions of this Declaration are not

respected, Turkey, upon the request of Iran, will return swiftly and unconditionally Iran's LEU to Iran.

Shortly after the agreement was struck, the three states held a press conference in Tehran announcing the breakthrough. The mood was jubilant, and a picture of Lula, Erdogan, and Ahmadinejad jointly raising their hands in a victorious gesture immediately went viral over the Internet. Davutoglu called the fuel swap deal a "historic turning point," and Erdogan and Lula both declared that the world no longer need consider further sanctions against Iran. Amorim proudly announced that the agreement accomplished all of the main objectives of the P5+1 and urged those countries to study it carefully. He also made clear that the agreement "serves as a confidence-building measure that prepares the situation for expanded dialogue on the broader issues of Iran's nuclear program." (The Brazilians also had another reason to be jubilant: through Amorim's mediation, the Iranians released the accused French spy Clotilde Reiss during Lula's state visit to Iran.)[29]

The Brazilians had been in contact with Mohammad ElBaradei, now the former director general of the IAEA, throughout their negotiations. Once the agreement was announced, he immediately gave it his blessing, calling the deal a "good agreement" that indicated that Iran is "changing its hand." UN secretary general Ban Ki-moon said the agreement was "an important initiative in resolving international tensions over Iran's nuclear program by peaceful means." The Tehran Declaration also won the support of Security Council member states such as Japan, which months earlier had pursued its own mediation efforts. Perhaps more important, this time around the Iranian political elite came out in support of the deal, unlike the Vienna negotiations in the fall. Two days after the agreement was struck, 234 out of the Iranian parliament's 290 members, including Speaker of the parliament—and Ahmadinejad's bitter enemy—Larijani, issued a public statement supporting the fuel swap. A group of Iranian national-religious political activists who were often sharply critical of the Iranian government also issued a statement in support of the declaration. In addition, key Green movement figures such as Ataollah Mohajerani also extended their blessing to the deal. Considering the divisions within Iran's political elite, which by no means had been resolved, the widespread support for the deal in Iran was noteworthy.[30]

Washington Chooses Sanctions over the LEU

Enthusiasm for the deal never spread to Washington. Unbeknownst to Turkey and Brazil, the Obama administration had secured final approval for the sanctions resolution from Russia and China only a day before Lula arrived in Tehran. A series of concessions had been made to Russia and China since early April to secure their Security Council votes for the sanctions, starting with a new nuclear disarmament treaty (START) on April 8. Immediately thereafter, Moscow signaled its support for sanctions in principle. As the deliberations at the UN continued, additional concessions were made, including the lifting of American sanctions against the Russian military complex; an end to NATO expansion; cancellation of the Russian sale of the S300 anti-aircraft missiles to Iran; and the scrapping of the proposed missile defense shield in Europe. There was, of course, also irritation in Beijing and Moscow over the failure of the negotiations in the fall; the fact that Iran had begun enriching to 19.75 percent; and Iran's failure to inform Russia and China about its planned enrichment facility in Qom.[31]

While the Turks and Brazilians characterized the Tehran Declaration as a breakthrough, the U.S. Department of State was "skeptical" and did not believe it represented "anything fundamentally new." State Department spokesperson P. J. Crowley derided the deal for having failed to address suspension of Iran's enrichment activities— something the swap agreement from the fall meetings did not intend to do either. "The joint declaration doesn't address the core concerns of the international community. Iran remains in defiance of five U.N.

Security Council resolutions, including its unwillingness to suspend enrichment operations," Crowley said. A day later, Clinton herself sounded the death knell for the deal in prepared remarks to the Senate while declaring that an agreement on a sanctions resolution at the UN had been reached. The choice of venue was not a coincidence. Between instituting sanctions and getting one bomb's worth of LEU out of Iran, Washington had chosen the former. "We have reached agreement on a strong draft with the cooperation of both Russia and China," Clinton told a Senate committee. "We plan to circulate that draft resolution to the entire Security Council today. And let me say, Mr. Chairman, I think this announcement is as convincing an answer to the efforts undertaken in Tehran over the last few days as any we could provide." That same day, Obama met with thirty-seven Jewish Democratic members of Congress for an hour and a half to assure them of his commitment to sanctions. A week later, Clinton raised the rhetorical volume even further, claiming that Turkey and Brazil's efforts had made "the world more dangerous."[32]

Washington was surprised by Turkey and Brazil's success. They were expected to fail and, in doing so, be forced to join the P5+1 in pushing for sanctions. At a White House meeting a week before Lula's trip to Tehran, an Obama administration official raised the question of "What if Iran agrees?" But the likelihood was deemed so low that the issue was dismissed and no further discussions preparing the U.S. for that scenario were held. But it was not just Brazil and Turkey's success that was surprising. The Obama administration's swift and undiplomatic rejection of the deal surprised a large number of officials within the U.S. government. The talking points prepared by the Iran Desk at the State Department were vague, designed to give the U.S. more time and maneuverability to handle the implications of the Tehran Declaration. But surprisingly, those talking points were not used by Crowley. Instead, the "spokesman of the State Department went to the podium and publicly destroyed it, which nobody was happy about," according to a former Iran Desk official.[33]

The debate within the administration was brief and rather one-sided. The principals at the State Department—Clinton, Undersecretary for Political Affairs William Burns, and Deputy Secretary of State Jim Steinberg—all opposed the Tehran Declaration. Deputy Assistant Secretary of State John Limbert, himself a former hostage in Iran, led the minority faction that favored exploring the deal, but the argument for patience did not have any takers at the top. Congress and, unsurprisingly, the American Israel Public Affairs Committee (AIPAC) were even more hawkish. Lawmakers tended to view Brazil and Turkey's mediation effort as an "annoyance," with some even preparing measures to punish Brazil by hitting its ethanol industry. According to a senior congressional aide, the attitude was: "Let's get the sanctions done. Let's get the ink dry. We can always come back to [the Tehran Declaration] later." Congress calculated that it was easier to recapture the diplomatic initiative than the momentum for sanctions. Consequently, the Tehran Declaration never became more than a blip on Congress's radar (where few, if any, at the time knew about Obama's letter to Lula). AIPAC, in turn, immediately applauded Clinton's announcement that the United States would move forward with sanctions at the UN and called for crippling sanctions to press Tehran to immediately suspend all nuclear activity.[34]

The other P5+1 states were also dismissive of the Tehran Declaration, stating clearly that the agreement would not affect the march toward sanctions. The British viewed it as a "distraction," and junior British foreign minister Alistair Burt said that the declaration did not address Iran's obligation to make clear its peaceful intentions. "Until Iran takes concrete actions to meet those obligations, that work [on a new UN sanctions resolution] must continue," he said. The French, who at best had been lukewarm about the fuel swap idea, took the opportunity to shoot down the entire concept. "Let us not deceive ourselves, a solution to the [fuel] question, if it happens, would do nothing to settle the problem posed by the Iranian nuclear program," spokesperson Bernard Valero said in a statement. For the French, there was never a question of the Tehran Declaration affecting the sanctions resolution. Deal or no deal, France would have pushed for a vote on the sanctions. Only a full suspension of nuclear activities could have changed the minds of decision makers in Paris. There was visible irritation at Turkey and Brazil as well among other EU officials, who accused them of naïveté for thinking that Iran would honor the agreement and that Tehran was going along with it solely to delay sanctions. "I think that they've been taken for a ride," a senior EU official told me. The Israelis shared that assessment and rejected the idea that the agreement could serve as an opening. "I don't think we can look at it as an opportunity," Israel's deputy foreign minister told me. "It was a blatant ploy by the Iranians. Unfortunately there were some in the international community that fell into the trap, namely here Brazil and Turkey. . . . It was just a measure of deceit and procrastination by Iran."[35]

More surprisingly, perhaps, was the reaction of Russia and China. Though they publicly welcomed the deal and commended Brazil and Turkey for their efforts, neither Moscow nor Beijing showed any inclination to withdraw its support for the sanctions resolution or even to review the decision. "The Russians and the Chinese didn't blink," an EU diplomat told me in regard to the swiftness of the Security Council's dismissal of the deal. Moscow was focused on the agreement with the U.S. at the Security Council, and, just as with the French, the Turkish-Brazilian efforts were not going to undo their deal with Washington. The Obama administration had given too many concessions to Moscow, so reconsidering the sanctions simply was not an option. Iran reacted angrily to what it considered to be a betrayal by Russia. "We do not like to see our neighbor supporting those who have shown animosity to us for 30 years," Ahmadinejad said. "This is not acceptable for the Iranian nation. I hope they will pay attention and take corrective action." The episode showed that Iran could "no longer rely on Russia the way it did before," a hard-line Iranian newspaper wrote. Absent U.S. pressure, however, it is not clear that Russia, China, and many of the EU states would have joined Washington in rejecting the deal. According to one senior EU diplomat, the EU would have welcomed the deal had Washington expressed its support for it. A minority within the EU, led by the EU's principal sanctions skeptic, Sweden, favored the Turkey-Brazilian deal and resisted the pressure from the U.S.[36]

Washington presented a mixture of public arguments against the deal, ranging from distrust of Iran and deficiencies in the deal to the introduction of completely new demands, such as requiring that Iran suspend all enrichment. On the technical side, the Obama administration pointed out that 1,200 kilograms of LEU constituted roughly 75 percent of Iran's total stockpile in October 2009. If the swap had taken place at that time, Iran's stockpile would have been less than the amount needed for a single bomb, which would have granted the White House valuable time and political space. By May 2010, however, 1,200 kilograms of LEU constituted only roughly 50 percent of Iran's LEU and would leave the country with still enough uranium in Iran for one bomb. As a result, the benefits of the swap had been significantly reduced. In the words of one Obama administration official, Turkey and Brazil had "missed the sell-by date" for the deal since the relative value in terms of nonproliferation and confidence-building had declined.

Moreover, the Iranians had begun enriching to 19.75 percent in February 2010. An implicit component of the original 2009 swap deal was that Iranian enrichment would be recognized or accepted in return for limiting it to below 5 percent—meaning Iran would not engage in any higher enrichment—in other words, 19.75 percent—but the Tehran Declaration did not address this issue. "One of the main difficulties is that [the Tehran Declaration] does nothing to address Iran's recent decision to enrich uranium up to 20 percent," a senior Obama administration official said. In their numerous previous meetings with Brazilian and Turkish officials, both French and American officials had indicated that a swap deal at this point should address the higher enrichment levels and the growth in Iran's LEU stockpile. From a purely technical perspective, these developments had made the Tehran Declaration far less attractive to Washington

than the original fuel swap, even though the three key components—
that the LEU would be sent out in one shipment, that the swap
would take place outside of Iran, and that it would not be instantane-
ous—had been set. "It certainly wasn't nearly as good of a deal for
us," a State Department official told me.[37]

The administration also listed arguments that put the concept of
a fuel swap in question more so than the Tehran Declaration per se.
Recognizing Iran's right to enrich, for instance, contradicted several
Security Council resolutions, the administration argued (this was
particularly problematic for the French, who for a long time had
argued that there was no such thing as a right to enrich). Yet, so did
the swap deal from the fall of 2009; in fact, the administration had
presented the deal's implicit recognition of Iranian enrichment as
one of its strengths. Similarly, the White House argued that since the
Tehran Declaration was "simply a confidence-building measure"
that did not address "the core issues surrounding Iran's defiance of
the UN Security Council," the deal fell "short of what's necessary"
and the pursuit of sanctions should continue. An acceptable swap
deal could not be a substitute for the core issue, but had to be linked
to the Security Council's concerns about Iran's nuclear program.
This line of argument also contradicted the Obama administration's
own terms set forth in the U.S.-and-Russian-led swap deal. In fact,
arguments made by critics of that fall 2009 swap deal were now being
rehashed by the administration to reject the Tehran Declaration.[38]

Moreover, the White House also put forward general mistrust of
Iran as a motivation for their rejection of the Tehran Declaration.
Iran was not serious, the argument read, and was engaging in a game
of deception only to delay or stave off the sanctions. "I think Iran's
main interest was to have a proposal in play that would reduce
momentum toward a sanctions resolution. I think that was the main
motivation of the Iranians," a senior Obama administration official
said. Another round of sanctions was needed to make Iran serious
about negotiations, continued this line of reasoning. Administration
officials said that they detected a pattern in Iranian behavior where

Tehran tended to, at critical moments, make a small move that had the effect of dividing the international community and, as a result, considerably delay any punitive measures. The Tehran Declaration fit that pattern and, mindful of the criticism against the White House's engagement policy—that the Obama administration had fallen into a trap where Iran simply was playing for time—it was imperative not to fall for Iran's latest stunt. This perspective was, arguably, even more fervently held by some of the EU actors due to their experience in negotiating with Iran since 2003. "If you look at the timing of the Tehran Declaration, it was done at the eve of the vote," Germany's UN ambassador told me. "Is that a very credible sign? So the whole timing, the way it was brought about and the phrasing of this declaration did not inspire any confidence. . . . The P-5 didn't want any monkey business at that time."[39]

The Western powers perceived that Brazil and Turkey had dragged Iran against its will and pushed it to go along with the agreement, and they interpreted that as a sign of Tehran's lack of sincerity. But the problem ran deeper. An EU diplomat conceded that the mistrust was so entrenched that had the roles been reversed—that is, had Iran dragged Brazil and Turkey to go along with the agreement—the conclusion would have been the same: Iran was insincere and only vying for time. If Iran had agreed willingly to the deal, then the deal would be a trick. Had it agreed to it reluctantly, then the deal was suspicious on other grounds. The mistrust was so deep that any new development was interpreted to fit, vindicate, and reinforce preexisting beliefs and suspicions. To the West, Iran was insincere and made tactical deals only to buy time. Despite the Obama administration's initial opening to Iran, the White House had retreated into a mode of "reading the other side's motives in the worst possible way," according to a senior Obama administration official. The sense was that "the Iranians [were] not interested in making a deal. They [were] just interested in putting off sanctions." To the Iranians, the West was out to deprive Iran of its independence, rights, and potential, whether it pursued diplomacy or confrontation.[40]

Lula's Revenge

Washington's swift and harsh dismissal of the Tehran Declaration infuriated Brazil and Turkey. Erdogan and Lula's personal investment in the Tehran Declaration made its dismissal nothing short of a rebuke of their leadership. And it was coupled with an aggressive campaign in the U.S. media accusing the two heads of state of vanity, megalomania, and anti-American and anti-Israeli sentiments. "There were two things that shocked us," Amorim told me. "First was the speed, or the rapidity between the agreement and the reaction." Lula had called Sarkozy from Tehran immediately after the agreement was reached. The second person the Brazilians spoke to was Clinton. Amorim called her during a stopover while flying back to Brasilia immediately following the press conference in Tehran. Only five hours had passed since the declaration had been announced, but the secretary of state made it absolutely clear to Amorim that the U.S. would continue pursuing sanctions. "So we were really taken aback not by the fact that they were negotiating sanctions, but that they wanted to make so clear the point that there was no room for negotiation," one of Lula's senior advisers told me. The other shock was "that no interval was left between the delivery of the comments of the Vienna Group and the sanctions." (As requested, Tehran did provide a written acceptance of the Tehran Declaration to the IAEA within seven days. The Vienna Group's official rejection of the declaration came only five hours before the Security Council was scheduled to vote on the sanctions resolution, giving Brazil and Turkey no time to react to their response).[41]

Brazil and Turkey fiercely defended their deal in the media. The Turks threatened to withdraw from the Tehran Declaration and to prohibit the Iranian LEU from being escrowed on its territory if the Security Council adopted a new round of sanctions on Iran. The U.S.-led push for fresh sanctions on Tehran was creating an "absurd situation," the Turks argued. They made clear that they had been in "constant contact" with American and French authorities, and that they had been "told" that the sanctions push would disappear if Iran agreed to the deal. At a press conference in Istanbul the day after the deal, Davutoglu said Turkey had "done its duty," convincing Iran to sign on, and expected reciprocal "flexibility" from Washington. Davutoglu and Amorim wrote in the *New York Times* that neither the Tehran Declaration nor the original fuel swap deal aimed to resolve the entire nuclear issue but that their efforts had succeeded in providing the key component missing in the 2009 talks: trust. "In the presence of deep mutual mistrust there will always be those who display skepticism about the feasibility of any negotiated outcome. But there is now sufficient substance to give negotiations a chance. Missing it may well be regretted for generations to come," they wrote. Privately, however, even the most seasoned Brazilian and Turkish diplomats could not conceal their ire. "What is the true meaning of engagement with Iran? Where is the engagement? There is no engagement. U.S. should do and deliver on what they say. . . . Obama has only changed America's conduct in words," a senior Turkish diplomat told me. The Turks and Brazilians categorically rejected the argument that Washington was unaware of their activities. In their view, they had followed Washington's "instructions" and had delivered what had been asked for: after all, 1,200 kilograms of LEU in a single shipment outside of Iran were American—and not Turkish or Brazilian—benchmarks, they pointed out. Nor did the Turks and Brazilians accept criticism against the Tehran Declaration's recognition of Iran's right to enrich. The Declaration was a document between Turkey, Brazil, and Iran. It expressed only the common points between these states. Acceptance of the Declaration would not mean that all states had to recognize this right but rather acknowledge that Iran, Turkey, and Brazil did so.[42]

Other international actors shared some of this frustration. El-Baradei, who had fought hard to convince the Iranians to agree to the original fuel swap, dismissed Washington's skepticism as "a dead end street." "Look, you can either choose to see the glass half full or half empty," he said. "To dismiss this move as window dressing is unhelpful." ElBaradei was not surprised by Turkey and Brazil's success, but he did express surprise at Washington's response. "I was frankly not surprised that the offer came through, I was surprised at the reaction that some countries would continue to say that they want to apply sanctions. . . . [Washington is] not accepting yes for an answer." The former head of the IAEA also dismissed the objection regarding Iran's expanded enrichment work and the fact that the fuel swap did not resolve the full nuclear issue, comparing it to the Bush administration's insistence that Iran suspend enrichment before talks could begin. "In fact, that insistence to get everything before you start negotiating, the result of that was six years of wasted time on resolving the Iranian issue," he said. In his view, the Tehran Declaration was fundamentally no different from the earlier fuel swap in terms of building confidence. The difference was that Iran's domestic situation did not enable it to respond positively in time. "It took Iran quite a while because of the domestic political situation to reciprocate."[43]

Washington's public motivations for the dismissal were particularly frustrating to Brazil and Turkey since they believed they had followed Obama's letter "sentence by sentence." The letter, however, was not public, and as a result very few, including only a handful of individuals within the Obama administration, knew about the apparent contradictions between Washington's public stance and the content of Obama's letter. Visibly angered by the Obama administration's treatment, the Brazilians leaked the letter to a local newspaper. Within hours, the U.S. media picked it up. The letter cast new light on the Obama administration's objections to the Tehran Declaration on the grounds that it did not address the growth in Iran's LEU stockpile and the issue of 19.75 percent enrichment. Neither issue was raised in the letter as a deal breaker. Clinton objected to the deal on these grounds in one of her conversations with Amorim. Amorim replied by saying that "these points are not part of President Obama's letter." A long silent pause followed, as Clinton had no response.[44]

The administration immediately shot back at Brazil and Turkey, saying that the letter only summarized Washington's position on the fall 2009 episode and was not a conclusive description of the Obama administration's position. Nor was it a guideline or a set of instructions for talks with Iran. Moreover, though the letter did not mention the issue of 19.75 percent enrichment, U.S. officials had in their numerous deliberations with Brazil and Turkey stated clearly that the swap deal had to be updated to reflect these changes on the ground. Turkish and Brazilian officials acknowledge that U.S. officials did raise these issues with them prior to the talks in Tehran but argue that they were not presented as deal breakers. The issue of 19.75 percent was, however, raised in Tehran, but Turkey and Brazil quickly concluded that the Iranians were not ready to compromise on that point before the P5+1 had accepted the Tehran Declaration. Tehran indicated to Brazil and Turkey, however, that once the Declaration had been accepted, they would be open to giving up higher-level enrichment. "We viewed the Tehran Declaration as the beginning of the deal, not the end of the deal," a Brazilian diplomat explained. As a result, this issue was saved for a later round of talks, the Brazilians and Turks argued. But perhaps more important, both states viewed the letter from the president of the United States as the final and authoritative document spelling out the U.S. position. Turkey and Brazil believed that the letter resolved whatever contradictions and mixed messages that had plagued their conversations with U.S. officials prior to the Tehran talks.[45]

In retrospect, U.S. officials have recognized that the letter was unclear, and that mixed messages had been sent to Turkey and Brazil. They have also acknowledged that it was a mistake to keep the October swap deal on the table (a week prior to Lula's visit to Tehran, a White House official reiterated that the deal was still valid). The letter should have been withdrawn in January when, in Washington's view, it expired. But it was kept on the table because there was a fear that if it was withdrawn, Washington would come across as the intransigent party that was unwilling to negotiate. The very concept of a dual-track approach would have been defeated if Washington admitted that diplomacy had been deactivated. "[The letter] shouldn't have been so polite," a senior State Department official told me. "We should have made clear we don't want you getting involved in this."[46]

A Divided Council

Once Iran formally notified the IAEA of its acceptance of the Tehran Declaration, the ball was back in the Vienna Group's court. At this point, there was no doubt that the sanctions would be adopted, but the manner in which the sanctions decision was taken further divided the Security Council. The Vienna Group gave their formal rejection of the Tehran Declaration only five hours before the scheduled vote on sanctions at the council on June 9, 2010. This gave the Brazilians and Turks little time to review the basis for the rejection, and pushed the parties even further apart. Washington's desire for the two to join the sanctions push was now reduced just to securing their abstentions. The night before the vote, Obama called Erdogan to urge him to abstain. The Turkish leader would not budge but agreed to study the issue (only six weeks earlier, the U.S. ambassador to Ankara, James Jeffrey, had publicly declared that Washington would view an abstention as a negative vote).[47]

The next day, the deliberations continued. The vote at the council had to be delayed, because Turkey and Brazil had not yet decided their votes. That morning, Obama spent forty minutes on the phone with Lula, urging Brazil to abstain. After speaking with Obama, Lula called Ahmadinejad and was told that if Brazil abstained, Iran would immediately denounce the Tehran declaration. As the Brazilian UN ambassador Maria Luiza Ribeiro Viotti went to the Security Council meeting, she had two statements in her hands—one announcing Brazil's abstention and one announcing its negative vote. She did not know which statement she was supposed to read. Her cell phone rang only moments before the meeting began. Ahmadinejad's tough bargain had worked. After speaking with the American and Iranian presidents, Lula and Erdogan spoke with each other and jointly decided to go against Obama.[48]

When the vote finally was cast, the victory was bittersweet for the Obama administration. Though Resolution 1929 passed, Brazil and Turkey voted against it while Lebanon abstained. Of all the sanctions passed against Iran at the UN, this resolution had the weakest support. Obama's predecessor had, with no effort to engage the Iranians diplomatically, imposed three sets of UN sanctions on Iran; two were unanimously adopted, and one suffered an abstention. For the first time, negative votes had been cast against a sanctions resolution on Iran. For the Brazilians, after their mediation efforts and their success in securing Tehran's signature, voting in favor of the sanctions was not really an option. "We couldn't vote in favor of the resolution, it would have been incoherent," a senior Brazilian diplomat explained. The Brazilians' resolve in opposition to sanctions was hardened by Clinton's comments at the Senate hearing the day after the Tehran Declaration had been signed, and by Brazil's conclusion that the Obama administration was never really going to forgo the sanctions in favor of diplomacy even if Tehran succumbed to the pressure. In Brazil's view, Washington was pursuing sanctions for the sake of sanctions. And for Brazil the negotiation process for the sanctions resolution represented all that was wrong with the current structure of the Security Council. The negotiations were not a debate over the substance of the measure, but rather a bargaining over various measures that had no direct relationship to the issue at hand—how to ensure that Iran does not build a nuclear weapon. The bargaining ensured that none of Russia or China's economic interests would be affected by the sanctions, but this also eliminated much of the bite of the sanctions. The end result was that a Brazilian company could not enter the Iranian energy sector, but the exemptions enabled Chinese and Russian companies to freely invest in Iran, and even to power up a nuclear reactor there. Inevitably, this increased Iran's dependence on these countries and pushed Tehran further away from the West. "This is the strangest thing," Amorim said, pointing out the long-term damage this approach did to the West's leverage over Iran.[49]

For Turkey, the matter was not as clear-cut. Ultimately, Turkey decided to vote against the sanctions since Iran guaranteed that it would not withdraw from the tri-party agreement if Turkey and Brazil cast a negative vote. To keep the Tehran Declaration alive, Turkey needed to oppose the sanctions resolution. At the end of the day, the Turks calculated, no one would remember their vote on this resolution. But everyone would remember the Tehran Declaration because it was the first agreement that Iran had committed itself to and put its signature on. Between the Declaration and sanctions, Turkey chose the Declaration. At the vote, Turkey made clear its displeasure with the swift rejection of the deal. The "Tehran Declaration provides a new and important window of opportunity for diplomacy," Turkey ambassador to the UN Ertugrul Apakan said. "Sufficient time and space should be allowed for its implementation. We are deeply concerned that adoption of sanctions would negatively affect the momentum created by the Declaration and the overall diplomatic process. . . . It is rather unhelpful that the responses of the Vienna Group were received only a few hours ago. The fact that the response has a negative nature and that it has been sent on the day of the adoption of the sanctions resolution had a determining effect on our position. Our position demonstrates our commitment to the Tehran Declaration and to the diplomatic efforts."[50]

Two weeks later, Congress passed the gasoline sanctions on Iran with an overwhelming majority, 408–8 in the House and 99–0 in the Senate. Obama signed the bill into law at a ceremony in the White House on July 1. Ultimately, he succeeded in scoring important domestic political points. He managed to put off the congressional sanctions until after the UN had acted, and he managed to convince China and Russia to support punitive measures in the Security Council. The reality was that the Obama administration was not going to abandon the sanctions push for a nuclear deal at that point, primarily for reasons that had little to do with either the technical details of the Tehran Declaration or the substance of the Iranian nuclear file per se. "There was nothing that the Iranians could do" to stop the sanctions push, a former State Department official said. The Tehran Declaration was problematic precisely because it revealed that imposing sanctions had superseded the objective of getting the LEU out of Iran and kick-starting diplomacy. Had Iran agreed to stop enrichment at 19.75 percent, it would have made matters even more difficult for Washington and its allies. "If they did agree to [halting higher-level enrichment], it would put us in quite a tricky situation," a senior EU diplomat told me, because "it would slow the march to sanctions."[51]

A mixture of political factors, management of relations with other permanent members of the council, and prestige made serious diplomacy a non-option by the time Washington had committed itself to the sanctions track. First, the political investment in the sanctions track was immense, including acts such as personal calls from Obama to other world leaders and high-level visits. The failure of the talks in Vienna was not only a defeat for Obama's nonproliferation agenda; it was also a major blow to his political standing. Undersecretary Burns told another Security Council member state that Obama had proffered an open hand to the Iranians and had nothing to show for it. "He needs something to take back to the American public," Burns purportedly said, according to a Western official. Diplomacy with America's political foes was a critical component of Obama's foreign policy platform during the presidential campaign, an issue that separated him not only from Senator John McCain and the Republicans but also from his main opponent in the Democratic primary, Hillary Clinton. Recognizing the political risk diplomacy with Iran would entail, the Obama team hedged its bets by arguing that the mere attempt at diplomacy would make it easier to mobilize international backing for sanctions if diplomacy failed. With its diplomatic outreach having done just that, the administration felt that it had to at least deliver on sanctions in order to justify the gamble on diplomacy.[52]

Second, the heavy investment in the sanctions process helped to turn the matter into one of prestige. Not imposing sanctions would have been hailed as a victory by Iran and condemned by Israel and its allies in the U.S. as a sign of Obama's weakness and indecisiveness. And the more Iran pushed against the sanctions, the harder the U.S. pushed back and the more important the imposition of sanctions became. Paradoxically, Iran's resistance to the sanctions strengthened the Obama administration's commitment to this punitive measure because of the prestige factor.

Third, moving forward with the sanctions in a swift manner was necessary in order to sustain consensus among the P5+1, and ensure that the various deals and concessions that had been made to secure the sanctions would be upheld. These deals and agreements between primarily the U.S. and Russia were not so much subject to the Iranian nuclear file as they were a rubric for U.S.-Russian relations and Washington's reset with Moscow. They were contingent upon Russian support for a sanctions resolution. If sanctions were sidelined by diplomacy, not only could the deals be jeopardized, but, in case the Tehran Declaration fell apart down the road, the sanctions process would start anew and all the deals and arrangements would have to be renegotiated. The imposition of sanctions on Iran had essentially become the organizing principle for alliance management within the P5+1, as well as with U.S. allies in the region such as Israel and some of the Sunni monarchies. By imposing sanctions, the Obama administration knew it likely would not achieve desirable results on the nonproliferation front, but it would demonstrate that it was in control of the Security Council and the alliance against Iran. This was particularly important since Congress would move forward with unilateral sanctions targeting other P5 states regardless of the UN outcome. This would pit the P5 nations against each other rather than against Iran.[53]

Fourth, and perhaps most importantly, the Obama administration had simply run out of political space domestically to accept the Tehran Declaration. Congress was coming at the Obama administration like a steamroller, and the White House did not believe that investing capital in expanding the political space for the deal would be a politically wise move. The political maneuverability Obama enjoyed on Iran when he first took office had by now been completely eaten away by pressure from Israel and Congress, the fallout from the June 2009 Iranian presidential election, and Iran's refusal to accept the Russian-American swap proposal in October 2009. U.S. diplomats had even raised this as an argument for sanctions in the Security Council, making the case that sanctions were needed in order for the U.S. to be able to gain space for diplomacy down the road. The White House believed that a nuclear deal could be sold domestically only if Iran was first punished through a new round of sanctions. Only then would there be receptivity in Washington for a nuclear agreement with Tehran. Hence, any nuclear deal that came before a new round of sanctions would complicate the Obama administration's domestic challenges. A deal without punishment—even a good deal—simply would not be enough. "The impression, right or wrong, that was created was that we could not take yes for an answer," a former senior Obama administration official told me. "That was not what I would call a triumph of public diplomacy."[54]

Eleven

Trapped in a
Paradigm of Enmity

Our Iran diplomacy was a gamble on a single roll of the dice.
  —Senior State Department official, July 2010

year and a half into his presidency, President Barack Obama was celebrating not the diplomatic victory he had been seeking, but rather the imposition of sanctions he had hoped to avoid. Despite extensive outreach, clear strategic benefits, and an unprecedented opportunity for engagement, Obama found himself stuck in the same confrontational relationship with Iran as that of other American presidents before him. And, as many officials in his administration had suspected, while sanctions might have been politically imperative from a domestic standpoint and could make life more difficult for the Iranians, they were not a solution to the standoff with Iran. "While Iran's leaders are feeling the pressure, the sanctions have not yet produced a change in Iran's strategic thinking about its nuclear program," Special Advisor for Nonproliferation and Arms Control Robert Einhorn told an audience at the Arms Control Association in Washington, D.C., on March 9, 2011. Instead, under Obama's watch, the cycle of escalation and counterescalation continued with no sign of a solution in the offing.[1]

A week after the UN Security Council imposed a third round of sanctions on Iran, Tehran announced that it was building a new nuclear reactor. When Obama signed new congressional sanctions into law, Iran responded by postponing, and putting conditions on, any new dialogue with the permanent members of the UN Security Council and Germany (P5+1). A new front in the confrontation with Iran had opened up with an increasing number of cyber attacks and other sabotage efforts, and the Obama administration found remarkable success in the push for tougher EU sanctions. But even with all the additional pressures, Tehran has displayed no detectable change in its policies or its determination. Much to Washington's disappointment, the pain imposed on Iran has not translated into a softening of Tehran's position. This was made abundantly clear during the latest meeting between the P5+1 and Iran in Istanbul in January 2011. Rather than negotiating from a position of weakness and succumbing to U.S. demands, the Iranians perceived themselves to be strong and upped the ante, worsening the situation in the interim and sharpening America's options. Their nuclear program, the Iranians insisted, was not on the agenda and Iran would agree to discuss its nuclear activities only if the P5+1 first recognized Iran's right to enrichment and lifted all sanctions. And stalemate has reigned since.[2]

From Extended Hand to Clenched Fist

While most of Obama's domestic critics opposed his pursuit of diplomacy on the grounds that talking with Iran was useless and morally questionable, a few voices also disapproved of his engagement policy as being insincere and aimed only at paving the way for sanctions. Neither criticism is well grounded. Diplomacy was not only a strategic necessity, but also the least costly avenue to address the tensions with Iran. And rather than being a well-designed conspiracy, the president's vision for diplomacy was genuine, as was his initial outreach. But faced with overwhelming resistance from Israel, Congress, Saudi Arabia, and other Arab allies, skeptics within his own administration and, most importantly, the actions of the Iranian government itself, the president's vision and political space were continually compromised. In the end, the diplomacy Obama pursued was only a shadow of the engagement he had envisioned.[3]

Obama's vision for engagement met stiff resistance from the outset. Whether the pressure was to impose unrealistic deadlines on diplomacy (which only fueled suspicion that the other side was not serious—or that some fear diplomacy more than they fear war), set unachievable goals for diplomacy (such as demanding that Iran give up rather than limit its enrichment program), or push for sanctions to be imposed before talks began, the end result was the same: Obama's already limited political space and maneuverability were slowly but surely chipped away. The Iranians themselves, however, dealt the biggest blow to Obama. The election fraud and ensuing human rights violations strengthened the arguments of Obama's domestic critics and made the administration all the more reluctant to defend its engagement policy. These events also bolstered the critics of engagement within the administration who viewed the election fallout as vindication of their skepticism. "You have the rigged elections of June 2009. Then the protests. And then, in a way, the moment was lost," David Miliband, then–foreign secretary of the United Kingdom, told me. The elections had a deep psychological impact on the administration. Though it stuck to its engagement policy and refused to come out in favor of the Green movement, its willingness to take bold steps on Iran essentially ended. Engagement started to become too risky and, with no immediate political benefits for the president domestically, the inclination was to revert to one's comfort zone. "When you don't know what's going on, and you don't feel like you have somebody you can communicate with on the other side of the table, you are going to revert back to what's safe," a State Department official explained. "And what's safe in the Iran context is demonization and just general negativity." By the time engagement finally could begin, in October 2009, Obama's room for maneuverability—and his political will to fight for greater flexibility —were almost nonexistent. He desperately needed a quick victory to create more time and space for diplomacy. But precisely because of his loss of maneuverability, he had little flexibility in negotiations and the discussions quickly turned into a "take-it-or-leave-it" proposition—the very approach that was doomed to fail.[4]

In Vienna, the Iranians dealt a second blow to Obama by refusing to accept the Russian-American swap proposal without any revisions. Though administration officials recognized that the primary reason for Iran's refusal was paralysis caused by political infighting at home, the impact was the same: Obama had nothing to show for his outreach. His own party was revolting against him in Congress on this issue; many in his administration felt uneasy about the portrayal of the White House as insensitive to the plight of Iranian prodemocracy protesters defying the Islamic Republic's repression; and the Israeli government was reportedly turning to high-level Democratic donors to exert additional pressure on Obama to forsake diplomacy in order to save the Democratic Party in the upcoming midterm elections. Moreover, Iran's continued political paralysis made the potential for additional diplomacy unclear at best. Once the decision was made to activate the sanctions track, diplomacy had disappeared in all but name. That first became evident when Washington informed Tokyo that its efforts to mediate a solution were no longer welcome, and occurred again when Brazil and Turkey's successful bid to convince Tehran to agree to the Obama administration's terms for the fuel swap was brusquely rejected. Obama's open hand had turned into a clenched fist.[5]

No Good Wishes from Tehran

Throughout this period, despite the Iranian recognition of Obama's political dilemma at home, a combination of factors caused Tehran to refrain from helping create more space for engagement. On the one hand, doubts about Obama's intentions and abilities made an already risk-averse leadership in Tehran more disinclined to take a gamble for peace. "I don't think the Iranians quite knew what to make about the

American outreach," Miliband said. "I think that it was such a change
for them, that they didn't quite know how to handle it." Even if the
Iranians maintained the assumption that Obama genuinely wished to
resolve the tensions between the two countries, they still doubted his
ability to break with long-standing American policies on Iran in order
to confront the forces of the status quo in Washington and beyond.
Investing in an American president whose intentions and abilities
were questionable was a tough sell in Tehran. The hard-line Iranian
newspaper *Kayhan* called Obama "impotent" and asked rhetorically,
"Who is wearing the trousers within the U.S. political hierarchy?"
Supreme Leader Ali Khamenei's insistence that Washington offer
signs of real strategic change rather than just a change in tone was
partly aimed at testing Obama's intentions and abilities for this very
purpose. When I challenged one of Iran's nuclear negotiators on the
Islamic Republic's deep skepticism of Obama and the unique opportunities Tehran risked missing as a result, the official was unapolo-
getic. "The U.S. should resolve its domestic political issues itself," he
said. As time passed and Tehran increasingly perceived Obama as
"no different from Bush in action," Iran's attitude hardened and the
absence of action to help Obama turned into a desire to see him fail.
Obama's opposition to war, it was said, was due not to a desire for
peace but rather to America's lack of capability for war as a result of its
engagements in Iraq and Afghanistan.[6]

Iran's skepticism was further fueled by the lack of clarity on
America's desired endgame with diplomacy more generally, and its
desired endgame on the nuclear issue more specifically. Was Washington seeking a strategic shift in its relationship with Iran, trans-
forming the enmity into a partnership, or was the Obama administration tactically seeking to reduce tension with Iran in order to benefit
from Iranian assistance in Iraq and Afghanistan? Was the administration ready to accept enrichment on Iranian soil, or was the purpose
of the nuclear talks to achieve the same objective as the Bush administration—zero-enrichment—by using different means? According to
a former Iranian diplomat who maintains close contact with the

leadership in Tehran, the Iranians still "regarded U.S. engagement as another means to get Iran to surrender." And after the failure in Vienna, where the Iranians concluded that accepting the fuel swap would not end the demand for Iran to suspend its enrichment activities, the Iranian takeaway message was that America's position on Iran had not changed much. "What had been a precondition under Bush—the suspension of enrichment—had become a postcondition under Obama," said Mohammad Khazaee, Iran's ambassador to the UN. But rather than engaging in deliberate deception, the Obama administration simply had not settled on a desired endgame with Iran, on the nuclear issue or otherwise. For the Obama White House, the destination of diplomacy was simply a function of the journey. Still, the lack of clarity on the endgame was not just a point of criticism by Iran or by the president's domestic opponents. Even senior Obama administration officials were unclear on the strategy and the endgame, as evidenced by the leaked three-page memo, signed by Secretary of Defense Robert Gates, that warned of the U.S. lack of a coherent, long-term plan to deal with Iran's steady progress toward a nuclear capability. The memo came to light in April 2010 but was penned in January of that year—just as the U.S. was embarking on the sanctions track.[7]

But the Iranians, who were already deeply distrustful of the U.S., found in Obama a more complex and sophisticated adversary than they had with President Bush. The complexity, however, came with less clarity, which further fueled Tehran's mistrust. In their assessment, the mistrust between the U.S. and Iran grew under Obama's tenure. "Let's say at least everybody knew what Bush is aiming at. It was clear with him," Ambassador Ali Asghar Soltanieh commented. The depth of Iran's paralyzing mistrust of the U.S. became clear during the talks in Vienna. As a goodwill gesture, Washington offered to upgrade the safety of the Tehran Research Reactor. This would be a major step that would make the U.S. directly involved in Iran's nuclear program. The Iranians, however, were not impressed and viewed the offer with great suspicion. "It's a mistake to underestimate how deeply distrustful the Iranians are of us, and vice versa," a top Obama administration official said, reflecting on the two sides' inclinations to assign negative intentions to each other's actions. The odds of limited diplomacy succeeding in what former International Atomic Energy Agency (IAEA) Director General Mohammad El-Baradei called an "environment of total distrust" were slim.[8]

Finally, there is the question of whether the Iranian government actually desires a deal with the United States. A common school of thought in Washington states that enmity with America—the "Great Satan"—is one of the uncompromising pillars of the Islamic Republic. As a result, Tehran cannot come to terms with Washington without risking an internal identity and legitimacy crisis. The state ideology of the regime requires enmity with the U.S., and without it the internal contradictions of the Islamic Republic would reach a breaking point. Iran's periodic reluctance to engage with the U.S. is grounded in this ideological rigidity rather than in internal divisions in Iran, mistrust of the U.S., or disinterest in the specific deals the U.S. has put on the table. The main obstacle to a diplomatic breakthrough is not the manner of the diplomacy or its extent or lack thereof, or the specifics of the deal, but rather the regime's DNA.

The calculations of the Iranian hard-liners are, however, not so mysterious and incomprehensible that analysts have to resort to genetics to make sense of them. Part of the reluctance of hard-liners in Iran to negotiate with the U.S. has been rooted not necessarily in these ideological factors but in the fear that any relationship with the U.S. would force Iran to adopt policies in the region that are aligned with those of Washington and, to a certain extent, Israel. Iran would lose its independence and, much like Egypt after the Camp David agreement, its bid for leadership in the region. Moreover, by aligning with the U.S., Iran would be forced to invest in the survival of pro-American Arab dictatorships rather than pursuing policies that would win it soft power on the Arab street. Because the Iranian hard-liners have calculated that the Arab street will ultimately overthrow the monarchial and pro-American regimes in the region, Iran's long-term security would be best achieved by aligning itself with the populace. Consequently, agreeing to any engagement with Washington—on its terms and designed to rehabilitate Iran as a compliant U.S. ally—would contradict Iran's long-term security interests in the region. Likely cementing the hard-liners' view of the U.S. as an increasingly irrelevant power incapable of adjusting to the new realities of the region are the continued decline of the U.S. in the Middle East, the Arab spring of 2011, and the downfall of the regimes in Egypt, Tunisia, and beyond. Any realization that an opportunity was lost with Obama in 2009 probably has yet to sink in. "What happened is clearly proving what our officials including Supreme Leader said," Soltanieh said. "The Americans come sometimes with the good words but in practice they might have a knife to [stick] in your back."[9]

Iran's suspicions and mistrust, whether justified or not, were paralyzing. What the Iranians failed to appreciate was that Obama's ability to drive the policy and "wear the pants" within the U.S. government was partly a function of how willing Iran was to take the same risk for peace that it had grown accustomed to taking for a continuation of the long-standing "no-war, no-peace" stalemate. In retrospect, once George W. Bush took office in 2001 and adopted a confrontational approach to Iran, reformists in former president Mohammad Khatami's circle came to regret their failure to reciprocate President Bill Clinton's outreach. The unprecedented willingness of the Obama administration to reach out to Iran and embark on a cautious reconciliation process, even if inadequate, is unlikely to be re-created by any later U.S. administration for some time. Likewise, the opportunity Iran had with Obama in the first months of his presidency will likely not be fully appreciated by the decision makers in Tehran until much later.

Why Was Diplomacy Not Fully Pursued?

Obama's attempt at diplomacy clearly did not bring about the desired results. But the question is not why diplomacy fell short, but rather why it was never fully pursued and exhausted. Seeking to pin the failure on either side does not offer a better understanding of the complexity of the conflict. At times, both sides showed goodwill, but at other times both were overtaken by their suspicions and fears. Both sides miscalculated and made mistakes, and both sides felt that the other side was taking a smaller share of the risk for peacemaking. Both sides were interested at different times in some sort of a deal; the question was and remains whether they have been seeking the same deal. Only through sustained, persistent, and patient diplomacy can that question be answered. Recent reconciliation efforts involving the U.S. itself provide a useful example.

For instance, the United States and Libya's journey toward ending their pre–Arab spring feud lasted almost seven years. Libya entered secret negotiations with the U.S. as early as May 1999, with an initial focus on the UN sanctions related to terrorism. However, negotiations between the U.S. and Libya were suspended during the 2000 U.S. presidential election and were not resumed until after September 11, 2001. In March 2003, Libyan officials contacted the British government to begin talks about "dismantling its WMD program in return for removing sanctions and normalizing relations." This led to the opening of a U.S. interest section at the Belgian embassy in Tripoli in 2004 and then-president Bush's executive order that lifted most of the U.S. sanctions against Libya. On May 15, 2006, almost seven years after diplomatic talks had begun, the Bush administration announced its intention to restore full diplomatic relations with Libya and to rescind Libya's listing as a state sponsor of terrorism. Full diplomatic relations were restored on May 31, when the United States upgraded its liaison office in Tripoli to embassy status.[10]

In the case of the United States and Vietnam, negotiations aimed at normalization of relations took four years—and another six years passed before a bilateral trade agreement between the two nations was signed. In April 1991, the U.S. laid out a road map to normalization, which began with the opening of a U.S. office in Hanoi to deal with prisoner-of-war and missing-in-action (POW/MIA) issues, a U.S. pledge for $1 million in humanitarian aid, and the easing of restrictions on Vietnamese diplomats traveling to and from the U.S. In January 1994, Congress passed authorizing legislation to lift the economic embargo on Vietnam, and the following year Vietnam and the U.S. settled bilateral and diplomatic claims and opened liaison offices. In 1995, the Treasury Department announced it was lifting all restrictions on those accounts with Vietnamese interests, and the U.S. established ambassadorial-level relations with Vietnam. Although some controversy remained in Congress concerning the POW/MIA issues, Pete Peterson was confirmed as ambassador to Vietnam in 1997.[11]

Even successful *mediation* efforts undertaken by the United States have been lengthy and exhausting. The Belfast Agreement, which ended fighting in Northern Ireland, for instance, was reached after seven hundred days of painstaking negotiations led by former senator George Mitchell, in which one of the main actors in the conflict—the Sinn Fein—refused to come to the table for much of that period. "I was in Northern Ireland for five years," Mitchell said on *Charlie Rose* in January 2010. "For 700 days one side said, 'We will never agree to new institutions between north and south Ireland.' The other side said for 700 days, 'We will never agree to a new Northern Ireland assembly.' And on the 701st day they both agreed to what they said they wouldn't agree to." However difficult and taxing, these peace agreements would never have been reached had the will and persistence not existed on both sides. Diplomacy between the U.S. and Iran between 2009 and 2011 did not exhibit any of these qualities.[12]

In Vienna, the Obama administration was so fearful that negotiations would drag along that it was unwilling to entertain any compromise on the central modalities of the deal. What was initially proposed as a negotiated solution quickly turned into an ultimatum—not necessarily by design, but by the virtue of the pressures the Obama administration was facing from Congress, Israel, and some EU states. "We essentially made it a take-it-or-leave-it proposition," said a senior Senate staffer supportive of the Obama administration. Once it was clear that the Iranians would not respond favorably to the U.S.-Russian swap proposal, the U.S. relied on the intervention of Brazil, Turkey, and Japan to explore last-ditch opportunities. At that point, the Obama administration had become open to the idea of doing the swap in two batches, but only if the Iranians agreed to another meeting at the political level. However, numerous attempts by the Europeans to reach out to Iran and schedule another political meeting were left unanswered. When confronted, the Iranians claimed not to have received the messages. "It was like high school," a State Department official told me. "It was ridiculous."[13]

Moreover, the singular focus on the nuclear issue at the expense of other pressing issues (such as the possibility of U.S.-Iran cooperation in Afghanistan, stability in Iraq, and the human rights situation in Iran) turned the negotiations into single variable bargaining, which is the toughest form of negotiations—particularly in an already difficult political climate (the Iranian proposition for an expansive agenda for the negotiations was viewed by the U.S. as an attempt to play for time). Had the agenda been wider from the outset, progress on one issue could have been used to break the deadlock on another issue. Larger agendas can provide greater maneuverability for creative solutions.

In addition, though the fuel swap was supposed to be a confidence-building measure, it soon turned into a precondition for continued diplomacy; unless Iran agreed to the swap, no other diplomatic activity would take place. This approach, which in essence confused the *strategic* goal of establishing a functioning and sustainable diplomatic process with the *tactical* benefit of the fuel swap as a trust-building measure, was highly problematic. It ensured that failure to agree on what was supposed to be a confidence-building measure would lead to a grinding halt of the entire agenda of U.S.-Iran negotiations. Usually in negotiations, if one trust-building measure does not work, another is put to the test. These measures are not treated as the endgame of negotiations. In the case of the Vienna Group and Iran, however, the confidence-building measure became the endgame. Rather than leapfrogging the interim deal, the Obama administration instead chose to abandon diplomacy over the failure to agree on it.

In contrast, the success of the Tehran Declaration can be partly explained by Turkey and Brazil's approach to diplomacy—an approach that differed from that of their American and European counterparts. Their starting point was of course more favorable. As developing countries with no recent history of hostility toward Iran, no atmosphere of mistrust existed between Turkey, Brazil, and Iran. Instead, there was an atmosphere of respect because diplomacy was conducted on the "basis of equality" with a focus on problem solving rather than coercion. "When you put intimidation and coercion ahead of respect, it falls apart," a senior Turkish diplomat explained. "Iran listens to us because we respect them." Brazil and Turkey circumvented the issue of trust, which had been so paralyzing in the dealings between Iran and the United States. Rather than putting their trust in Iran, they put their trust in the agreement, with the expectation that the agreement would provide the guarantees that would help generate trust. "It's not about trusting anyone," an adviser to Brazilian president Lula da Silva told me, "It's about generating the mechanics under which people can prove that they deserve that trust. That's what it's about."[14]

Moreover, the Brazilians and Turks did not search for a singular authentic channel to Iran, but rather recognized that diplomacy had to be conducted with all major Iranian power centers. Just as they engaged with the White House, State Department, Pentagon, and Congress on the U.S. side, they recognized that no major decision was likely to be made in Iran unless a range of key stakeholders was brought into the discussion. As a result, they spent considerable time in face-to-face meetings building confidence with all relevant Iranian power centers, including the *Majles* (Iranian parliament), the Supreme Leader's office, and other political centers and factions. "There is one country that resembles the Iranian power structure," Turkish veteran journalist

Cengiz Candar told me. "It's the United States of America. So talking to the president is not enough. You have to talk to them all." And perhaps most importantly, Brazil and Turkey's pursuit of a diplomatic solution was far more persistent and deliberate, perhaps a task they could undertake because they faced no major political obstacles at home. Between November 2009 and 2010, Brazil and Turkey spent more time in talks with Tehran than did the entire P5+1 combined. Clearly, the specifics of the Tehran Declaration were more attractive to the Iranians—such as the explicit recognition of their right to enrich— but that alone does not explain the success of Turkey and Brazil in securing Iran's agreement. Their approach to and persistence with diplomacy are of critical importance.[15]

Ultimately, the failure of diplomacy between the U.S. and Iran came down to insufficient political will and the atmosphere of mistrust that granted neither side any margin for error. The proposals put on the table may have been flawed; at different points either side may have played for time or sought to delay talks; and goodwill measures may not have been reciprocated. But these phenomena do not make U.S.-Iran talks unique; they are common features in almost all negotiations. Talks that succeed do not do so because the proposals are flawless and because both sides play fair. Rather, they succeed because the many flaws associated with the talks are overcome by the political will to reach a solution.

The will for a diplomatic solution must be strong enough to overcome every last hurdle. In the case of the U.S. and Iran, diplomacy was in effect abandoned at the first hurdle. And though the desire for diplomacy was genuine, the administration's lack of confidence in its chances of succeeding—several high-level officials in the Obama administration told me separately that they did not believe diplomacy would work—raises the question as to whether the White House would fully invest in a policy it believed would fail. Lack of political will also plagued the bureaucracy. After the June election in Iran, in particular, a combination of fear and "old think"—sticking to old patterns because they were comfortable and less risky—set in and helped reduce the will to see diplomacy through. "People are just afraid of their own shadows," a senior State Department official said. "You propose something and people all scurry for cover. . . . There is a collective inability to break the patterns of the past and the principles of the past. I mean, thirty years of doing something in a certain way is pretty powerful." This "collective inability," which is also present on the Iranian side but not necessarily for the same reasons, is what makes U.S.-Iranian tensions more than just an antagonistic relationship. It is an *institutionalized enmity*.[16]

Faced with these obstacles, Obama adopted a strategy that would not expend political capital to expand his maneuverability, but rather would pursue what the political landscape in Washington permitted. As that landscape became more hostile as a result of the Iranian government's actions and pressure from both Congress and some of Washington's key allies, Obama's prospects for success decreased accordingly. Obama never really fought at home to get the political space he needed to succeed. The administration rarely reached out to lawmakers for help, and even when senior political allies in Congress offered to provide the president with political cover to pursue a "bolder diplomatic strategy," the White House declined because pushing for more political room on Iran did not carry with it any domestic political benefits. Ayatollah Khamenei has pursued a similar approach in Iran. At the same time that he has opposed talks with the U.S. to rob his political rivals of credit, he has also approached any dealings with the U.S. with utmost skepticism and backed down from any initiative if faced with opposition at home. Iran's failure to agree to the U.S.-Russian swap proposal in October 2009 is one such example. In this paradigm, both sides— perhaps as a result of their respective "collective inability" to change —have proven themselves more capable of mustering political will for confrontation than for reconciliation, and more willing to accept risks in conflict than risks for peacemaking.[17]

This institutionalized enmity between the U.S. and Iran tends to ensure that domestic political considerations trump strategic imperatives. In the words of a senior U.S. State Department official, Iran is the "third rail" of U.S. politics and very much a domestic political issue—not because the average American cares about or has a sense of involvement in the U.S.-Iran conflict, but because a few interest groups manage to have a decisive impact on the formulation of America's Iran policy by turning the issue into a domestic political football. Any compromise with Iran must have the support of a few key domestic constituencies in the U.S., of which some are reflexively against a deal with Iran—period. A similar phenomenon exists in Iran. Tehran's fractured politics have often paralyzed its ability to pursue a conciliatory policy toward the U.S. in a sustained fashion. Paradoxically, most factional groups—including the hard-liners— oppose the idea of another faction securing an agreement with Washington more so than the idea of reconciling with the U.S. itself.

Thus far, both sides have at various times shown an interest in resolving their conflict. Both sides have taken risks and launched initiatives to overcome their differences. But their abilities to reach out have rarely been synchronized; when one has been looking outward, the other has been looking inward. And rarely have they been able to sustain the necessary political will for a solution. Because of the American political system's susceptibility to outside influence, and because of Iran's fractured politics, the ability of both states to muster sufficient will and persistence at the same time has been limited. In the case of Obama's outreach to Iran, it was genuine but short-lived. It had to succeed immediately or not at all. "Our Iran diplomacy was a gamble on a single roll of the dice," a senior State Department official told me. While Tehran and Washington need not bet the farm, more than beginner's luck is needed to break free from the paradigm of enmity that currently entraps them.[18]

Twelve

Epilogue

An Uncertain Future

Uncertainty is the only certainty there is, and knowing how to live with insecurity is the only security.

—John Allen Paulos

With popular unrest sweeping away dictatorial regimes in the Arab world, strategists in the White House must take into account far greater uncertainty as they address Iran going forward. Splits within the conservative camp in Iran have widened, and the power struggle between President Mahmoud Ahmadinejad and Supreme Leader Ali Khamenei has reached a climax as the former becomes increasingly marginalized within the regime and inches closer to what may be a lame duck term. This power struggle is symptomatic of a larger competition between the Islamic Republic's old guard and a new generation of Iranian politicians who were the foot soldiers of the revolution thirty years ago. The impact of this power struggle on Iranian foreign policy remains to be seen, but it raises the possibility of certain shifts while increasing the unpredictability of Iranian behavior in the near term.

The Arab world as a whole is undergoing the most dynamic transformation since World War I, when Sir Mark Sykes and François Georges-Picot first divided the region into colonized spheres of influence. Washington was at first taken aback when the Arab spring swept through the Middle East and North Africa. The fall of the

Mubarak regime in Egypt—a pillar of the American order in the region—could spell disaster for the U.S. and significantly advance Iran's regional position. But while Tehran has long cherished the day when the pro-American regimes in the Middle East would fall, it too was taken by surprise, not only because of the swift collapse of the Mubarak regime, but also by the lack of an anti-American dimension in the Egyptian "revolution." Tehran had projected that the populations of these pro-American regimes would rise and direct their anger against both the autocrats and their American backers. This, in turn, could provide Iran with an inroad to expand its regional influence.[1]

Thus far, Tehran's projection has not materialized. Instead, Washington has found an opportunity to reinvent its leadership in the region by recognizing that the status quo is untenable, and that a new bargain—based on a new order—must be struck between America and the governments *and* populations of the Middle East. If such an agreement is reached, it could put Tehran on the defensive and significantly reduce its ability to position itself as indispensable to U.S. interests in Iraq, Afghanistan, and beyond. But the road to such a new covenant is long and arduous. It will require a tectonic shift in how the U.S. approaches the region, and cannot be achieved through visionary speeches alone. It will require tangible changes in policy, not just platitudes. Washington's public admission that the status quo is untenable has already created tensions with Israel and Saudi Arabia, two of its key allies in the region—both of which benefited from the previous order and desperately want Washington to reinstate it. Martin Kramer of Israel's conservative Shalem Center put his finger on this central point of contention during the February 2011 Herzliya Conference in Israel. Questioning America's assertion that the regional status quo is unsustainable, Kramer was unabashed: "In Israel, we are for the status quo. Not only do we believe the status quo is sustainable, we think it's the job of the U.S. to sustain it."[2]

Paranoia and defiance in Riyadh were no less palpable. The Saudis were infuriated by Washington's decision to abandon Mubarak. To the Saudi royal family, the Arab spring is an existential threat to their regime. With the Obama administration backing the Arab populace's desire for change, decision makers in Riyadh believe that Washington violated its long-ago promise to guarantee the security of the House of Saud. This perception prompted the Saudis to take matters into their own hands. Scuttling a mediation effort by the U.S. between the Bahraini regime and its opposition, Saudi troops moved into the tiny Persian Gulf kingdom on March 15, 2011, and crushed the prodemocracy uprising. Fearing that regime change in Bahrain would repeat the Iraqi experience—where a Sunni Arab dictator was replaced by a democratically elected Shia government with close ties to Tehran—the Saudis were determined to push back against what they perceived to be an opportunity for Iran to expand its influence in the Persian Gulf region and beyond. According to an Arab official who was briefed on talks between President Obama and King Abdullah, the Saudi monarch was unwavering: "King Abdullah has been clear that Saudi Arabia will never allow Shia rule in Bahrain —never." Moreover, the Saudis began forming an anti-Iran alliance consisting of Arab and Muslim states, a move that Washington worried could bring the region to the brink of war. More than ever before, the U.S. is now forced to balance its interests (positive relations with Israel and Saudi Arabia) with its values (democracy and human rights).[3]

America's Options

Washington is facing an unprecedented situation in the region where its own position has weakened; its interests and those of its close regional allies are diverging, and, though it has not become an irrelevant superpower, its leadership is increasingly questioned and disregarded. In the meantime, the Iranians are also losing their momentum—due partly to the Arab spring and partly to their own internal divisions. While this does not undermine the strategic utility of resolving U.S.-Iran tensions, the immediate benefits are less certain and there is a perception of even greater risk involved in any efforts to engage Tehran. These developments will continue to limit Washington's options on Iran. In the short run—more specifically, the period leading up to the 2012 U.S. presidential election—no space will exist for any constructive initiative.

Instead, Obama's Iran policy will likely become a target of Republican campaigns in the upcoming election. With the president's success in eliminating Osama Bin Laden, and the absence of a unified Republican position on the Arab spring and the intervention in Libya, Iran stands out as the easiest and most unifying foreign policy target for the Republicans. Obama will likely try to "out-hawk" the Republicans and emphasize his administration's success in creating a strong international coalition for sanctions on Iran. This is, however, an inherently weak position because the Iranian nuclear program nevertheless continues to advance. The administration's efforts have raised the cost of the program and have succeeded in slowing it down, but Obama's efforts have not changed the direction of the Iranian program. It continues to progress, albeit at a slower pace.

Playing a dangerously hawkish game with the Republicans will betray the foreign policy values Obama promised to bring to the White House in 2008—and is unlikely to succeed. Regardless of how tough Obama presents himself, there will always be a Republican political opponent who can up the ante even further. Indeed, Democrats have failed in this game in the past. In the 1990s Republicans in Congress dismissed the sanctions on Saddam Hussein's Iraq and forced President Bill Clinton to adopt more extreme measures, including making regime change official U.S. policy and providing funding for the now-disgraced Iraqi "opposition" groups through the Iraq Liberation Act of 1998. Clinton's attempts to push back against this pressure by out-hawking the Republicans helped only to create a false binary choice between accepting a nuclear Saddam or taking military action. The parallels with developments with Iran today are plenty. And as the president enters this game, he limits his ability to pursue more constructive policies down the road. A reelection strategy based on intensifying the paradigm of enmity rather than breaking free from it will render any future diplomatic initiative in a second Obama term only more difficult. Moreover, this approach will also strengthen the false narrative of exhausted diplomacy and painful but insufficient sanctions, which have added artificial weight to the position that the only remaining option is some form of military strike. As Israel's Deputy Foreign Minister Danny Ayalon told me: "If diplomacy fails and the economic sanctions fail, [then] everybody understands that all options are on the table."[4]

The military option remains highly questionable and risky. Beyond the humanitarian disaster that war brings about, its key weaknesses—the unpredictable regional and global repercussions, and the likelihood that it would increase rather than decrease an Iranian desire for a nuclear bomb—become even more glaring in the aftermath of the Arab spring. Discussions of a possible military strike become more precarious when taking into account the potential impact it will have on the continued spread of popular uprisings in the region, and America's increased military overextension as a result of operations in Libya. It has also become clearer that Israel, the main proponent of U.S. military action, is unlikely to attack Iran and that its bluster for the past decade has been primarily aimed at spurring the U.S. to exercise its military option. "Our time would be better spent lobbying Barack Obama to do this, rather than trying this ourselves," an Israeli general told Jeffrey Goldberg of the *Atlantic*. Goldberg's piece "Point of No Return" was arguably the starting salvo of the latest Israeli campaign to present the American president with the binary choice of either bombing Iran or leaving Israel to do so itself. In Goldberg's assessment, the Obama administration "knows it is a near-certainty that Israel will act against Iran soon if nothing or no one else stops the nuclear program." But secret State Department cables reveal that the U.S. government treated Israeli worst-case assessments on the Iranian nuclear program with some skepticism, recognizing that Israel might be trying to augment Washington's sense of urgency.[5]

While the Israelis were telling the Obama administration that

"America must attack Iran or Israel will have no choice but to do so itself," they were reassuring the Russians that no such plans for an attack existed. According to Russian president Dmitry Medvedev, Israeli officials had assured him that they were not planning a military strike on Iran. "My Israeli colleagues told me they were not planning to act in this way, and I trust them," Medvedev told CNN in September 2009. Even publicly, some former Israeli officials have started rescinding the frequent threats to attack Iran. Former military intelligence chief Aharon Ze'evi-Farkash told a March 2009 security conference in Israel that "Israel cannot deal with the Iranian threat on its own. It can only take part in a course of action." Speaking even more forcefully, Meir Dagan, former chief of Mossad, Israel's national security agency, made headlines in mid-2011, stating that Israel could not withstand a regional conflict ignited by an Israeli strike of Iran's nuclear facilities, and that Israel possessed the capability only to delay Tehran's nuclear ambitions, not to stop them. In Dagan's view, the possibility of a future Israeli attack on Iranian nuclear facilities was "the stupidest thing I have ever heard . . . if anyone seriously considers [a strike] he needs to understand that he's dragging Israel into a regional war that it would not know how to get out of. The security challenge would become unbearable."[6]

The Israeli bluff, however, was effective. Congress used it to push sanctions onto the Obama administration. The argument read that the only measure that could prevent war was the imposition of sanctions. No longer were the choices between diplomacy, sanctions, and military action, but between sanctions and military action only. And even though Obama was aware of Israel's intent behind the bluster, it did not prevent the administration from using the same false argument to strong-arm Russia, China, and other skeptics in the Security Council into supporting sanctions. Dagan's recent statements, however, suggest that the sense of urgency for sanctions was fabricated; Israel was not on the verge of attacking Iran. On the contrary, at most it only intensified its efforts to convince Washington to start a war that it itself could not wage. Indeed, contrary to their common rhetoric, the Israelis recognize that while a nuclear Iran would carry numerous strategic negatives for Israel, the Iranians are not likely to attack the Jewish state. "I don't think the Iranians, even if they got the bomb, [would] drop it in the neighborhood," Israel's defense minister, Ehud Barak, said in February 2010. "They fully understand what might follow. They are radical but not totally crazy. They have a quite sophisticated decision-making process, and they understand reality." Barak has also publicly stated that Iran does not pose an existential threat to Israel.[7]

Furthermore, from the Israeli perspective, sanctions and (American) military action are not either-or options. Rather, they are complementary. While sanctions systematically weaken Iran and reduce its capabilities, including its ability to muster nuclear advances, American military action is needed to push back Iran if it reaches important nuclear milestones. Sanctions can slow down Iran's nuclear advances, but military action can set the nuclear program back. Alone, neither approach is satisfactory for Israel. Only when the two are combined will the Jewish state feel confident that the balance of power is securely locked in its favor. The Obama administration's sanctions effort has been very helpful to the Israeli government—it has put a wedge between Russia, China, and Iran, while pressuring more individual states to adopt unilateral sanctions against Iran that go well beyond the UN sanctions.[8]

But if the U.S. and its allies continue to pursue an approach to Iran that is centered around sanctions, it could turn into a de facto strategy predicated on the assumption that Iran will eventually go nuclear, and that the West's best option from a nonproliferation perspective is to look beyond Iran. In other words, it should make the cost of reaching a nuclear threshold so high that if or when Iran becomes a nuclear power, sanctions will have so devastated the country's economy and infrastructure that no other country would choose to mimic Iran's path to a bomb. The lesson to other would-be proliferators is clear: although proliferation cannot be completely stopped, your nuclear status will not be accepted ultimately and you can achieve the bomb only at the expense of the complete political and economic devastation of your country. While making an example out of Iran may deter other potential proliferators, the cost-benefit analysis of this policy must also take into consideration additional effects that the devastation of Iran's economy will have. This includes but is not limited to: the impact on Iran's indigenous pro-democracy movement; the risk of Iran turning into a failed state and the destabilizing effect this would have on the Middle East as a whole (see: Pakistan); the deleterious humanitarian impact on innocent Iranians; and the dangers associated with a vengeful and isolated nuclear power. Furthermore, escalating sanctions will exacerbate divisions within the Security Council and among some of America's allies. It will risk further breaking the international consensus against Iran. Russia, for instance, already believes that Washington's approach to sanctions is that, at best, they are pursued to create discontent inside the country in an attempt to usher in a new regime—or, at worst, they have become an end in and of themselves.[9]

This containment option is attractive in Washington because neither the U.S. nor Iran currently has the political will (and, by extension, the political space) for sustained diplomacy, and because the military option is too risky. In numerous conversations with me senior U.S. officials have alluded to Libya "not being the name of the game" when it comes to Iran. That is, at this point the American strategy is not to utilize diplomacy and direct negotiations to reach a nuclear compromise, but rather to win time by postponing the climax of the nuclear dispute as much as possible through sanctions, sabotage, and containment. "Iran is not the top of the agenda at the moment for a number of reasons," said David Miliband, who served as the foreign secretary of the United Kingdom from 2007 to 2010. "One is that its program has not proceeded in a way that Iran had hoped. And part of the reason for that are the sanctions."[10]

But containment—and the "crippling" sanctions that inevitably follow—is not a new policy; it is precisely the Iran policy that America has pursued since 1979, with occasional augmentations of a more

aggressive regime change strategy or of brief episodes of engagement. But Iran's nuclear advances and America's increased involvement in the region raise the question as to whether containment is
any longer a stable, sustainable policy. On the one hand, containment absent mechanisms for de-escalation creates a situation in
which small incidents can escalate uncontrollably into a larger conflict—the smallest spark can ignite the U.S.-Iranian powder keg. On
the other hand, with the domestic political burden in Washington
and Tehran to increase the pressure on one another constantly, their
ability to counter this force for escalation is limited. Unlike the Cold
War, when there was recognition of the existential dangers of a
nuclear confrontation, the necessary cautionary impulses that conse
quently existed between the U.S. and the Soviet Union—manifested
in extensive direct diplomacy, a hotline between the two capitals, an
incident at sea agreement, among other measures—do not exist between Washington and Tehran. Direct contact remains a rarity rather
than the norm. As a result, containment without a sustained effort to
resolve their conflict puts the U.S. and Iran permanently on the verge
of war, with little to no guarantee that tensions will not spill over into
a mutually undesirable confrontation. Moreover, Washington's containment option is entirely predicated on pressure-inducing tools
such as covert action, cyber warfare, and other forms of sabotage.
While covert action can and probably has been effective in damaging
Iran's nuclear program, it further reduces the stability of containment and increases the risk of an unwanted escalation. Iran will likely
respond in kind, by targeting American interests in Iraq, Afghanistan, and elsewhere in the region.

Moreover, the political realities in Tehran and Washington belie
the argument that containment is stable and won't escalate into a
military confrontation because going to war doesn't lie in the interest
of either state. This argument assumes a level of rationality that is
increasingly absent in the policy-making process in Iran and the
U.S., the result of factional politics and the increasingly scorched-
earth nature of American politics, respectively.

Despite the inherent difficulties and struggles, sustained diplomacy is the only policy that remains largely unexplored *and* that has a likelihood of achieving results amounting to more than simply kicking the can down the road. However, as long as U.S. policy focuses on military action and containment, which instead of resolving the nuclear dispute merely slow down or set back Iran's program at best, it exacerbates rather than addresses other points of tension such as Iraq, Afghanistan, human rights, and Iran's wider role in the region. Successful diplomacy, however, can *resolve* these conflicts rather than reconfigure them. But Washington is likely to pursue sustained diplomacy in just three scenarios. The first is in response to an unexpected development that creates an opportunity for diplomacy that either suddenly increases the strategic necessity of talks and pushes the cost of not engaging to a tipping point or significantly reduces the risk of engagement. To a certain extent, the September 11 terrorist attacks did create one such opportunity, as did Saddam Hussein's invasion of Kuwait in 1990. The fall of the current Iranian theocracy could also create such an opportunity. The second scenario involves a dramatically changed domestic political landscape in America in which political forces against engagement are weakened. This situation could create the necessary political space to pursue diplomacy in a more systematic and sustained fashion—the same way that American diplomacy functions nearly everywhere else in the world. But because of the industry that has been created around sanctions and conflict with Tehran, this scenario remains unlikely. Under the third scenario, the president of the United States musters the political will to pursue diplomacy due to its strategic benefits *regardless* of the domestic political cost.

The first scenario is impossible to predict. The last two scenarios remain unlikely, particularly considering that they are required just for diplomacy to be *pursued* by Washington, not for it to be *successful*. To succeed, similar changes must simultaneously occur in Iran, and Ayatollah Khamenei must overcome his contradictory desire to prevent any other Iranian figure from reaping the political benefits of resolving outstanding issues with the United States, while at the same time maintaining sufficient distance from any negotiations to evade the repercussions should they fail. And he doesn't trust the political figures distant enough from him to provide plausible deniability to lead the talks without stealing credit. Those sufficiently close to and trusted by him cannot provide the desired remoteness to retain Khamenei's above-the-political-fray illusion—which has already been shattered by his actions surrounding the contested 2009 Iranian presidential election and its aftermath.

Lessons Learned: How to Make Diplomacy Succeed

Ambassador John Limbert, a former hostage in Iran who later served as deputy assistant secretary of state for Iran in the Obama administration, has bemoaned the inability of Iran and the United States to overcome their enmity. As the hostility has become institutionalized, Limbert argues, a few ineffectual "rules" have emerged that guide and sustain it. First, "never walk through an open door. Instead, bang your head against a wall." Second, "never say yes to anything the other side proposes. Doing so will make you look weak." Third, assume that the "other side is infinitely hostile, devious, domineering and irrational. It is the embodiment of all that is evil." Consequently, "anything the other side proposes must contain some kind of trick. Its only purpose in life is to cheat you." And last but not least, "whenever you seem to be making progress, someone or some diabolical coincidence will mess it up." Limbert argues that before diplomacy can succeed, these rules must be abolished.[11]

Several points can be added to Limbert's thoughtful suggestions. First, sanctions neither complement diplomacy nor provide an alternative to engagement. Rather than being an alternative policy, sanctions have become an alternative *to* policy. If diplomacy is pursued again, it must succeed for the sake of resolving the conflict, not for the sake of creating an impetus for more sanctions. While sanctions can potentially play a role during specific phases of an engagement policy, a sanctions-centric policy that places diplomacy on the margins is unlikely to succeed. The opposite is more likely to yield results—that is, a policy centered on diplomacy whereby sanctions can be used on the margins as one of many instruments rather than as the bedrock of the policy. A sanctions-centric policy also runs the risk of putting undue pressure on the Iranian prodemocracy movement. Green movement leaders have repeatedly stated publicly that sanctions will hurt rather than aid their struggle, even though they blame the Iranian government for having put the country on this confrontational path against the international community. "Although we think this situation arose from tactless and adventurous foreign policies, we are against it because it will affect people's lives," former prime minister and unsuccessful 2009 presidential candidate Mir Hussein Mousavi said in May 2010. Privately, Green movement leaders have pointed out that sanctions tend to harm the Iranian middle class, which constitute the core of the prodemocracy movement. A similar pattern can be found in other countries, where the key agent for democratic change was also the middle class. Weakening this important socioeconomic segment of the population does not strengthen the prodemocracy movement, it strengthens the authoritarian regime, they argue.[12]

Second, do not put unnecessary limitations on U.S. diplomats. Obama administration officials recognize that, on numerous instances in the fall of 2009, opportunities to salvage the fuel-swap deal existed if only the United States and Iran could have spoken to each other directly. Efforts should be made to establish such a channel quickly. And the belief that dialogue is possible only if a singular authentic channel to Iran is found must be discarded. Such a channel does not exist. There are many power centers in Iran, all of which need to be included in the process. If direct engagement with these political centers and factions is not immediately possible, negotiators must be willing to give them time so as to neutralize these stakeholders' inclinations to scuttle a deal of which they were not a part. Pressing Iran's fractured political system to give a quick "yes" usually results instead in "no." Before another major diplomatic effort is made, the "no contact" policy that prohibits U.S. diplomats from interacting with their Iranian counterparts should be revised.[13]

Third, progress on the nuclear issue is unlikely unless Washington and the EU clarify their ambiguity on the enrichment issue. Negotiating whether Iran can or cannot have enrichment is no longer in the cards. At this stage the only feasible negotiations are those regarding how enrichment in Iran can be inspected, verified, limited, and controlled. Negotiations over control of Iranian enrichment would require, at a minimum, a clear acceptance of enrichment *inside* Iran—a step the West has either refused to acknowledge or sought to postpone until the end of negotiations. This approach has backfired and only widened the gulf between the West and Iran. It has also contributed to the difficulties in devising a common strategy between the permanent members of the UN Security Council. In late summer 2010, Russian and American diplomats jointly drafted a few ideas on how to restart negotiations with Iran. The ideas centered on various forms of a road map that entailed several reciprocal steps between Iran and the Security Council, including limitations to Iran's enrichment program that would be followed by the lifting of some UN sanctions. But like all road maps, it needed to lead somewhere. Enrichment in Iran was inescapable, Moscow believed, and as a result the Russians were ready to commit to such a destination. Washington, however, could not commit upfront to any end goal, leaving Moscow and Washington with no agreement on how to proceed.[14]

Fourth, reducing thirty years of wide-ranging U.S.-Iran tensions to a single-variable negotiation is not a formula for success. Specifically, limiting it to the nuclear dispute has proved a failure. Not only should other security issues be put on the agenda, but perhaps more importantly Washington should also give the human rights situation in Iran significant prominence. The human rights violations committed by the Iranian government in the aftermath of the June 2009 presidential election were a clear offense of Iran's international obligations—regardless of whether there was election fraud, regardless of who had won the election, and, indeed, regardless of whether there had been any election. The Arab spring has demonstrated that the old formula of cutting security deals with authoritarian regimes while neglecting their human rights abuses and democracy deficits is no longer a viable strategy. The fear of aiding an undemocratic regime by negotiating with it is a valid concern when those negotiations are limited to security issues and exclude human rights and democratization from the agenda. This is a point that several prominent figures in the Green movement have emphasized. The pro-democracy movement inside Iran does not oppose U.S.-Iran dialogue if human rights are addressed alongside other issues. This is due partly to the belief that Obama's less threatening tone helped create an atmosphere in Iran that enabled the Green movement to emerge. "Obama offered a dialogue with Iran," prominent pro-democracy activist Akbar Ganji said, "and this change in discourse immediately gave rise to that [indigenous] outpouring of sentiment against the Islamic Republic [in 2009]. . . . The mere fact that Obama didn't make military threats made the Green movement possible." The opposition fears that when faced with an opportunity to secure a nuclear deal, Washington's instincts would be to sacrifice the human rights issue. The setup appears analogous to the state of relations that existed under the shah: a relationship centered on security at the expense of basic freedoms, and the cardinal sin that has poisoned relations between the two countries to this day. While Green movement leaders have avoided direct contact with the Obama White House, they have made clear that they wish to see far greater focus from the international community on the plight of human rights in Iran. "Please do support human rights in Iran," Ganji told a Washington audience in May 2010. "I believe that this is not too much to ask." His message has been echoed by numerous recognized figures in the movement, including Mousavi's external spokesperson, Ardeshir Amirarjomand.[15]

Treating the human rights situation in Iran as a strategic issue is in America's long-term interest. A healthy, sustainable relationship with Iran cannot be built if the current reservoir of American soft power among the Iranian population is squandered for the sake of a nuclear deal. Just as Iranians' respect and admiration for American achievements, values, and culture would be jeopardized in the event of a military attack on Iran, silence on human rights will likewise deplete this crucial strategic asset. This is particularly important because an Iranian opening to the United States will likely be accompanied with a tightening of domestic restrictions, as the government will not want its policy to be understood as a sign of weakness.[16]

Fifth, utilize the help of states that can bridge the trust gap between Iran and the UN Security Council generally, and Iran and the U.S. specifically. Iran's relationship with each of the P5 + 1 countries ranges from bad to worse. There is a huge reservoir of mistrust, suspicion, and hostility. Resolving the nuclear dispute through a mechanism almost completely void of trust is a formidable task. Although the Security Council process cannot be sidestepped, relying on states that, due to their cordial relations with both the permanent members and Iran, can inject trust into the diplomatic process will complement it. Washington showed little appreciation for Turkey and Brazil's efforts to breathe life into the fuel-swap deal, but their rapport and trust with Iran can be used to Washington's benefit.

Turkey in particular is poised to be a key player in the unfolding U.S.-Iranian drama. While Washington has been uncomfortable with Turkey's perceived leniency toward Tehran, it has overlooked how Turkey's maneuvering has checked Iran's attempts to fill the vacuum created by America's decline in the region. Rather than pursuing Iran's isolation and the imposition of additional sanctions, Turkey has taken a page out of the post–World War II American playbook and has sought to bring Iran into a variety of international agreements and treaties and, by doing so, gradually eliminate Iran's use of destabilizing policies for the purpose of asserting its influence. Washington should be able to relate to the Turkish approach since it is partly inspired by how the allied powers dealt with Germany after

World War II. And much like America and Europe's dealings with postwar Germany, Turkey fears that its ability to avoid a later confrontation with Iran will decrease if this approach is discarded. Instead of treating Turkey's approach with suspicion, Washington and the EU should utilize Turkey's ability to elicit Iranian cooperation. Not only is this a more effective strategy in addressing Iran's nuclear program, but Ankara's efforts to shift the security paradigm in the Middle East toward collective security can also be instrumental in ensuring the full potential of the Arab spring. After all, democracy does not produce peace in and of itself. Only when combined with collective security thinking can a region plagued by war find a path to peace.

Finally, Washington must play the long game, with a focus on the long-term benefits of engaging Iran and the dangers of noncommunication. As Admiral Mike Mullen, the seventeenth Chairman of the Joint Chiefs of Staff (CJCS), said on the eve of retiring: "We haven't had a connection with Iran since 1979. Even in the darkest days of the Cold War, we had links to the Soviet Union. We are not talking to Iran, so we don't understand each other. If something happens, it's virtually assured that we won't get it right—that there will be miscalculation which would be extremely dangerous in that part of the world."

Washington must be willing to make the political investment necessary to give the process a chance to succeed. If the Obama administration is going to retreat at the first sign of Iranian intransigence or congressional opposition—both of which are inevitable—then it might be better not to embark on a new round of diplomacy at all. An institutionalized enmity that has taken three decades to build will not be undone through a few meetings over the course of a few weeks. Neither side should expect that its first overture will be accepted. Success will come only if diplomats put a premium on patience and long-term progress rather than on quick fixes aimed at appeasing skeptical and impatient domestic political constituencies, whether in Tehran or in Washington.[17]

Notes

Chapter One.
A Peace of Necessity

1. "Iran: Hardline Daily Dismisses Saudi Plan for Recognizing Israel," *Resalat,* February 26, 2002.

2. Guy Dinmore, "Washington Hardliners Wary of Engaging with Iran," *Financial Times,* March 16, 2004.

3. Gordon Corera, "Iran's Gulf of Misunderstanding with U.S.," BBC News, September 25, 2006, http://news.bbc.co.uk/2/hi/middle_east/5377914.stm. Interview with Lawrence Wilkerson, October 16, 2006.

4. Gareth Porter, "Burnt Offering," *American Prospect,* June 6, 2006.

5. Gareth Porter, "Cheney-Led 'Cabal' Blocked 2003 Nuclear Talks with Iran," *IPS,* May 28, 2006. Interview with Lawrence Wilkerson, October 16, 2006.

6. Porter, "Burnt Offering."

7. Glenn Kessler, "In 2003, U.S. Spurned Iran's Offer of Dialogue," *Washington Post,* June 18, 2006. Interview with Lawrence Wilkerson, October 16, 2006. Bernard Gwertzman, "Leverett: Bush Administration 'Not Serious' About Dealing with Iran," *Council on Foreign Relations,* March 31, 2006.

8. "U.S. Admiral Urges Caution on Iran," BBC News, July 2, 2008, http://news.bbc.co.uk/2/hi/7486338.stm. James Sturcke, "U.S. Admiral Warns Israel Against Opening Iran 'Third Front,' " *Guardian,* July 3, 2008.

9. James A. Baker III and Lee H. Hamilton, *The Iraq Study Group Report,* United States Institute for Peace, December 2006.

10. "Five Ex-secretaries of State Urge Talks with Iran," Associated Press, September 15, 2008.

11. Democratic Debate Transcript, Austin, Texas, Council on Foreign Relations, February 21, 2008.

Chapter Two.
With Friends Like These . . .

1. Telephone interview with senior non-EU3 diplomat, September 2, 2010. Interview with Ambassador Andreas Michaelis, director-general for Middle Eastern Affairs and North Africa, German Foreign Ministry, September 14, 2010. Interview with Pierre Vimont, ambassador of France to the United States, July 26, 2010. Interview with senior EU official, May 27, 2010. Interview with senior EU official involved in the negotiations with Iran, July 14, 2010. Telephone interview with two European officials, June 8, 2010. Interview with senior French diplomat, June 15, 2010.

2. Interview with senior EU diplomat, September 14, 2010. John Vinocur, "Europe Is Waiting to See How Obama Plays Iran," *New York Times,* November 24, 2008. Interview with senior French diplomat, June 15, 2010.

3. Transcript of President-elect Obama's first press conference, November 7, 2008.

4. William Luers, Thomas Pickering, and James Walsh, "How to End the U.S.-Iran Standoff," *New York Times,* March 3, 2008. Ali Scotten, "NIAC Conference: Blix, Pickering Propose Nuclear Compromise," April 8, 2008, http://www.niacouncil.org/site/News2?page=NewsArticle&id=6091.

5. Interview with senior EU diplomat, May 27, 2010. Interview with senior EU diplomat, September 14, 2010. Francois Murphy, "France, UK Push for EU Sanctions on Iran—Report," Reuters, January 19, 2009. Alex Barker, Najmeh Bozorgmehr, and Guy Dinmore, "EU Trio Targets Tougher Iran Sanctions," *Financial Times,* February 25, 2009. Interviews with senior EU3 and non-EU3 diplomats, May 27, 2010, June 15, 2010, and September 10, 2010.

6. Interview with two senior non-EU3 diplomats, September 2 and 10, 2010.

7. "Arabs Lament Lack of Dialogue on Iran Nuclear Crisis," AFP, November 9, 2008.

8. Interview with Rayed Krimly, November 25, 2010.

9. "Arabs Lament Lack of Dialogue." Classified U.S. State Department cable, "Scenesetter for Ambassador Ross' Visit to Egypt," April 28, 2009. Daniel Brumberg, "Obama's Overtures to Iran," *Washington Post,* March 20, 2009. Howard Schneider and Glenn Kessler, "Israel Puts Iran Issue Ahead of Palestinians," *Washington Post,* April 22, 2009. Abdullah Alshayij, "Arab Countries Worry About Improved U.S.-Iran Relations," Gulf News, May 11, 2009. Interview with Prince Turki bin Faisal Al Saud, December 2, 2010. Krimly expanded on this point, saying: "Saudi Arabia has no problem in giving Iran a larger regional role for clearly this is normal given the importance of Iran in the region. The issue then is not about Iran assuming a leading role in the region but is whether its leading role would be to enhance stability, security, and prosperity in the region or to promote conflicts and instability so that Arab countries become merely an arena for the intervention of others." Interview with Rayed Krimly, November 25, 2010. Classified U.S. State Department cable, "Abu Dhabi Crown Prince Reiterates Iran Concerns for S/SRAP Holbrooke," April 5, 2009.

10. Alshayij, "Arab Countries Worry About Improved U.S.-Iran Relations."

11. Classified U.S. State Department cable, "Counterterrorism Adviser Brennan's Meeting with Saudi King Abdullah," March 22, 2009. Robert Worth, "Gaza War Exposes Rift Between Pro-Western Arab States and Iran-led Alliance," *New York Times,* December 31, 2008. Classified U.S. State Department cable, "Abu Dhabi Crown Prince Talks Iran Concerns with General Moseley," February 7, 2007. Roula Khalaf, "U.S. Has Others to Please as It Engages Iran," *Financial Times,* April 13, 2009.

12. Jonathan Spyer, "Gaza War Exposes Rift Between Pro-Western Arab States and Iran-led Alliance," *Jerusalem Post,* December 31, 2008. Liz Sly, "Outcome of Gaza Conflict Will Echo in Iran," *Chicago Tribune,* January 11, 2009.

13. Spyer, "Gaza War Exposes Rift." "Iran's Ahmadinejad Presses Egypt on Gaza

Stance," Reuters, January 10, 2009. "Egypt Attacks Iran and Allies in Arab World," Reuters, January 28, 2009. Sly, "Outcome of Gaza Conflict Will Echo in Iran."

14. Classified U.S. State Department cable, "Abu Dhabi Crown Prince Talks Iran Concerns with General Moseley." Classified U.S. State Department cable, "Saudi King Abdullah and Senior Princes on Saudi Policy Toward Iraq," April 20, 2008. Comments by State Department officials in these cables reveal that Saudi diplomats tended to advise the U.S. against war, whereas senior members of the royal family were far more bellicose. Classified U.S. State Department cable, "Saudis on Iran Ref Upcoming NAM FM Meeting," July 22, 2008.

15. Matthew Fisher, "Israel's Livni Blasts Obama's Iran Plan," Canwest News Service, November 6, 2008.

16. Interview with Ali Reza Alavi Tabar, Tehran, August 21, 2004. Interview with former Deputy Foreign Minister Abbas Maleki, Tehran, August 1, 2004. Interview with former Iranian official, Tehran, August 2004.

17. Gary Sick, *October Surprise* (New York: Random House, 1991), 114. "Sharon Reveals Arms Supplies to Iran," BBC, May 28, 1982. "Israel Sends Military Equipment to Iran," Associated Press, May 28, 1982.

18. Nader Entessar, "Israel and Iran's National Security," *Journal of South Asian and Middle Eastern Studies* 4 (2004): 7; Samuel Segev, *The Iranian Triangle* (New York: Free Press, 1988), 43. "There was a big Israeli fear that Iraqi divisions would descend on Israel together with other Arab armies," Shmuel Bar of the Israeli think tank Interdisciplinary Center in Herzliya explained. Interview with Shmuel Bar, Tel Aviv, October 18, 2004. Interview with David Kimche, Tel Aviv, October 22, 2004. Segev, *Iranian Triangle,* 22. General Raphael Eytan, the chief of staff of the Israeli army at the time, explained Iran's inability to pose a threat to Israel: "If Iran decided to invade Israel, first her forces should cross Iraq and then, they should cross Jordan; in order to get to Israel they should destroy these two countries and when they reach Israel, they would realize that we are neither Iraq nor Jordan and to overcome us would not be possible." Behrouz Souresrafil, *Khomeini and Israel* (London: Researchers, 1988), 79. Interview with David Menashri, professor at Tel Aviv University, Tel Aviv, October 26, 2004. According to Yuval Ne'eman, a right-wing Knesset member, though Iran was not a friendly state, "as far as Israel's security is concerned, Iraq is a far greater danger." Ruth Sinai, "Israel Helps Iran for Strategic and Economic Reasons," Associated Press, December 1, 1986.

19. Interview with Itamar Rabinovich, former adviser to Rabin and Israeli ambassador to the United States, Tel Aviv, October 17, 2004. Interview with Kimche, October 22, 2004. Malcolm Byrne, *The Chronology* (New York: Warner, 1987), 116. Interview with former National Security Adviser Robert McFarlane, Washington, D.C., October 13, 2004. "In strict geopolitical terms, if you don't consider regimes, our friend should be Iran, and we should never forget that," argued Itamar Rabinovich, Israel's U.S. ambassador 1993–96 and a close adviser to Rabin. Interview with Jess Hordes, director of the Anti-Defamation League's Washington office, Washington, D.C., March 24, 2004.

20. Segev, *Iranian Triangle,* 7. Interview with David Kimche, October 22, 2004.

21. AFP, February 12, 1993. Interview with Itamar Rabinovich, Tel Aviv, October 17, 2004.

22. Interview with former Assistant Secretary of State Martin Indyk, Washington, D.C., March 4, 2004.

23. "Israel Focuses on the Threat Beyond the Periphery," *New York Times,* November 8, 1992.

24. See, for instance, Classified U.S. State Department cable, "Israeli Intentions Regarding the Iranian Nuclear Program," March 17, 2005. Interview with Ranaan Gissin, Jerusalem, October 31, 2004.

25. Interview with Ephraim Sneh, former Israeli deputy minister of defense, Tel Aviv, October 31, 2004.

26. Interview with Professor Gerald Steinberg, Jerusalem, October 28, 2004. Leslie Susser, "Israel Facing Grim Threat Assessment for '09," Jewish Telegraphic Agency, November 24, 2008. Joshua Mitnick, "Israel Warms to Obama's Pledge of Talks with Iran," *Washington Times,* November 26, 2008.

27. Classified U.S. State Department cable, "Israeli Intentions Regarding the Iranian Nuclear Program." Interview with Danny Ayalon, October 4, 2010. Conversation with senior Israeli diplomat, August 3, 2010.

28. Dudi Cohen, "Former General: Israel Can't Defeat Iran," Ynet, December 18, 2008. Classified U.S. State Department cable, "Israeli Intentions Regarding the Iranian Nuclear Program." Aluf Benn, "Iran—An Attack Is Still Possible," *Haaretz,* October 5, 2008.

29. Jonathan Steele, "Israel Asked U.S. for Green Light to Bomb Nuclear Sites in Iran," *Guardian,* September 25, 2008.

30. "U.S. Puts Brakes on Israeli Plan for Attack on Iran Nuclear Facilities," *Haaretz,* August 13, 2008. Steele, "Israel Asked U.S. for Green Light." David Ignatius, "The Tea Leaves Say America Is Not About to Attack Iran," *Daily Star,* August 2, 2008. Israeli defense minister Ehud Barak confirmed America's resistance to military action in an interview with Israeli Army Radio. "Iran MPs Slam Ahmadinejad's Aide over Pro-Israeli Remarks," AFP, August 14, 2008. Daniel Dombey, Andrew Ward, and Harvey Morris, "Mullen Warns of 'Third Front' for U.S.," *Financial Times,* July 3, 2008. "U.S. Army Chief: Israeli Strike on Iran Would Destabilize Mideast," *Haaretz,* July 2, 2008.

31. Classified U.S. State Department cable, "U/S Burns' August 17 Meeting with Israeli Mossad Chief Meir Dagan," August 31, 2007.

32. James Besser, "Dems See Domestic Agenda Blunting Stubborn Age Gap," *Jewish Week,* June 14, 2008. Jim Hoagland, "Countering Iran in Gaza and Beyond," *Washington Post,* January 4, 2009. Joshua Mitnick, "Israel Warms to Obama's Pledge of Talks with Iran," *Washington Times,* November 26, 2008. Prime Minister Olmert even publicly urged Jewish Americans to lobby their government to impose more sanctions on Iran two weeks after Obama had been elected. "Each and every one of us needs to play a role—lobby your government, lead your organization or identify a project that can exert additional pressure on Iran," he said. Allison Hoffman, "Olmert: U.S. Must Take Lead Against Iran," *Jerusalem Post,* November 16, 2008.

Chapter Three.
"He Is with Us"

1. Laura Rozen, "Revealed: Recent U.S.-Iran Nuclear Talks Involved Key Officials," ForeignPolicy.com, January 30, 2009, http://thecable.foreignpolicy.com/posts/2009/01/29/americas_secret_back_channel_diplomacy_with_iran. "Joseph Rotblat, Won Nobel Prize for Nuclear Arms Fight," Associated Press, September 2, 2005.

2. Per the invitation of Pugwash, I participated in several of these meetings in my capacity as an independent scholar.

3. Translation of Ahmadinejad's Letter, *Washington Post,* November 6, 2008.

4. Interview with senior Iranian nuclear negotiator, May 27, 2010.

5. Jim Muir, "Tehran: Obama Quashes Iran's Hopes for Change," BBC News, November 9, 2008, http://news.bbc.co.uk/2/hi/americas/us_elections_2008/7718603.stm. Hadi Nili, "Iranians' Hope for U.S. Policy Shift Dims," *Washington Times,* January 11, 2009.

6. Press conference with President-elect Barack Obama and Vice President–elect Joseph Biden, November 7, 2008.

7. "Larijani Prefers Obama to Win," Persia House News Brief, November 17, 2008.

8. "Obama's Right Hand Man in Relation to Iran," *Raja News,* August 30, 2008 (Shahrivar 9, 1387).

9. "War in the Mid East, McCain's Trump Card," *Aftab,* July 29, 2008 (Mordad 8, 1387).

10. Interview with Ataollah Mohajerani, 19 September 2010.

11. Roshanak Taghavi, "Iranians Unsure What U.S. Election Will Bring," *Wall Street Journal,* November 5, 2008.

12. Nahid Siamdoust, "Iranians Hope Obama Lives Up to His Name," *Time,* November 2008. Muir, "Obama Quashes Iran's Hopes for Change."

13. Gareth Porter, "Iranian Leaders Split over Obama's Policy Freedom," Inter Press Service, December 10, 2008. Interview with Ataollah Mohajerani, 19 September 2010. Interview with Maziar Bahari, August 16, 2010.

14. Interview with former Iranian ambassador, June 30, 2010. Interview with senior Iranian nuclear negotiator, May 27, 2010.

15. "Who negotiates?" *Aftab,* August 6, 2008 (Mordad 16, 1387). Robert Dreyfuss, "Inside the Head of Mahmoud Ahmadinejad," *Nation,* September 25, 2008. Interview with Ambassador Khazaee, June 15, 2010.

16. Amir Mohebian, editorial, *Resalat News,* November 6, 2008.

17. Interview with senior adviser to former president Mohammad Khatami and opposition leader Mir Hossein Mousavi, July 23, 2010.

18. Roshanak Taghavi, "Iranians Unsure What U.S. Election Will Bring," *Wall Street Journal,* November 5, 2008.

19. Interview with Professor Ahmad Sadri, August 10, 2010.

20. Scott Peterson, "Is Iran Prepared to Undo 30 Years of Anti-Americanism?," *Christian Science Monitor,* February 6, 2009.

21. Classified U.S. State Department cable, November 26, 2008. Interview with senior adviser to former president Mohammad Khatami and opposition leader Mir Hossein Mousavi, July 23, 2010. *Aftab,* August 3, 2008 (Mordad 13, 1387).

22. Thomas Erdbrink, "Facing Obama, Iran Suddenly Hedges on Talks," *Washington Post,* November 13, 2008. Porter, "Iranian Leaders Split over Obama's Policy Freedom." Hadi Nili, "Iranians' Hope for U.S. Policy Shift Dims," *Washington Times,* January 11, 2009. "Obama's Inexperience," *Raja News,* August 27, 2008 (Shahrivar 6, 1387). "Bush and Obama: For as Long as American Policy Does Not Change, There Is No Difference Between You," Fars News, November 7, 2008 (Aban 17, 1387). Mohebian, editorial. Interview with senior adviser to former President Mohammad Khatami and opposition leader Mir Hossein Mousavi, July 23, 2010. Interview with Ambassador Khazaee, June 15, 2010.

23. Porter, "Iranian Leaders Split Over Obama's Policy Freedom."

24. Scott Peterson, "Iranians Wary of Obama's Approach," *Christian Science Monitor,* February 5, 2009. Ross's appointment also sparked a debate in Washington, prompting some experts to question whether he was in line with Obama's foreign policy vision. Steve Clemons of the New America Foundation wrote, "Ross is much more hawkish on Iran than I am. While I'm impressed with his ability to simultaneously sell conflicting themes—like on one hand he wants to bomb Iran and undermine any engagement with Hamas while on the other he desires the sort of dovish position advocated by Search for Common Ground—Dennis Ross is much more comfortable with neoconservatives than realists or liberal internationalists" (TheWashingtonNote .com, November 25, 2008).

25. Islamic Republic News Agency, March 2, 2009 (Esfand 12, 1388). Interview with former Iranian ambassador, June 30, 2010. Criticism against Obama's foreign policy team was also common among progressives in the United States, who argued that Obama had put too many foreign policy hawks in key positions. Jeremy Scahill, "This Is Change? 20 Hawks, Clintonites and Neocons to Watch for in Obama's White House," AlterNet, November 20, 2008. Interview with senior adviser to former President Mohammad Khatami and opposition leader Mir Hossein Mousavi, July 23, 2010.

26. Nathan Guttman, "Iran Emerges as Wedge Issue for Jewish Voters," *Jewish Daily Forward,* August 28, 2008, http://www.forward.com/articles/14104/.

27. Erdbrink, "Facing Obama, Iran Suddenly Hedges on Talks." Islamic Republic News Agency, November 8, 2008.

28. Farideh Farhi, "U.S.-Iran: The More Things Change . . . ," Inter Press Services, February 5, 2009. Jahan News, September 15, 2008 (Shahrivar 24, 1387).

29. Robert Tait and Ewen MacAskill, "Revealed: The Letter Obama Team Hope Will Heal Iran Rift," *Guardian,* January 29, 2009.

30. Matt Morre and Alexander G. Higgins, "Israeli Candidate at Davos Warns on Iran," Associated Press, January 29, 2009.

31. Farhi, "U.S.-Iran." Erdbrink, "Facing Obama, Iran Suddenly Hedges on Talks." Islamic Republic News Agency, November 8, 2008. Jahan News, December 4, 2008 (Azar 14, 1387).

32. Kenneth Pollack, *The Persian Puzzle* (New York: Random House, 2004), 346–47.

33. Speech by Ambassador James Dobbins to the New America Foundation, Washington, D.C., August 24, 2006. Interview with Javad Zarif, Iran's ambassador to the UN, New York, October 12, 2006. Pollack, *Persian Puzzle,* 347.

34. Ali Ansari, *Confronting Iran* (New York: Basic, 2006), 186–87.

35. Scott Peterson, "Pragmatism May Trump Zeal as Iran's Power Grows," *Christian Science Monitor,* July 6, 2006.

36. The "deputies committee" consisted of Stephen Hadley, who served as chairman, Undersecretary Dick Armitage, Deputy Secretary of Defense Paul Wolfowitz, and a deputy to CIA director George Tenet. Gareth Porter, "Burnt Offering," *American Prospect,* June 6, 2006. Scott Ritter, "On the Eve of Destruction," TruthDig.com, October 22, 2007, http://www.truthdig.com/report/item/20071022 on the eve of destruction.

37. Peterson, "Iranians Wary of Obama's Approach."

38. Corbett Daly, "U.S. Brands Anti-Iran Kurdish Group Terrorist," Reuters, February 4, 2010.

39. Interview with Ataollah Mohajerani, September 19, 2010.

40. Interview with Ali Ansari, September 17, 2010

Chapter Four.
The Review

1. "Seven Questions: Hans Blix," *Foreign Policy Magazine,* April 29, 2009. Jonathan Tirone, "IAEA Chief ElBaradei Seeks Stop to Iran 'War Drums,'" Bloomberg, September 7, 2007.

2. Simon Hooper, "Iran: Ready to Work with Obama," CNN, January 30, 2009.

3. Roger Cohen, "Realpolitik for Iran," *New York Times,* April 13, 2009.

4. Jay Solomon, "Obama Team Plots Opening of Iran Ties," *Wall Street Journal,* March 12, 2009.

5. Sue Pleming, "Clinton Doubts Iran Will Respond to Overtures," Reuters, March 2, 2009.

6. Interview with senior EU official, September 14, 2010. Interview with senior EU diplomat, June 2, 2010.

7. Interview with former U.S. State Department Iran Desk officer, June 14, 2010.

8. Interview with senior U.S. State Department nonproliferation officer, July 21, 2010. Interview with former U.S. State Department Iran Desk officer, June 14, 2010.

9. Sue Pleming, "Analysis—Obama Likely to Take Cautious Approach on Iran," Reuters, January 26, 2009. "Iran: Assessing U.S. Strategic Options," Center for a New American Security, September 2008. Glenn Kessler, "Writings Offer Look at Administration Debate on Iran," *Washington Post,* January 30, 2009. Adam Graham-Silverman, "Special Adviser on Iran Hopes for 'Just Right' Engagement Approach," *Congressional Quarterly,* March 16, 2009.

10. Helene Cooper and David E. Sanger, "Obama's Message to Iran Is Opening Bid in Diplomatic Drive," *New York Times,* March 21, 2009. David E. Sanger, "After Israeli Visit, a Diplomatic Sprint on Iran," *New York Times,* May 20, 2009.

11. Oded Eran, Giora Eiland, and Emily Landau, "Let Russia Stop Iran," *New York Times,* December 21, 2008.

12. Classified U.S. State Department cable, "Action Request: Russia S-300 Missile to Iran," February 18, 2009. Charles Clover and Andrew England, "Saudis Seek Russian Pledge on Missiles," *Financial Times,* September 29, 2009.

13. Dennis Ross and David Makovsky, *Myths, Illusions & Peace: Finding a New Direction for America in the Middle East* (New York: Viking, 2009), 221.

14. David E. Sanger and Mark Landler, "China Pledges to Work with U.S. on Iran Sanctions," *New York Times,* April 12, 2010.

15. Interview with former U.S. State Department Iran Desk officer, June 14, 2010. Also based on author's conversations with U.S. officials at the time of the review. Jay Solomon, "Obama Team Plots Opening of Iran Ties," *Wall Street Journal,* March 12, 2009. Classified U.S. State Department cable, "Codel Cardin Discusses Iran, Syria, Palestinians, and Israel Election with Benjamin Netanyahu," February 26, 2009.

16. David E. Sanger and William J. Broad, "Allies' Clocks Tick Differently on Iran," *New York Times,* March 15, 2009.

17. "Iran Nuclear Arms Bid Unclear: U.S. Intel Chief," AFP, February 12, 2009. Roger Cohen, "Realpolitik for Iran," *New York Times,* April 13, 2009.

18. Interview with former U.S. State Department Iran Desk officer, June 14, 2010. Classified U.S. State Department cable, "Codel Cardin Discusses Iran, Syria, Palestinians, and Israel Election with Benjamin Netanyahu," February 26, 2009. Conversation with senior Israeli diplomat, August 2010. "Tel Aviv Wants Time Limit on N-talks with Tehran," *Arab Times Online,* April 10, 2010. Yaakov Katz, "Ya'alon: West Must Stand Up to, Confront Iran," *Jerusalem Post,* April 27, 2009. Sanger and Broad, "Allies' Clocks Tick Differently on Iran."

19. Trita Parsi, "Netanyahu and Threat of Bombing Iran—The Bluff That Never Stops Giving?," Huffington Post, April 7, 2009, http://www.huffingtonpost.com/trita-parsi/netanyahu-and-threat-of-b_b_183822.html.

20. Interview with Vice President Biden, *The Situation Room,* CNN, April 8, 2009. Interview with former U.S. State Department Iran Desk officer, June 14, 2010.

21. "National Security Through Diplomacy," *Before the House Appropriations Subcommittee on State, Foreign Operations and Related Programs,* 111th Cong. (April 23, (2009) (statement of Hillary Clinton, Secretary of State), http://www.state.gov/secretary/rm/2009a/04/122098.htm

22. Conversation with senior Israeli diplomat, August 2010. Aluf Benn, "Obama Team Readying for Clash with Netanyahu," *Haaretz,* April 8, 2009. Katz, "Ya'alon."

23. Howard Schneider and Glenn Kessler, "Israel Puts Iran Issue Ahead of Palestinians: Shift on One Tied to Progress on Other," *Washington Post,* April 22, 2009.

24. David Sanger, "Iranian Overture Might Complicate Relations with Israel," *New York Times,* February 11, 2009.

25. Interview with senior EU negotiator, June 14, 2010. David Sanger, "U.S. May Drop Key Conditions for Talks with Iran," *New York Times,* April 14, 2009.

26. Erika Niedowski, "U.S. Wants Iranian Involvement in Conflict Resolution," *The National* (Abu Dhabi), January 29, 2009. Slobodan Lekic, "NATO Leader Urges

Engagement with Iran," Associated Press, January 27, 2009. Golnar Motevalli, "Analysis—U.S. Needs Iran's Help to Fight Afghan War," Reuters, February 1, 2009. Interview with former U.S. State Department Iran Desk officer, June 14, 2010. "Q&A with Iran's Deputy Foreign Minister for Americas Affairs," *Wall Street Journal,* April 1, 2009. Interview with Ambassador Mohammad Khazaee, June 15, 2009.

27. Robert Dreyfuss, "Hillary & Iran & Dennis & Israel," Agence Global, March 6, 2009. "Iran and U.S. Hold 'Cordial' Talks," BBC News, March 31, 2009, http://news.bbc.co.uk/2/hi/south_asia/7975079.stm. Anne Gearan, "U.S., Iranian Diplomats Break the Ice at Conference," Associated Press, March 31, 2009.

28. Jay Solomon, "U.S., Allies Set October Target for Iran Progress," *Wall Street Journal,* May 14, 2009.

29. Robin Wright, "Stuart Levey's War," *New York Times Magazine,* November 2, 2008. Interview with former U.S. State Department Iran Desk officer, June 14, 2010.

30. Interview with senior U.S. State Department nonproliferation officer, July 21, 2010. Interview with former U.S. State Department Iran Desk officer, June 14, 2010. Classified U.S. State Department cable, "Codels Ackerman and Casey Meetings with Prime Minister Netanyahu," June 2, 2009. "Senators Mull Iran Nuclear Threat, Diplomatic Efforts," AFP, March 4, 2009.

31. Interview with senior U.S. State Department nonproliferation officer, July 21, 2010. Telephone interview with senior non-EU3 diplomat, September 2, 2010. Daniel Dombey, "U.S. Senator Opens Iran Nuclear Debate," *Financial Times,* June 10, 2009. Interview with senior U.S. Senate staffer, August 20, 2010.

32. Interview with Ambassador Andreas Michaelis, director-general for Middle Eastern Affairs and North Africa, German Foreign Ministry, September 14, 2010. Interview with senior EU official involved in the negotiations with Iran, July 14, 2010. Interview with former U.S. State Department Iran Desk officer, June 14, 2010.

33. Adam Graham-Silverman, "Special Adviser on Iran Hopes for 'Just Right' Engagement Approach," *Congressional Quarterly,* March 16, 2009.

34. Sue Pleming, "Clinton Doubts Iran Will Respond to Overtures," Reuters, March 2, 2009. Borzou Daragahi, "Obama Overture Elicits Cautious Response from Iran," *Los Angeles Times,* March 21, 2009. "Gates Prefers Sanctions to Diplomacy for Iran," AFP, March 29, 2009.

35. Interview with former U.S. State Department Iran Desk officer, June 14, 2010.

36. Farideh Farhi, "And Happy Nowruz to You Too Mr. Obama!," Informed Comment: Global Affairs, March 20, 2009, http://icga.blogspot.com/2009/03/and-happy-nowruz-to-you-too-mr-obama.html.

37. Interview with Maziar Bahari, August 16, 2010.

38. Farideh Farhi, "On Khamenei's Response to Obama," Informed Comment: Global Affairs, March 22, 2009, http://icga.blogspot.com/2009/03/on-khameneis-response-to-obama.html. Interview with Farideh Farhi, June 7, 2010.

39. "Text of Khamenei's Speech to U.S. President," BBC, March 22, 2009.

40. Rasool Nafisi, e-mail message to author, March 22, 2009.

41. *Asr-e Iran,* March 21, 2009. Interview with senior adviser to former president Mohammad Khatami and opposition leader Mir Hossein Mousavi, July 23, 2010.

42. "The Nuances of Iran's Response to Obama's Nowruz Message," Persia House News Brief, March 27, 2009. "Iran Senior Cleric Calls U.S. to Show Its 'Goodwill in Practice,'" BBC, March 28, 2009. "America Resents Iran's Military and Scientific Progress," Islamic Republic News Agency, April 1, 2009.

43. "Iranian President Welcomes Honest, Fair Talks with U.S.A.," BBC Worldwide Monitoring, April 9, 2009, http://www.iranalmanac.com/news/lastnews.php?newsid=10131. Nazila Fathi, "Iran Responds Cautiously to Obama's Gesture," *New York Times,* April 9, 2009.

44. Interview with Ambassador Mohammad Khazaee, June 15, 2010.

45. Roula Khalaf, "U.S. Has Others to Please as It Engages Iran," *Financial Times,* April 13, 2009.

Chapter Five.
Israel and Obama Clash

1. "Peres to Iran: Reclaim Your Rightful Place Among 'Enlightened Nations,'" *Haaretz,* March 21, 2009.

2. "With Obama to Iran," *Haaretz,* March 24, 2009.

3. Interview with former Israeli negotiator, July 20, 2010. E-mail correspondence with Marsha Cohen, March 25, 2009. Helene Cooper and David E. Sanger, "Obama's Message to Iran Is Opening Bid in Diplomatic Drive," *New York Times,* March 21, 2009.

4. Classified U.S. State Department cable, "Codel Kyl's Meeting with Prime Minister Netanyahu: What Will the U.S. Do About Iran?," April 28, 2009.

5. Sean Lengell, "Senators Target Firms Doing Business with Iran," *Washington Times,* April 13, 2009.

6. Ron Kampeas, "AIPAC Policy Conference to Push Iran Bills," Jewish Telegraphic Agency, April 28, 2009.

7. Press Release, "Stand with Obama on Israel and Iran," J Street, Washington, DC, April 30, 2009, available at http://www.mepeace.org/group/jstreet/forum/topics/stand-with-obama-on-israel. Ali Gharib, "Hawks Soften Rhetoric on Iran," *Asia Times Online,* April 30, 2009.

8. Nathan Guttman, "AIPAC Confronts a New Reality as Obama's Agenda Becomes Clear," *Forward,* May 7, 2009, http://www.forward.com/articles/105680/.

9. Press Release, "Berman Introduces Legislation to Prevent Iran Nuclear Weapons Capability," House Foreign Affairs Committee, April 29, 2009.

10. Andrew Glass, "AIPAC Launches Push for Iran Sanctions," Politico, May 4, 2009, http://www.politico.com/news/stories/0509/22086.html. Guttman, "AIPAC Confronts a New Reality." Interview with senior Senate staffer, September 2, 2010.

11. Reuters, "Clinton Plays Down More U.S. Sanctions on Iran Now," May 20, 2009.

12. Guttman, "AIPAC Confronts a New Reality."

13. Herb Keinon, "Iran Talks Should Last 12 Weeks Max," *Jerusalem Post,* December 18, 2008. UPI, "Israel Calls for Time-limit on Iran Talks," May 7, 2009.

14. Jeremy Ben-Ami and Trita Parsi, "How Diplomacy with Iran Can Succeed," Huffington Post, June 11, 2009, http://www.huffingtonpost.com/jeremy-benami/how-diplomacy-with-iran-c_b_214407.html.

15. The Israeli press reported in early May that Israel had received a confidential report recounting a meeting between Dennis Ross and a senior EU official, in which Ross stated that the administration had set early fall 2009 as the deadline for the first round of talks. Barak Ravid, "U.S. Puts October Deadline on Iran Talks," *Haaretz,* May 11, 2009. Transcript of State Department Press Briefing, May 14, 2009.

16. Jim Lobe, "Despite Smiles, Obama, Netanyahu Seem Far Apart," Inter Press Service, May 19, 2009.

17. Transcript of Remarks by President Obama and Prime Minister Netanyahu, May 18, 2009.

18. Sheryl Gay Stolberg, "Obama Tells Netanyahu He Has an Iran Timetable," *New York Times,* May 19, 2009. Lobe, "Despite Smiles."

19. Classified U.S. State Department cable, "Codels Ackerman and Casey Meetings with Prime Minister Netanyahu," June 2, 2009.

20. David Sanger, "After Israeli Visit, a Diplomatic Sprint on Iran," *New York Times,* May 20, 2009.

Chapter Six.
Fraud

1. Interview with former Press TV producer, July 13, 2010.

2. "Powerful Reformer to Run Against Iran's President," Associated Press, March 10, 2009.

3. Mark Phillips, "Who Is Mir Hossein Mousavi?," CBS, June 18, 2009. "Profile: Mir Hossein Mousavi," BBC News, June 16, 2009, http://news.bbc.co.uk/2/hi/middle_east/8103851.stm. Mehrzad Boroujerdi and Kourosh Rahimkhani, "Iran's Political Elite: The Iran Primer," United States Institute of Peace, December 2010. Farideh Farhi, "New Hardships Intensify Debate over Iran Iraq War," Tehran Bureau, August 5, 2010. Mehrzad Boroujerdi, "The Potato Revolution," *Foreign Policy,* May 13, 2009.

4. Interview with former Iranian reformist lawmaker, September 17, 2010.

5. Interview with former U.S. State Department Iran Desk officer, June 14, 2010.

6. "Mousavi: I Stand Firm on Principles/Diplomacy Will Relieve Tensions," Mehr News Agency, April 6, 2009 (Farvardin 17, 1388).

7. Interview with campaign worker at Mousavi's headquarters, July 28, 2009. "Iran Reform Candidate Says Open to U.S. Negotiations," AFP, April 6, 2009.

8. "Mousavi: I Stand Firm on Principles." Interview with campaign worker at Mousavi's headquarters, July 28, 2009. Parisa Hafezi, "Iran Candidate Backs Nuclear Talks with the West," Reuters, May 29, 2009.

9. "Iran Reform Candidate Says Open to U.S. Negotiations." Hafezi, "Iran Candidate Backs Nuclear Talks with the West."

10. Barbara Slavin, "Iran's Unlikely Hero," *Washington Times,* June 17, 2009. Interview with senior adviser to former president Mohammad Khatami and opposition

leader Mir Hossein Mousavi, July 23, 2010. Interview with campaign worker at Mousavi's headquarters, July 28, 2009. "We need a comprehensive plan from him. . . . If Obama makes a practical gesture, Iran would immediately respond," Mousavi's chief foreign policy adviser Sadegh Kharrazi—one of the authors of the 2003 negotiation proposal—told the *Nation* (Robert Dreyfuss, "Iran's Election, Obama's Challenge," *Nation,* June 10, 2009).

11. Interview with senior adviser to former president Mohammad Khatami and opposition leader Mir Hossein Mousavi, July 23, 2010.

12. Scott Peterson, "Lincoln-Douglas Debates, Iranian Style," *Christian Science Monitor,* June 3, 2009.

13. Interview with senior adviser to former president Mohammad Khatami and opposition leader Mir Hossein Mousavi, July 23, 2010. Muhammad Sahimi, "New Evidence of Fraud in 2009 Election," Tehran Bureau, August 11, 2010. Farideh Farhi, "Is Commander Jafari Stupid?," Informed Comment: Global Affairs, September 4, 2009, http://icga.blogspot.com/2009/09/is-commander-jafari-stupid.html.

14. Interview with senior adviser to former president Mohammad Khatami and opposition leader Mir Hossein Mousavi, July 23, 2010. Interview with campaign worker at Mousavi's headquarters, July 28, 2009.

15. For studies on the elections and documentation of the irregularities, see Ali Ansari, ed., *Preliminary Analysis of the Voting Figures in Iran's 2009 Presidential Election* (London: Chatham House, 2009), http://www.chathamhouse.org/sites/defa ult/files/public/Research/Middle%20East/iranelection0609.pdf.

16. Robert Dreyfuss, "A Disgusting Fraud," *Nation,* June 21, 2009.

17. "Iran Bars Foreign Media from Reporting on Streets," Associated Press, June 16, 2009.

18. Trita Parsi, "Who's Fighting Who in Iran's Struggle?," *Time,* June 16, 2009.

19. Nazila Fathi and Alan Cowell, "Iran's Top Leader Dashes Hopes for a Compromise," *New York Times,* June 19, 2009.

20. "Larijani Criticizes the Guardian Council, IRIB," Press TV, June 21, 2009, http://edition.presstv.ir/detail/98645.html.

21. "Iran Leader Rafsanjani Rallies Opposition," *Washington Times,* July 19, 2009.

22. "Iran Prisoner Beaten to Death, Coroner Says," CNN, September 1, 2009. Kahrizak was ordered closed by Iran's Supreme Leader Ayatollah Ali Khamenei in late July amid reports that the facility did not meet required standards.

23. Farnaz Fassihi, "Tehran Court Tries Top Reformists," *Wall Street Journal,* August 4, 2009. "Moussavi, Khatami Blast Iran Trials," CNN, August 2, 2009.

24. Interview with former Iranian diplomat who advises the Iranian government, June 30, 2010. Interview with senior adviser to former president Mohammad Khatami and opposition leader Mir Hossein Mousavi, July 23, 2010.

25. Interview with former U.S. State Department Iran Desk officer, June 14, 2010. Interview with senior EU diplomat, May 27, 2010.

26. Laura Rozen, "The Iran Chessboard, as Seen by Team Obama," ForeignPol icy.com, June 26, 2009, http://thecable.foreignpolicy.com/posts/2009/06/26/the_iran

_chessboard_as_seen_by_team_obama. Obama's former national security advisor, General Jim Jones, addressed the Russian-Iranian angle in a speech at the Iran's Nuclear, Terrorist Threats and Rights Abuses conference in Washington, D.C., on January 20, 2011: "I would tell you that the rapprochement between Russia and the United States started very early on in 2009, and that Iran was one of the central reasons for that rapprochement."

27. Scott Wilson, "Muted Response Reflects U.S. Diplomatic Dilemma," *Washington Post,* June 15, 2009. Iason Athanasiadis, "Iran Protest Biggest Since Revolution," *Washington Times,* June 16, 2009. Interview with Michael Ratney, August 10, 2010.

28. Interview with senior EU diplomat, May 27, 2010. Interview with two EU officials, June 8, 2010.

29. David Weigel, "Neocons, House GOPers Demand Obama Take Moussavi's Side," *Washington Independent,* June 16, 2009. Manu Raju, "GOP Tries to Find Its Pitch on Iran," Politico, June 17, 2009, http://www.politico.com/news/stories/0609/23827.html. Anne Flaherty, "House Condemns Tehran Crackdown on Protesters," Associated Press, June 19, 2009. Wilson, "Muted Response Reflects U.S. Diplomatic Dilemma." Moreover, several Republicans pressured the White House to halt any effort for dialogue with Iran in response to the election mayhem. Though there was some Democratic pushback—Rep. Howard Berman (D-CA), chair of the House Foreign Relations Committee, said that the president is "correct in continuing to pursue a policy of engagement"—there did not seem to be much political will in the White House to take on the Republicans in public on this issue ("Iran: Recent Developments and Implications for U.S. Policy," *Before the House Foreign Relations Committee,* 111th Cong. [July 22, 2009] [Howard Berman, committee chair]).

30. Interview with former Iranian lawmaker and prodemocracy activist, September 17, 2010. Interview with senior adviser to former president Mohammad Khatami and opposition leader Mir Hossein Mousavi, July 23, 2010.

31. Interview with Professor Ahmad Sadri, August 10, 2010. Interview with senior adviser to former president Mohammad Khatami and opposition leader Mir Hossein Mousavi, July 23, 2010.

32. Borzou Daragahi, "Ahmadinejad Calls for Prosecution of Iran's Opposition Leaders," *Los Angeles Times,* August 28, 2009.

33. Interview with campaign worker at Mousavi's headquarters, July 28, 2009. Trita Parsi, "What Obama Must Do Now on Iran," *Christian Science Monitor,* June 22, 2009. Interview with Professor Ahmad Sadri, August 10, 2010. Interview with Maziar Bahari, August 16, 2010.

34. Parsi, "What Obama Must Do Now on Iran."

35. Azadeh Moaveni, "Iranians to Obama: Hush," Daily Beast, June 17, 2009, http://www.thedailybeast.com/articles/2009/06/17/iranians-to-obama-hush.html.

36. "Obama Ratchets Up Language on Iran Violence," Associated Press, June 23, 2009. "Obama Condemns Iran Violence as 'Outrageous,' " CBC News, June 26, 2009. Author was invited to the White House to advise the Obama administration during the turmoil in Iran.

37. "Human Rights Violations in Iran Worst for 20 Years: Amnesty," Reuters, December 10, 2009.

38. Interview with senior EU diplomat, May 27, 2010. Interview with senior EU official, June 14, 2010.

39. Borzou Daragahi, "Iran: Report of Second Letter from Obama to Tehran," *Los Angeles Times,* September 2, 2009. Interview with senior Obama administration official, October 27, 2010. Interview with senior Senate staffer, August 20, 2010.

40. Conversations with various Obama administration officials throughout 2009 and 2010. Interview with senior EU diplomat, May 27, 2010. Interview with senior EU official, June 14, 2010. Interview with two EU officials, June 8, 2010. Interview with former U.S. State Department Iran Desk officer, June 14, 2010.

41. Interview with Professor Ahmad Sadri, August 10, 2010. Interview with Maziar Bahari, August 16, 2010. Interview with former Iranian reformist lawmaker, September 17, 2010. Interview with senior adviser to former president Mohammad Khatami and opposition leader Mir Hossein Mousavi, July 23, 2010.

42. Interview with Michael Ratney, August 10, 2010.

Chapter Seven.
Sanctions Versus Diplomacy

1. Interview with senior congressional staffer, August 31, 2010.

2. "FAQs: The Iran Refined Petroleum Sanctions Act," American Israel Public Affairs Committee (AIPAC), September 1, 2009, www.aipac.org. Classified U.S. State Department cable, "Codels Ackerman and Casey Meetings with Prime Minister Netanyahu," June 2, 2009. Interview with senior Senate staffer, September 2, 2010.

3. "Iran: Recent Developments and Implications for U.S. Policy," *Before the House Foreign Relations Committee,* 111th Cong. (July 22, 2009) (Howard Berman, committee chair).

4. Interview with senior congressional staffer, August 31, 2010. Interview with senior Senate staffer, September 2, 2010. Interview with senior Obama administration official, October 27, 2010.

5. Interview with State Department official, October 7, 2010. Interview with State Department official, September 17, 2010. Interview with former U.S. State Department Iran Desk officer, June 14, 2010.

6. Interview with State Department official, September 17, 2010. "There is no reason to believe that additional sanctions will result in increased support for the regime. The people of Iran—especially in light of the brutal crackdown—are more likely to oppose the regime, not rally around it." "FAQs: The Iran Refined Petroleum Sanctions Act." Interview with senior congressional staffer, August 31, 2010. Brad Sherman, "New Sanctions on Iran Must Be Enforced," *The Hill,* August 9, 2010.

7. Interview with State Department official, September 17, 2010. Hossein Askari and Trita Parsi, "Throwing Ahmadinejad a Lifeline," *New York Times,* August 14, 2009.

8. Ibid. Interview with State Department official, September 17, 2010.

9. Interview with State Department official, October 7, 2010. Interview with State Department official, September 17, 2010. Interview with senior Obama administration official, October 27, 2010.

10. Interview with senior Senate staffer, August 20, 2010. Interview with State Department official, September 17, 2010. Ongoing conversations with lawmakers and congressional staffers throughout 2009 and 2010.

11. Interview with senior Senate staffer, September 2, 2010. Interview with senior Senate staffer, October 5, 2010.

12. Interview with senior Senate staffer, August 20, 2010. Interview with senior Senate staffer, October 5, 2010.

13. Interview with senior congressional staffer, August 31, 2010. Interview with senior Senate staffer, August 20, 2010. Interview with former U.S. State Department Iran Desk officer, June 14, 2010.

14. Interview with senior adviser to former president Mohammad Khatami and opposition leader Mir Hossein Mousavi, July 23, 2010.

15. Interview with Maziar Bahari, August 16, 2010. Interview with Ahmad Sadri, August 10, 2010. Interview with Ataollah Mohajerani, September 18, 2010.

16. According to Ahmad Sadri, a reformist close to the Karroubi camp, none of the more vocal individuals outside the U.S. "have a smidgen of legitimacy in Iran." The "ridiculous" statements of these "self-appointed leaders of the Green movement . . . finally motivated Mr. Mousavi to come out and denounce [them]." Interview with Ahmad Sadri, August 10, 2010. Interview with senior adviser to former president Mohammad Khatami and opposition leader Mir Hossein Mousavi, July 23, 2010. Conversations with individuals close to Mousavi and former president Mohammad Khatami throughout the summer and fall of 2009.

17. "Iran's Mousavi Opposes Sanctions Against Tehran," AFP, September 28, 2009. Ramin Mostaghim and Borzou Daragahi, "Iranian Cleric Rises to Become Voice of Opposition," *Los Angeles Times*, September 8, 2009.

Chapter Eight.
The Confidence-Building Measure

1. Mark Fitzpatrick, *Iran's Nuclear, Chemical and Biological Capabilities* (London: International Institute for Strategic Studies, 2011).

2. Interview with senior State Department official, July 22, 2010. Interview with State Department official, July 21, 2010.

3. Thomas Erdbrink and William Branigin, "In Iran, Nuclear Issue Is Also a Medical One," *Washington Post*, December 20, 2009. Interview with Ambassador Ali Asghar Soltanieh, June 30, 2010. "IAEA Obligated to Supply Nuclear Fuel," *Tehran Times*, February 10, 2010.

4. Interview with Ambassador Peter Wittig, July 7, 2010. Interview with senior State Department official, July 22, 2010. Interview with State Department official, July 21, 2010. Interview with senior EU official, June 14, 2010.

5. Interview with State Department official, July 21, 2010. Interview with senior

EU diplomat, May 27, 2010. Interview with senior EU official, June 14, 2010. Interview with senior State Department official, October 27, 2010. Interview with Iranian nuclear negotiator, May 27, 2010.

6. Interview with senior EU official, June 14, 2010. Interview with Ambassador Peter Wittig, July 7, 2010. Interview with senior State Department official, July 22, 2010. Interview with senior EU diplomat, June 15, 2010.

7. The French had also been left disappointed over Washington's decision not to single out Iran at the upcoming Non-Proliferation Treaty review conference. Interview with Ambassador Gérard Araud, June 15, 2010. Another EU official pointed out the French opposition to the TRR deal and preference for sanctions. "They were always on the accelerator through the whole process," he said. Interview with senior EU diplomat, September 14, 2010. Classified U.S. State Department cable, "France's Position on Nuclear Issues in the Run-up to the NPT Revcon," July 31, 2009. To a certain extent the UK also shared a preference for moving faster on sanctions. In midsummer 2009 the UK was seeking to convince Sweden, which held the presidency of the EU at the time, to begin preparing sanctions discussions within the EU even though diplomacy had not yet begun. Sweden pushed back, arguing that the discussions should be kept at a general level "because if the Iranians (or the Russians or the Chinese) became aware of the EU doing 'specific' and 'legal' work on additional sanctions, then they would complain that the EU was never serious about giving Iran time to respond to the P5 1 offer." Classified U.S. State Department cable, "GAERC July 26–7 Agenda: Sweden's Preliminary Items," July 14, 2009. Interview with EU diplomat, July 6, 2010.

8. "Israeli Officials: Iran Vote Shows Growing Threat," Associated Press, June 13, 2009. Interview with Deputy Foreign Minister Danny Ayalon, October 4, 2010. Interview with senior EU official, June 14, 2010. Interview with senior State Department official, October 27, 2010. Interview with senior State Department official, July 22, 2010.

9. Interview with Ambassador Peter Wittig, July 7, 2010. Interview with State Department official, July 21, 2010. Interview with senior State Department official, July 22, 2010. Interview with senior EU diplomat, May 27, 2010. "It is not just about the humanitarian assistance, it's not just about the fuel to a reactor in Iran," ElBaradei said. "It's about the first step in a very long growth toward finally normalization between Iran and the United States. . . . Iran could be a very positive element in the stable Middle East. Iran could be absolutely essential to stability in Afghanistan, in Iraq, Syria, Lebanon, Palestinian territories" (Charlie Rose, PBS, November 6, 2009).

10. Interview with senior State Department official, July 22, 2010. Background discussion with senior Obama administration official, October 5, 2010. E-mail exchange with senior State Department official, February 24, 2011.

11. Jim Jones's remarks at Iran's Nuclear, Terrorist Threats and Rights Abuses conference, January 20, 2011. Interview with senior State Department official, October 27, 2010. Interview with State Department official, July 21, 2010. Interview with senior State Department official, July 22, 2010.

12. Interview with Russian diplomat, August 26, 2010. Marc Champion, "Russia Rejects New Iran Sanctions," Wall Street Journal, September 10, 2009. Classified U.S.

State Department cable, "FM Lavrov Discusses Missile Defense and Iran with Codel Levin," April 29, 2009. Classified U.S. State Department cable, "Israeli FM Lieberman in Moscow," June 5, 2009. Interview with senior State Department official, July 22, 2010.

13. Interview with Iranian nuclear negotiator, May 27, 2010. Interview with senior State Department official, July 22, 2010. Interview with Ambassador Ali Asghar Soltanieh, June 30, 2010.

14. Interview with senior State Department official, October 27, 2010. Interview with State Department official, July 21, 2010. Classified U.S. State Department cable, "U/S Tauscher's Meetings with FS Miliband and Other HMG Officials," September 22, 2009.

15. Interview with Ambassador Ali Asghar Soltanieh, June 30, 2010. Interview with State Department official, July 21, 2010. Interview with Ambassador Gérard Araud, June 15, 2010. E-mail and phone exchange with Olli Heinonen, February 21, 2011. A final agreement between the IAEA and Iran on providing the agency with access and information about the site was reached on October 4, 2009, during ElBaradei's visit to Tehran.

16. Michael D. Shear and Karen DeYoung, "Iran Reveals Existence of Second Uranium Enrichment Plant," *Washington Post,* September 25, 2009. Scott Ritter, "Keeping Iran Honest," *Guardian,* September 25, 2009. Interview with Ambassador Ali Asghar Soltanieh, June 30–July 1, 2010. Interview with Ambassador Gérard Araud, June 15, 2010. E-mail exchange with James Acton of the Carnegie Endowment for International Peace, September 26, 2009.

17. Interview with State Department official, July 21, 2010.

18. Interview with Ambassador Gérard Araud, June 15, 2010. Interview with French diplomat at the French UN Mission, June 15, 2010.

19. Statements by President Obama, President Sarkozy, and Prime Minister Brown on Iranian Nuclear Facility, September 25, 2009.

20. Ibid. "Berman Calls Iran Nuclear Plant News Disturbing, Says It Reinforces His Determination to Have Committee Consider Sanctions Legislation," news release, House Foreign Affairs Committee, Washington, D.C., September 25, 2009. Classified U.S. State Department cable, "Medvedev, Putin, and Russia's Iran Policy," October 6, 2009.

21. Glenn Kessler, "U.S. Aims to Isolate Iran If Talks Fail," *Washington Post,* September 29, 2009. Tom Doggett, "U.S. Lawmakers Vote to Punish Iran's fuel?," Reuters, October 1, 2009. Eric Fingerhut, "Getting a Yes on Iran Advocacy Day," Jewish Telegraphic Agency, September 11, 2009. Mark Landler, "U.S. Is Seeking a Range of Sanctions Against Iran," *New York Times,* September 29, 2009.

22. Laura Rozen, "U.S. Previews Geneva Talks, as Iranian Foreign Minister Visits DC," Politico.com, September 30, 2009, http://www.politico.com/blogs/laurarozen/0909/US_previews_Geneva_talks_as_Iranian_foreign_minister_visits_DC.html. Mark Landler and Steven Erlanger, "As U.S. Plots Iran Strategy, Envoy's Visit Hints at a Thaw," *New York Times,* October 1, 2009. "The US Is Working Hard to Talk to Iran," Jahan News, October 3, 2009.

23. Interview with Michael Ratney, August 10, 2009. Classified U.S. State Department cable, "Ideas on How to Pressure the Regime on Human Rights Without Risking Our Broader Agenda," October 16, 2010. Interview with senior EU diplomat, May 27, 2009. Interview with senior State Department official, October 27, 2010.

24. Steven Erlanger and Mark Landler, "Iran Agrees to Send Enriched Uranium to Russia," *New York Times,* October 2, 2009. Interview with senior EU official, June 14, 2010. Interview with senior State Department official, July 22, 2010.

25. Ibid. Interview with senior State Department official, October 27, 2010. Interview with State Department Iran Desk officer, June 14, 2010. Interview with Iranian nuclear negotiator, May 27, 2010.

26. Interview with State Department official, October 7, 2010. Interview with State Department Iran Desk officer, June 14, 2010. Interview with senior State Department official, July 22, 2010. Interview with senior EU official, June 14, 2010. Erlanger and Landler, "Iran Agrees to Send Enriched Uranium to Russia." Interview with Ambassador Ali Asghar Soltanieh, June 30, 2010. E-mail and phone exchange with Olli Heinonen, February 21, 2011. Interview with Ambassador Gérard Araud, June 15, 2010.

27. Erlanger and Landler, "Iran Agrees to Send Enriched Uranium to Russia." Interview with senior EU official, June 14, 2010. Introductory remarks by Javier Solana, EU High Representative for the Common Foreign and Security Policy, October 1, 2009.

28. "Cleric Terms Geneva Talks Victory for Iran," Fars News Agency, October 9, 2009. "Ahmadinejad Optimistic About Future of Iran Talks with 5+1," Fars News Agency, October 12, 2009. "MP: Negotiations Progressing in Iran's Interest After Geneva Talks," Fars News Agency, October 6, 2009.

29. Remarks by President Obama, October 1, 2009. Erlanger and Landler, "Iran Agrees to Send Enriched Uranium to Russia." Interview with senior EU official, June 14, 2010. Interview with senior State Department official, October 27, 2010. The French had a slightly different and more pessimistic read on the Geneva talks. "To some extent maybe there was a slight difference of interpretation of what went on in Geneva," Pierre Vimont, France's ambassador to the U.S., said. "We had the impression that at some point our American colleagues were more, a little bit more optimistic at the end of their conversation with the Iranians in Geneva. They had the impression that the head of the Iranian delegation was rather straightforward in giving them the feeling that this deal could be a good deal and that he could sell it in Iran" (interview with Ambassador Pierre Vimont, July 26, 2010).

30. Interview with senior EU official, June 14, 2010.

31. Jay Solomon, "U.S., Allies Confer on New Iran Sanctions," *Wall Street Journal,* October 9, 2009.

32. "Minimizing Potential Threats from Iran: Administration Perspectives on Economic Sanctions and Other U.S. Policy Options," *Before the Senate Banking Committee,* 111th Cong. (October 6, 2009) (Testimony of James Steinberg, Deputy Secretary of State).

33. Interview with French diplomat, July 6, 2010. Interview with Ambassador Ali Asghar Soltanieh, June 30, 2010. Interview with senior EU diplomat, June 15, 2010.

Interview with senior State Department official, October 27, 2010. Interview with senior State Department official, July 22, 2010.

34. Interview with Ambassador Ali Asghar Soltanieh, June 30, 2010. Interview with senior State Department official, July 22, 2010.

35. Interview with senior EU diplomat, June 15, 2010. Interview with Ambassador Ali Asghar Soltanieh, June 30, 2010. Interview with senior EU official, June 14, 2010. Interview with French diplomat, July 6, 2010. In 1974, Iran lent $1 billion to the French Atomic Energy Commission to build the Eurodif plant. This entitled Iran to buy 10 percent of the enriched uranium produced by Eurodif. Three years later, Iran paid another $180 million for future enrichment services. Yet, Eurodif never delivered any nuclear fuel to Iran. In the ensuing legal battle, Iran demanded repayment of its original $1-billion loan, plus interest. At the end of 1991, Iran won the suit and was reimbursed a total of $1.6 billion. The settlement came just as Iran demanded delivery of enriched uranium based on the old contract. Paris maintained that the contract had expired in 1990. By that time, Iran was already subject to Western sanctions. France refused to deliver the fuel even though Tehran still held an indirect share in Eurodif. Oliver Meier, "Iran and Foreign Enrichment: A Troubled Model," *Arms Control Today,* January/February 2006.

36. Interview with Ambassador Ali Asghar Soltanieh, June 30, 2010. Interview with senior State Department official, July 22, 2010.

37. Interview with Iranian nuclear negotiator, May 27, 2010. Interview with Ambassador Ali Asghar Soltanieh, June 30, 2010. Interview with senior EU diplomat, June 15, 2010. Interview with senior State Department official, July 22, 2010.

38. Hillary Mann Leverett, "Pragmatists in Tehran," *Foreign Policy,* October 28, 2009. Interview with Iranian nuclear negotiator, May 27, 2010. Relations between Russia and Iran have historically been very tense. There has always been concern that Russia would seek territorial or political concessions or break promises to Iran at the last minute. In the nineteenth century, Iran did lose its foothold—as well as territory—in central Asia to Russia. In 1911, the Russians shelled the Iranian parliament and a venerated and important mosque in the city of Mashad. The Russian czar Peter the Great's famous quote that Russia "should get to warm waters by Persian Gulf. Russia would be a true empire with such an achievement" has perpetuated a strongly held suspicion toward Moscow in Iran. Hadi Nili, "Iran Still Holds Bitter Memories of Russia," *Washington Times,* September 11, 2008.

39. Interview with Ambassador Ali Asghar Soltanieh, June 30, 2010. Interview with Iranian nuclear negotiator, May 27, 2010. Interview with senior State Department official, July 22, 2010.

40. Interview with Iranian nuclear negotiator, May 27, 2010. Interview with Ambassador Ali Asghar Soltanieh, July 1, 2010.

41. Interview with Ambassador Mohammad Khazaee, June 15, 2010. Interview with senior State Department official, July 22, 2010. Interview with Iranian nuclear negotiator, May 27, 2010. Interview with Ambassador Ali Asghar Soltanieh, July 1, 2010.

42. Ibid. Conversations with Obama administration officials, summer and fall of 2010.

43. Interview with senior State Department official, July 22, 2010. Interview with Ambassador Ali Asghar Soltanieh, July 1, 2010. Conversations with Obama administration officials, summer and fall of 2010. Interview with senior Senate staffer, August 20, 2010.

44. David Sanger, "Iran Agrees to Draft of Deal on Exporting Nuclear Fuel," *New York Times*, October 21, 2009.

45. International Atomic Energy Agency, "IAEA Statement on Proposal to Supply Nuclear Fuel to Iranian Research Reactor," news release, October 23, 2009, http://www.iaea.org/newscenter/pressreleases/2009/prn200912.html.

46. "West Trying to Trick Iran in Nuclear Deal: Larijani," *Tehran Times*, October 25, 2009. Richard Spencer, "Iran May Offer Compromise on UN Nuclear Deal," *Telegraph*, October 26, 2009. Borzou Daragahi and Ramin Mostaghim, "Iran's President Appears to Back Nuclear Proposal," *Los Angeles Times*, October 29, 2009.

47. International Atomic Energy Agency, "IAEA Receives Initial Iranian Response on Proposal to Supply Nuclear Fuel to Research Reactor," news release, October 29, 2009, http://www.iaea.org/newscenter/pressreleases/2009/prn200914.html. "U.S. Tells Iran Nuclear Deal Offer Won't Be Changed," Reuters, Nov 5, 2009. Interview with Ambassador Ali Asghar Soltanieh, June 30, 2010. Interview with senior EU official, June 14, 2010.

48. *Charlie Rose*, PBS, November 6, 2009. Classified U.S. State Department cable, "Moscow's Increasing Frustration with Tehran," December 14, 2009. Interview with Ambassador Peter Wittig, July 7, 2010. Interview with two EU officials, June 8, 2010. Interview with senior EU diplomat, September 2, 2010. Interview with senior EU official, June 14, 2010. Interview with senior EU diplomat, September 14, 2010. Interview with David Miliband, June 7, 2011.

49. *Charlie Rose*, PBS, November 6, 2009.

50. Interview with senior EU diplomat, June 15, 2010. Interview with senior EU diplomat, September 2, 2010. Interview with senior State Department official, July 22, 2010.

51. "China to Invest $2.5bn in Iran Oilfield," AFP, February 25, 2011. "Japan's Inpex Maintains 10% Share in Azadegan: Minister," *Tehran Times*, May 20, 2008. Interview with Japanese diplomat, June 22, 2010.

52. Laura Rozen, "Japan Emerges as Key Player on Iran," Politico, February 1, 2010, http://www.politico.com/blogs/laurarozen/0110/Japan_emerges_as_key_player _on_Iran.html. Interview with Japanese diplomat, June 22, 2010. Interview with former Iranian diplomat, June 30, 2010. Interview with senior State Department official, September 10, 2010.

53. Sabrina Tavernise, "Turkish Leader Volunteers to Be U.S.-Iran Mediator," *New York Times*, November 11, 2008. Hossein Jaseb, "Iran Says Won't Hinder Turkish Mediation with U.S.," Reuters, November 17, 2008. Zahra Hosseinian, "No Sign of U.S. Correcting Regional 'Mistakes': Iran," Reuters, March 11, 2009. Borzou Daragahi and Ramin Mostaghim, "Visit Raises Speculation over Turkish-mediated U.S.-Iran Talks," *Los Angeles Times*, March 10, 2009. Classified U.S. State Department cable, "Working Erdogan Back into the Fold on Iran," November 3, 2009.

54. *Charlie Rose,* PBS, November 6, 2009. Interview with senior State Department official, October 27, 2010. Classified U.S. State Department cable, "Turkey: A/S Gordon Presses FM Davutoglu on Iran," November 17, 2009. Interview with Ambassador Pierre Vimont, July 26, 2010.

55. Interview with Michael Ratney, August 10, 2009. Interview with senior non-EU3 official, September 10, 2010. Interview with two EU officials, June 8, 2010. Interview with senior EU diplomat, September 14, 2010.

56. Interview with former Iranian diplomat, June 30, 2010. Glenn Kessler, "As Standoff with Iran Continues, U.S. Prepares Targeted Sanctions," *Washington Post,* December 30, 2009.

57. Gareth Porter, "Iran's Fuel for Conflict," *Le Monde Diplomatique,* December 9, 2009. Classified U.S. State Department cable, "Turkey: A/S Gordon Presses FM Davutoglu on Iran," November 17, 2009. Interview with senior EU diplomat, September 14, 2010.

58. Mir Hossein Mousavi, statement, October 30, 2009, www.kalame.ir.

59. Robert F. Worth and Nazila Fathi, "Opposition in Iran Urges Continuing Challenge," *New York Times,* November 1, 2009. Interview with Maziar Bahari, August 16, 2010. Interview with senior adviser to former president Mohammad Khatami and opposition leader Mir Hossein Mousavi, July 23, 2010. Interview with Ahmad Sadri, August 10, 2010. Interview with former Iranian reformist lawmaker, September 17, 2010.

60. Interview with former Iranian diplomat, June 30, 2010. Interview with Ambassador Peter Wittig, July 7, 2010. Interview with senior State Department official, September 10, 2010. *Charlie Rose,* PBS, November 6, 2009. Interview with senior adviser to former president Mohammad Khatami and opposition leader Mir Hossein Mousavi, July 23, 2010.

61. Interview with Ahmad Sadri, August 10, 2010. Discussion with senior State Department official, November 9, 2010. Interview with former Iranian diplomat, June 30, 2010. Interview with William D. Wunderle, September 2, 2010. Interview with Professor Ali Ansari, September 17, 2010. *Charlie Rose,* PBS, November 6, 2009. Interview with Ambassador Peter Wittig, July 7, 2010. Interview with Ambassador Ali Asghar Soltanieh, June 30, 2010. Interview with David Miliband, July 7, 2011. Interview with senior State Department official, July 22, 2010.

Chapter Nine.
The Second Track

1. Interview with senior State Department official, September 12, 2010. Interview with Michael Ratney of the State Department, August 10, 2010. Interview with former Iran Desk officer at the State Department, June 14, 2010. Classified U.S. State Department cable, "Staffdel Kessler Discusses Iran with MFA, ENI, PD," January 22, 2010. Interview with Ambassador Pierre Vimont, July 26, 2010.

2. Interview with senior State Department official, September 12, 2010.

3. "Obama Accepts Nobel Prize," *Financial Times,* December 10, 2009.

4. Interview with EU diplomat, June 21, 2010. Interview with senior State Department official, September 12, 2010. Interview with Michael Ratney of the State Department, August 10, 2010.

5. Glenn Kessler, "As Standoff with Iran Continues, U.S. Prepares Targeted Sanctions," *Washington Post,* December 30, 2009.

6. Classified U.S. State Department cable, "Codel Skelton's Meeting with Prime Minister Netanyahu," December 23, 2009. Classified U.S. State Department cable, "U/S Tauscher's December 1–2 Visit to Israel," December 22, 2009. Dan Williams, "Israel Urges Iran Oil Embargo Even," Reuters, February 22, 2010. Roshanak Taghavi, "Iran, Bracing for Sanctions, Presses Its Parliament for Gas Money," *Christian Science Monitor,* January 5, 2010.

7. Classified U.S. State Department cable, "Staffdel Kessler Discusses Iran with MFA, ENI, PD," January 22, 2010. Classified U.S. State Department cable, "German MFA Hope Iran Sanctions Target Leaders Not Masses," January 21, 2010. Classified U.S. State Department cable, "Readout of January 20 U.S.-France Strategic Dialogue in Washington," February 17, 2010. Interview with senior EU official, June 14, 2010. Interview with two EU officials, June 8, 2010. *Charlie Rose,* PBS, November 6, 2009. Interview with David Miliband, June 7, 2011.

8. John Pomfret, "Oil, Ideology Keep China from Joining Push Against Iran," *Washington Post,* September 30, 2009. Kate Mackenzie, "Oil at the heart of Latest Iranian Sanction Efforts," *Financial Times,* March 8, 2010. Laurent Maillard, "China Takes Over from West as Iran's Main Economic," AFP, March 15, 2010.

9. Pomfret, "Oil, Ideology Keep China from Joining Push Against Iran." "Response to Taiwan Deal Oil at the Heart of Latest Iranian Sanction Efforts," *Financial Times,* March 8, 2010.

10. Kevin Bogardus, "House Readies Iran Sanctions on Gas Imports," *The Hill,* December 15, 2009. Interview with senior Senate staffer, August 20, 2010. Laura Rozen, "Berman: Iran Sanctions Bill Empowers Obama," Politico, December 15, 2009, http://www.politico.com/blogs/laurarozen/1209/Berman_says_Iran_sanctions_bill_empowers_Obama_Iran_policy.html. Howard Berman, speech given at Center for Strategic and International Studies, Washington, D.C., September 21, 2010. With J Street supporting the sanctions, Americans for Peace Now became the sole major Jewish organization opposing the sanctions measure. Ron Kampeas, "As Zero Hour Nears, Differences Emerge on Sanctions," Jewish Telegraphic Agency, January 5, 2010.

11. Josh Rogin, "Exclusive: State Department Letter to Kerry Outlines "Serious Substantive Concerns" with Iran Sanctions Bill," *Foreign Policy,* December 11, 2009. Interview with senior Senate staffer, August 20, 2010. Interview with senior Senate staffer, September 2, 2010.

12. Martin Matishak, "House Approves Gasoline Cutoff Bill on Iran Despite Warnings," Global Security Newswire, December 16, 2009.

13. "Iran Ayatollah: 'I Am Convinced That the Regime Will Collapse," *ABC News,* December 28, 2009. "Iran's Dissident Grand Ayatollah Montazeri Dies," BBC News, December 20, 2009, http://news.bbc.co.uk/2/hi/8423046.stm. "Shirin Ebadi Warns Against Iranian Sanctions," BBC News, March 4, 2010, http://news.bbc.co.uk/2/hi/

8549183.stm. Robert Tait, "Funeral of Iranian Cleric Montazeri Turns into Political Protest," *Guardian,* December 21, 2009. "Iran Website Says Mousavi Nephew Killed in Clashes," Reuters, December 21, 2009.

14. Josh Rogin, "Iran Sanctions Bill Update: Full Speed Ahead," *Foreign Policy,* January 19, 2010. Interview with senior Senate staffer, August 20, 2010. Josh Rogin, "Senators Pressure Obama on Iran Sanctions," *Foreign Policy,* January 27, 2010. Josh Rogin, "Iran Sanctions Bill Benefits from Joe-mentum," *Foreign Policy,* January 29, 2010. Howard Berman (chairman, U.S. House Committee on Foreign Affairs), "Iran: Addressing the Nuclear Threat" (speech, St. Regis Hotel, Washington, D.C., September 21, 2010).

15. Interview with senior Senate staffer, September 2, 2010. Interview with Ambassador Gérard Araud, June 15, 2010.

16. Interview with EU ambassador involved in the sanctions negotiations, June 2010. Interview with State Department Iran Desk officer, June 14, 2010.

17. Arshad Mohammed, "China to Send Lower-level Envoy to Talks on Iran," Reuters, January 14, 2010. Flynt Leverett and Hillary Mann Leverett, " 'Narrow Stripes of Rationality' on the Iranian Nuclear Issue," Race for Iran, January 19, 2010, http://www.raceforiran.com/%E2%80%9Cnarrow-stripes-of-rationality%E2%80%9D-on-the-nuclear-issue. Classified U.S. State Department cable, "Russia: Moving Beyond Bilateral Issues, Miliband Reopened Dialogue," November 5, 2009.

18. Mark Landler, "Despite Pressure, China Still Resists Iran Sanctions," *New York Times,* February 25, 2010. Charley Keyes, "U.S. Announces $6.4 Billion Arms Deal with Taiwan," CNN, January 29, 2010. Interview with Ambassador Gérard Araud, June 15, 2010. Interview with Xavier Chatel, June 15, 2010. Classified U.S. State Department cable, "Secretary of Defense Gates's Meeting with French Foreign Minister Kouchner," February 12, 2010.

19. "Iran to U.N.: We Will Increase Uranium Enrichment," Fox News, February 8, 2010. The letter to the IAEA can be found at http://graphics8.nytimes.com/packages/pdf/world/2009/IAEA-Letter.pdf. Helene Cooper, "U.S. Encounters Limits of Iran Engagement Policy," *New York Times,* February 16, 2010.

20. Classified U.S. State Department cable, "Saudi Foreign Ministry Pressing China to Stop Iranian Proliferation, Concerned About TSA Regulations," January 26, 2010. Classified U.S. State Department cable, "Scenesetter for Secretary Clinton's Feb 15–16 Visit to Saudi Arabia," February 11, 2010. Kate Mackenzie, "Oil at the Heart of Latest Iranian Sanction Efforts," *Financial Times,* March 8, 2010. Interview with Rayed Krimly, November 25, 2010. Interview with Ambassador Gérard Araud, June 15, 2010. Interview with Xavier Chatel, June 15, 2010.

21. "New Iran Sanctions Within a Month: Israeli Minister," AFP, January 3, 2010. Classified U.S. State Department cable, "Iran Dominates Netanyahu's Visit to Moscow," February 22, 2010.

22. Nathan Guttman, "U.S. Delays Iran Sanctions While Persuading Israel Not to Attack," *Jewish Daily Forward,* February 26, 2010, http://www.forward.com/articles/126305/. Josh Rogin, "Choose Your Own Iran Sanctions Adventure at the U.N.?," *Foreign Policy,* February 24, 2010. Nahum Barnea and Shimon Shiffer, "Iranian Nu-

clear Program Is a Threat to America," *Yedioth Ahronoth,* March 8, 2010. Interview with Ambassador Gérard Araud, June 15, 2010. Interview with senior State Department official, July 22, 2010. Interview with Ambassador Peter Wittig, July 7, 2010. Josh Rogin, "Congress Hot to Trot on Iran Sanctions," *Foreign Policy,* March 5, 2010.

23. Tim Starks, "Plenty of Push for Iran Sanctions Legislation, but Little Consensus Yet," *CQ Today,* March 15, 2010. Interview with senior Senate staffer, September 2, 2010. Interview with senor congressional staffer, August 31, 2010.

24. Interview with senior Senate staffer, September 2, 2010. Starks, "Plenty of Push for Iran Sanctions Legislation." Alastair Macdonald, "'Insulted' by Israel, U.S. Scrambles to Save Talks," Reuters, March 13, 2010. Daniel Nasaw, "Obama Aide Calls Israeli Settlement Announcement an 'Insult' to the US," *Guardian,* March 14, 2010. Mark Perry, "The Petraeus Briefing: Biden's Embarrassment Is Not the Whole Story," *Foreign Policy,* March 14, 2010. Barak Ravid, "Netanyahu's Brother-in-law: Obama Is an Anti-Semite," *Haaretz,* March 17, 2010.

25. American Israel Public Affairs Committee, "AIPAC Calls Recent Statements by the U.S. Government 'A Matter of Serious Concern,' " press release, March 14, 2010, http://www.aipac.org/~/media/Publications/Policy%20and%20Politics/Press/AIPA C%20Statements/2010/03/AIPAC_CALLS_ON_OBAMA_ADMIN_TO_DEFU SE_TENSION.pdf. J Street, "Statement on Escalation of US-Israel Tensions," press release, March 15, 2010, http://jstreet.org/blog/statement-on-escalation-of-us-israel-tensions/. Laura Rozen, "Israeli Ambassador: U.S.-Israel Relations in Crisis," Politico, March 15, 2010, http://www.politico.com/blogs/laurarozen/0310/Israeli_ambassador _USIsrael_relations_in_crisis.html.

26. American Israel Public Affairs Committee, "AIPAC Applauds Overwhelming Bipartisan House Letter," press release, March 26, 2010, http://www.aipac.org/~/ media/Publications/Policy%20and%20Politics/Press/AIPAC%20Statements/2010/03/ AIPAC_applauds_Hoyer_Cantor.pdf. David Corn, "Sen. Lindsey Graham: Any Attack on Iran Must Be Full-Scale," *Mother Jones,* March 24, 2010. Josh Rogin, "Senators Pressure Obama on Iran Sanctions," *Foreign Policy,* March 23, 2010.

27. Adrian Blomfield, "Obama Snubbed Netanyahu for Dinner with Michelle and the Girls, Israelis Claim," *Telegraph,* March 25, 2010. Laura Rozen, "Fierce Debate on Israel Underway Inside Obama Administration," Politico, March 28, 2010, http:// www.politico.com/blogs/laurarozen/0310/Fierce_debate_on_Israel_underway_in side_Obama_administration.html.

28. Chris Strathmann and Kate McCarthy, "Netanyahu Calls for 'Crippling Sanctions' Against Iran," *ABC News,* April 19, 2010.

29. "Russia, China Push Iran to Change Nuclear Stance," Reuters, March 24, 2010. "Iran's Top Nuclear Negotiator Heads to China," Associated Press, March 31, 2010. Julian Borger and Ewen MacAskill, "China Supports Barack Obama's Call for New Iran Sanctions," *Guardian,* March 31, 2010. Colum Lynch, "U.S. Urges U.N. Security Council to Impose Arms Embargo, Other Measures on Iran," *Washington Post,* April 15, 2010.

30. Interview with Ambassador Gérard Araud, June 15, 2010. Interview with Xavier Chatel, June 15, 2010. Michael D. Shear and Glenn Kessler, "Russia Supports

Iran Sanctions, but with Limits," *Washington Post,* April 9, 2010. Laura Rozen, "Iran Rundown in Prague," Politico, April 8, 2010, http://www.politico.com/blogs/laurar ozen/0410/Iran_rundown_in_Prague.html. Jonathan Weisman, "U.S., Russia Focus on Iran Sanctions," *Wall Street Journal,* April 9, 2010. "U.S., Israeli Attack on Iran Would Be 'Unacceptable'—Russian Military," RIA Novosti, April 12, 2010, http://en.rian.ru/russia/20100412/158538895.html.

31. Hiedeh Farmani, "Iran Is Obama's 'Only Chance' of Success: Ahmadinejad," AFP, April 13, 2010.

Chapter Ten.
The Art of Taking Yes for an Answer

1. Louis Charbonneau, "Obama, Medvedev Discuss 'Progress' on Iran sanctions," Reuters, May 13, 2010. "Brazil's Lula Arrives in Iran for Key Nuclear Talks," AFP, May 15, 2010. Viola Gienger, "Clinton Urges Action from Turkey, Brazil on Iran," Bloomberg, April 13, 2010.

2. Classified U.S. State Department cable, "Constraining Iranian Influence in Brazil," July 1, 2008. Classified U.S. State Department cable, "Brazil on Ahmadinejad, Iran's Nuclear Program, and Visas," November 6, 2009. Classified U.S. State Department cable, "Peres and Abbas Visits in Perspective," December 2, 2009.

3. Interview with Celso Amorim, July 15, 2010. Classified U.S. State Department cable, "Constraining Iranian Influence in Brazil," July 1, 2008.

4. Jay Solomon and John Lyons, "New Hurdles to Iran Sanctions," *Wall Street Journal,* March 4, 2010. Classified U.S. State Department cable, "Constraining Iranian Influence in Brazil," July 1, 2008.

5. "UN Says Sanctions Have Killed Some 500,000 Iraqi Children," Reuters, July 21, 2000, http://www.commondreams.org/headlines/072100-03.htm. Classified U.S. State Department cable, "Qom Report Gets the Brazilians Thinking," October 7, 2009. Classified U.S. State Department cable, "HMG Officials," September 23, 2009. Matias Spektor, "How to Read Brazil's Stance on Iran," Council on Foreign Relations, March 5, 2010, http://www.cfr.org/brazil/read-brazils-stance-iran/p21576. Sanctions would also affect the Brazilian economy negatively. Brazilian leaders were angered by the way Brazil's commercial relations with Iran were conditioned by decisions made in Washington, in addition to the fact that these extraterritorial sanctions on Iran had caused Brazil's trade ties with Iran to suffer. Interview with Brazilian diplomat, July 1, 2010.

6. Classified briefing for the Brazilian diplomatic corps by Celso Amorim, May 18, 2010. Interview with Celso Amorim, July 15, 2010. Interview with senior adviser to Lula, July 15, 2010.

7. Andrew Downie, "Brazil's Diplomacy on Iran Points to Larger Ambitions," *Los Angeles Times,* May 22, 2010. Interview with senior adviser to Lula, July 15, 2010. Interview with Brazilian diplomat, July 1, 2010. Spektor, "How to Read Brazil's Stance on Iran."

8. Classified U.S. State Department cable, "Brazil on Ahmadinejad, Iran's Nu-

clear Program, and Visas," November 6, 2009. Interview with Brazilian diplomat, July 1, 2010. Interview with Brazilian diplomat, July 7, 2010.

9. Classified U.S. State Department cable, "Brazil on Iran: A Soft Voice in the Chorus," September 18, 2009. Interview with Brazilian diplomat, July 1, 2010. Classified U.S. State Department cable, "Brazil on Ahmadinejad, Iran's Nuclear Program, and Visas," November 6, 2009. Classified U.S. State Department cable, "August 4–5 Visit of U.S. National Security Advisor to Brazil," September 18, 2009. Interview with Brazilian diplomat, September 4, 2010.

10. Classified U.S. State Department cable, "Qom Report Gets the Brazilians Thinking," October 7, 2009. Classified U.S. State Department cable, "Ahmadinejad Visit Readout: A Well-Scripted Affair," November 25, 2009. Classified U.S. State Department cable, "Peres and Abbas Visits in Perspective," December 2, 2009.

11. Classified briefing for the Brazilian diplomatic corps by Celso Amorim, May 18, 2010. Interview with Brazilian diplomat, July 1, 2010. Interview with Celso Amorim, July 15, 2010.

12. Şahin Alpay, "Ahmadinejad's Visit to Turkey Is Welcome," *Today's Zaman,* August 11, 2008. Sabrina Tavernise, "Turkish Leader Volunteers to be U.S.-Iran Mediator," *New York Times,* November 11, 2008. Borzou Daragahi and Ramin Mostaghim, "Visit Raises Speculation over Turkish-mediated U.S.-Iran talks," *Los Angeles Times,* March 10, 2009. Interview with Cengiz Candar, June 18, 2010.

13. "Turkey Chastises the West on Iran," BBC News, October 26, 2009, http://news.bbc.co.uk/2/hi/8325373.stm. "We watch the relations between Iran and U.S. with great concern," Mr. Erdogan said. "We expect such issues to be resolved at the table. Wars are never solutions in this age." Tavernise, "Turkish Leader Volunteers to Be U.S.-Iran Mediator." Classified U.S. State Department cable, "Turkey-Iran Relations: Motivations, Limitations, and Implications," December 4, 2009. A senior Turkish diplomat argued that war with Iran would have catastrophic consequences that would not even be comparable to Iraq. Interview with senior Turkish diplomat, July 13, 2010. Interview with senior Turkish diplomat, August 15, 2010.

14. Classified U.S. State Department cable, "Turkey-Iran Relations: Motivations, Limitations, and Implications," December 4, 2009. Classified U.S. State Department cable, "Turkey: A/S Gordon Presses FM Davutoglu on Iran," November 17, 2009. Interview with Cengiz Candar, June 18, 2010. Interview with senior Turkish diplomat, July 13, 2010.

15. Daragahi and Mostaghim, "Visit Raises Speculation over Turkish-mediated U.S.-Iran Talks." "Turkey Chastises the West on Iran." Classified U.S. State Department cable, "Turkey: A/S Gordon Presses FM Davutoglu on Iran," November 17, 2009. Classified U.S. State Department cable, "Israeli Ambassador Traces His Problems to Erdogan," October 27, 2009. Classified U.S. State Department cable, "Turkey-Iran Relations: Motivations, Limitations, and Implications," December 4, 2009. Interview with senior Turkish diplomat, July 13, 2010.

16. Interview with Cengiz Candar, June 18, 2010. Classified briefing for the Brazilian diplomatic corps by Celso Amorim, May 18, 2010. Interview with Celso Amorim, July 15, 2010.

17. Classified U.S. State Department cable, "Staffdel Kessler Engages the French on Iran, Sanctions and Afghanistan," January 22, 2010. Classified U.S. State Department cable, "Amb. Rices's Meeting with Brazilian PermRep," February 16, 2010. Classified U.S. State Department cable, "Brazil: Ambassador's Meetings with MRE Under Secretaries for Political Affairs," February 19, 2010. Interview with senior Brazilian diplomat, June 21, 2010.

18. Conversation with U.S. diplomat, March 8, 2010. Flynt Leverett and Hillary Mann Leverett, "Clinton Strikes Out in Brazil: A Security Council Divided on Iran Sanctions," Race for Iran, March 4, 2010, http://www.raceforiran.com/clinton-strikes-out-in-brazil-a-security-council-divided-on-iran-sanctions. Selcuk Gokoluk, "Turkey Rebuffs U.S. Call to Join Iran Sanctions," Reuters, March 24, 2010.

19. Interview with senior adviser to Lula, July 15, 2010. Interview with Celso Amorim, July 15, 2010. Interview with Iranian nuclear negotiator, May 27, 2010. Interview with senior Turkish diplomat, July 13, 2010. State Department, "Background Briefing on Nuclear Nonproliferation Efforts with Regard to Iran and the Brazil/Turkey Agreement," May 28, 2010, http://www.state.gov/r/pa/prs/ps/2010/05/142375.htm.

20. Viola Gienger, "Clinton Urges Action from Turkey, Brazil on Iran," Bloomberg, April 13, 2010. "I think we would view the Lula visit as perhaps the last big shot at engagement," a senior State Department official told reporters in Washington. Charbonneau, "Obama, Medvedev discuss 'progress' on Iran sanctions." Ilhan Tanir, "Turkey: 'There is no deadline for Iran,'" *Hurriyet Daily News,* April 16, 2010, http://www.hurriyetdailynews.com/n.php?n=turkey-there-is-no-deadline-for-iran-2010-04-16.

21. "Timeline: Brazil-Iranian Relations," Al Jazeera, May 16, 2010. "Iran Optimistic About Fuel Swap: Mottaki," April 28, 2010, http://www.campaigniran.org/casmii/index.php?q=node/9806. "Iran, Turkey to Discuss Fuel Swap Deal," Press TV, May 7, 2010. Thomas Erdbrink, "Iran Seeks to Persuade Security Council Not to Back Tough Nuclear Sanctions," *Washington Post,* April 21, 2010. Sylvia Westall, "Iran Tries Fuel Deal Counter-offer as Sanctions Loom," Reuters, April 28, 2010. "U.S. Diplomats Attend Iran Dinner in New York, *Haaretz,* May 6, 2010. Colum Lynch, "In Unusual Move, Iran's Foreign Minister Invites U.N. Security Council to Dinner," *Washington Post,* May 7, 2010.

22. Laura Rozen, "Obama WMD Czar Discusses Iran Nuclear Program," Politico, May 11, 2010, http://www.politico.com/blogs/laurarozen/0510/Obama_WMD_czar_says_Iran_nuclear_program.html. Charbonneau, "Obama, Medvedev Discuss 'Progress' on Iran Sanctions." Andre Soliani and Matthew Bristow, "Lula to Visit Iran as Chances for Nuclear Deal Fade," Bloomberg, May 14, 2010. Alexei Barrionuevo and Ginger Thompson, "Brazil's Iran Diplomacy Worries U.S. Officials," *New York Times,* May 15, 2010. Louis Charbonneau, "Turkey, Brazil Brokering Iran Nuclear Deal," Reuters, April 30, 2010. "Timeline: Brazil-Iranian Relations," Al Jazeera, May 16, 2010. *Raja News,* May 19, 2010 (Ordibehesht 29, 1389).

23. Letter from Barack Obama to Lula da Silva, Politica Externa Brasileira, April 20, 2010, http://www.politicaexterna.com/11023/brazil-iran-turkey-nuclear-negotiations-obamas-letter-to-lula.

24. Interview with Celso Amorim, July 15, 2010.

25. "Erdogan Calls a Trip to Iran 'Unlikely,' " BBC Persian, May 14, 2010. Interview with Celso Amorim, July 15, 2010.

26. Classified briefing for the Brazilian diplomatic corps by Celso Amorim, May 18, 2010. "The West has to come to their senses. They will never get [zero-enrichment]. This is completely unrealistic," a Brazilian diplomat added. Interview with Brazilian diplomat, July 1, 2010. Interview with Celso Amorim, July 15, 2010. Interview with EU diplomat, July 6, 2010.

27. "Erdogan Joins Tehran Nuclear Talks," AFP, May 16, 2010. Ladane Nasseri and Steve Bryant, "Erdogan Heads to Tehran for Nuclear Talks with Ahmadinejad, Brazil's Lula," Bloomberg, May 16, 2010. "Iran Will Never Agree to Fuel Exchange," *Jerusalem Post,* April 30, 2010. Interview with Celso Amorim, July 15, 2010. Interview with Iranian nuclear negotiator, May 27, 2010. Interview with senior Turkish diplomat, July 13, 2010. Interview with Mohammad Khazaee, June 15, 2010.

28. Celso Amorim, presentation at Carnegie Endowment for International Peace 2011, Carnegie International Nuclear Policy Conference, Washington D.C., March 28, 2011. Interview with Celso Amorim, July 15, 2010. Interview with Iranian nuclear negotiator, May 27, 2010.

29. Parisa Hafezi and Fernando Exman, "Iran Agrees Atom Fuel Deal with Turkey, Brazil," Reuters, May 17, 2010. "Brazil's FM to G5+1: Study Contents of Deal Carefully," Islamic Republic News Agency, May 17, 2010. The media never linked Reiss's release to Lula's visit, even though they coincided. When I asked Amorim whether Brazil was involved in securing her release, he smiled and responded with a question: "Do you believe in coincidence? I don't." Interview with Celso Amorim, July 15, 2010.

30. Stefan Simanowitz, "ElBaradei: To Dismiss Iranian Nuclear Agreement Would Be "a Dead End Street,' " Payvand, May 18, 2010, http://www.payvand.com/news/10/may/1209.html. Daren Butler, "U.N.'s Ban Hopes Iran Deal May Bring Atom Settlement," Reuters, May 21, 2010. Japan Backs Tehran Declaration," Press TV, May 21, 2010. "The Decisive Support of 234 MPs for the Nuclear Swap Deal," Islamic Republic News Agency, May 18, 2010. "Iranian Political Activists Support Nuclear Swap Agreement," Radio Zamaneh, May 17, 2010. Interview with former Iranian lawmaker and prodemocracy activist, September 17, 2010. Interview with Ataollah Mohajerani, September 18, 2010.

31. "Timeline: Brazil-Iranian relations," Al Jazeera, May 16, 2010. Peter Baker and David E. Sanger, "U.S. Makes Concessions to Russia for Iran Sanctions," *New York Times,* May 21, 2010. Interview with European diplomat, July 7, 2010. Interview with Russian diplomat, August 26, 2010. Conversation with senior U.S. diplomat, November 9, 2010.

32. Dan Robinson, "U.S.: Iran Nuclear Deal Will Not Slow UN Sanctions Drive," Voice of America, May 17, 2010, http://www.voanews.com/english/news/West-Skeptical-About-Irans-Fuel-Swap-Deal—93960164.html. "U.S. Eyes Sanctions as Iran, Turkey Forge Nuclear Fuel Swap," PBS, May 17, 2010. Peter Baker, "Major Powers Have a Deal on Sanctions for Iran, U.S. Says," *New York Times,* May 18, 2010. "Clinton Blasts

Brazil-Turkey Approach to Iran," Radio Free Europe/Radio Liberty, May 28, 2010. "Obama Talks Iran Sanctions, Israel with Jewish Lawmakers," AFP, May 19, 2010.

33. Interview with State Department official, September 17, 2010. Interview with former Iran Desk officer at the State Department, June 14, 2010. Interview with William D. Wunderle, September 2, 2010.

34. Interview with senior Senate staffer, October 5, 2010. Interview with senior Senate staffer, August 20, 2010. Interview with senior congressional aide, August 31, 2010. Interview with former Iran Desk officer at the State Department, June 14, 2010. "AIPAC Applauds Move Toward New UNSC Resolution: Imposition of Tough Sanctions Needed," American Israel Public Affairs Committee press release, May 18, 2010, http://www.aipac.org/~/media/Publications/Policy%20and%20Politics/Press/AIP AC%20Statements/2010/05/AIPAC_applauds_UNSCR_draft_agreement_5_18_2010.pdf.

35. Hafezi and Exman, "Iran Agrees Atom Fuel Deal with Turkey, Brazil." Interview with senior EU diplomat, May 27, 2010. Interview with French diplomat, July 6, 2010. Interview with senior EU official, June 14, 2010. Interview with Danny Ayalon, October 4, 2010.

36. Gareth Porter, "Fuel Swap Shakes Sanctions Draft, Prods U.S. on New Iran Talks," IPS, May 29, 2010, http://ipsnews.net/news.asp?idnews=51636. Ellen Barry, "Iran and Russia Exchange Acerbic Barbs on Sanctions," *New York Times,* May 26, 2010. Interview with EU diplomat, June 21, 2010. Interview with Russian diplomat, August 26, 2010. Interview with senior EU diplomat, September 15, 2010. Interview with senior EU official, September 10, 2010. *Raja News,* May 26, 2010 (Khordad 5, 1389).

37. The Federation of American Scientists (FAS) disputed this point and argued that the effort to enrich to 20 percent is modest and has a more political than technical meaning. FAS encouraged the Obama administration to accept the Tehran Declaration. "This whole deal was supposed to be a step forward for engaging Iran, not to stop its enrichment program," Ivan Oelrich of FAS said. State Department, "Background Briefing on Nuclear Nonproliferation Efforts with Regard to Iran and the Brazil/Turkey Agreement." Conversation with senior State Department official, November 9, 2010. Interview with State Department official, September 17, 2010. Interview with State Department official, October 7, 2010. Interview with senior EU official, June 14, 2010. Interview with senior State Department official, July 21, 2010. Interview with Pierre Vimont, July 26, 2010. Nathan Hodge, "Iran's Nuke Fuel Deal: Breakthrough or Bogus?," Wired, May 17, 2010, http://www.wired.com/dangerroom/2010/05/irans-nuke-fuel-deal-breakthrough-or-bogus/.

38. Interview with EU diplomat, July 6, 2010. State Department, "Background Briefing on Nuclear Nonproliferation Efforts with Regard to Iran and the Brazil/Turkey Agreement." Conversation with senior State Department official, November 9, 2010.

39. Interview with State Department official, September 17, 2010. Interview with senior EU diplomat, May 27, 2010. State Department, "Background Briefing on Nuclear Nonproliferation Efforts with Regard to Iran and the Brazil/Turkey Agreement." Interview with French diplomat, July 6, 2010. Interview with Peter Wittig, July 7, 2010.

40. Interview with senior EU diplomat, September 15, 2010. Interview with senior State Department official, September 10, 2010. Interview with EU diplomat, July 6, 2010. Interview with Ali Asghar Soltanieh, June 30, 2010. The Tehran Declaration's clause giving Iran the right to unconditionally take back its LEU from Turkey in case the provisions of the Declaration were not respected was particularly difficult for the West to accept given the depth of its mistrust of Iran.

41. Interview with senior Turkish diplomat, July 13, 2010. Interview with senior Brazilian diplomat, June 21, 2010. Interview with Brazilian diplomat, July 7, 2010. Interview with Celso Amorim, July 15, 2010. Interview with senior adviser to Lula, July 15, 2010.

42. "To be willing to dialogue means to run a risk?" one of Lula's advisers said. "To run a risk that you are going to make a gesture and you might fall flat on your face. The Americans are not willing to entertain this kind of scenario. Why? Because they're accustomed to having their way. Because might makes right. That's the whole issue." Interview with senior adviser to Lula, July 15, 2010. "Turkey Chides U.S. in Iran Row, Urges Support for Swap Deal," AFP, May 27, 2010. "Turkey to Withdraw from Nuclear Fuel Deal If West Imposes Sanctions on Iran," Bernama, May 18, 2010. Scott Peterson, "U.S. Answer to Iran Nuclear Swap: Overnight Deal on Sanctions," *Christian Science Monitor,* May 18, 2010. Ahmet Davutoglu and Celso Amorim, "Giving Diplomacy a Chance," *New York Times,* May 26, 2010. Interview with senior Turkish diplomat, July 13, 2010.

43. Simanowitz, "ElBaradei." "ElBaradei Supports the Iran-Turkey-Brazil Nuclear Deal, Warns Against Sanctions and Military Strikes," Race for Iran, May 20, 2010, http://www.raceforiran.com/baradei-supports-the-iran-turkey-brazil-nuclear-deal-war ns-against-sanctions-and-military-strikes. Roger Cohen, "America Moves the Goalposts," *New York Times,* May 20, 2010. The international outcry against Washington's swift dismissal of the deal forced the U.S. to recalibrate its approach. The harshness of the initial reaction made it "difficult not to appear irresponsible." While the Europeans by and large did not question the Obama administration's decision, even staunch supporters of the rejection were uncomfortable with Washington's tone. This was particularly true of Clinton's characterization of the deal as "dangerous." Interview with senior EU diplomat, September 15, 2010. Interview with two EU officials, June 8, 2010.

44. Interview with Japanese diplomat, June 22, 2010. Interview with Celso Amorim, July 15, 2010. Glenn Kessler, "U.S., Brazilian Officials at Odds over Letter on Iranian Uranium," *Washington Post,* May 28, 2010. For some of the Europeans, the letter became a problem as questions began to arise about the wisdom of rejecting the Tehran Declaration. "Even German parliamentarians asked why we didn't agree to it," an EU diplomat explained to me. "It was difficult not to appear irresponsible." Interview with senior EU diplomat, September 15, 2010.

45. Interview with senior Turkish diplomat, July 13, 2010. Interview with former Iranian diplomat, June 30, 2010. Interview with Celso Amorim, July 15, 2010. Interview with Brazilian diplomat, July 7, 2010. Interview with senior Obama administration official, October 27, 2010. Frustrated, Amorim also pointed out that the issue of 20 percent enrichment would not have emerged had the West been willing to sell Iran the

fuel rather than proposing the fuel swap in the first place. "The 20 percent enrichment dilemma only posed itself because the West did not want to sell the fuel to Iran. They preferred to pose this smart deal. . . . If it had just sold to Iran the fuel they were looking for, this problem would not have existed." Amorim, presentation at Carnegie Endowment for International Peace 2011.

46. Interview with senior Obama administration official, October 27, 2010. Interview with senior State Department official, July 21, 2010. Interview with Michael Ratney, August 10, 2010.

47. "U.S. Pressures Ankara to Not Abstain from Iran Sanctions Vote," *Hurriyet Daily News,* April 2, 2010, http://www.hurriyetdailynews.com/n.php?n=ankara-com es-under-us-pressure-against-abstention-vote-2010-04-27. Interview with Cengiz Candar, June 18, 2010. Interview with Russian diplomat, August 26, 2010.

48. Interview with Matias Spektor, June 17, 2011. Interview with senior Brazilian diplomat, June 21, 2010. Interview with Brazilian diplomat, July 7, 2010. Interview with Japanese diplomat, June 22, 2010. Interview with senior adviser to Lula, July 15, 2010. Interview with Celso Amorim, July 15, 2010.

49. Interview with senior Brazilian diplomat, June 21, 2010. Interview with Brazilian diplomat, July 7, 2010. Interview with Japanese diplomat, June 22, 2010. Interview with senior adviser to Lula, July 15, 2010. Interview with Celso Amorim, July 15, 2010. Amorim, presentation at Carnegie Endowment for International Peace 2011.

50. Interview with Cengiz Candar, June 18, 2010. Interview with senior Turkish diplomat, August 15, 2010. H. E. Ertugrul Apakan (Permanent Representative of Turkey), "Explanation of Vote," 6335th Meeting of the Security Council, New York, June 9, 2010.

51. Susan Cornwell, "U.S. Congress OKs Sanctions on Iran's Energy, Banks," Reuters, June 24, 2010. White House, "Remarks by the President at Signing of the Iran Sanctions Act," press release, July 1, 2011, http://www.whitehouse.gov/the-press-off ice/remarks-president-signing-iran-sanctions-act. Interview with senior Senate staffer, September 2, 2010. Interview with former Iran Desk officer at the State Department, June 14, 2010. Interview with senior EU diplomat, May 27, 2010. Interview with State Department official, September 17, 2010. Interview with senior adviser to Lula, July 15, 2010.

52. Interview with State Department official, September 17, 2010. Interview with senior adviser to Lula, July 15, 2010. Interview with former Iran Desk officer at the State Department, June 14, 2010.

53. Interview with William D. Wunderle, September 2, 2010. Interview with senior Obama administration official, October 27, 2010. Interview with French diplomat, July 6, 2010. Interview with senior adviser to Lula, July 15, 2010.

54. Trita Parsi, "Analysis: Iran's Nuke Deal Irritates Washington, ABCnews.com, May 18, 2010, http://abcnews.go.com/International/analysis-irans-nuclear-deal-turkey-brazil/story?id=10681106. Interview with senior Obama administration official, October 27, 2010. Interview with senior adviser to Lula, July 15, 2010. Interview with senior State Department official, September 10, 2010.

Chapter Eleven.
Trapped in a Paradigm of Enmity

1. See transcript at http://www.armscontrol.org/events/RoleSanctionsIranNuclear.

2. "Iran Starting Work on New Nuclear Reactor, Official Says," CNN, June 17, 2010. Justyna Pawlak, "Iran Ready for Nuclear Talks After November 10," International Business Times, October 30, 2010, http://uk.ibtimes.com/articles/77282/20101030/iran-ready-for-nuclear-talks-after-november-10.htm. Semira N. Nikou, "The Iran Primer: Timeline of Iran's Foreign Relations," United States Institute of Peace, http://iranprimer.usip.org/resource/timeline-irans-foreign-relations. Bruce Schneier, "The Story Behind the Stuxnet Virus," Forbes, October 7, 2010. Jonathan Tirone and Benjamin Harvey, "Iran Refuses to Talk About Nuclear Program at Istanbul Meeting," Reuters, January 21, 2011.

3. Flynt Leverett and Hillary Mann Leverett, "Have We Already Lost Iran?," New York Times, May 24, 2009.

4. Interview with former Iran Desk officer at the State Department, June 14, 2010. Interview with senior Senate staffer, August 20, 2010. After the 2009 elections, some senior Obama administration officials successfully argued that the consolidation of power under Iranian hard-liners created incentives for a quick resolution to the nuclear standoff. Others viewed that argument as wishful thinking. Interview with David Miliband, June 7, 2011.

5. Jeffrey Goldberg, "Point of No Return," Atlantic, September 2010.

6. Interview with Iranian nuclear negotiator, May 27, 2010. Interview with former Iranian diplomat, June 30, 2010. Kian Mokhtari, "The Hidden Cost," Kayhan, January 13, 2010. Interview with David Miliband, June 7, 2011.

7. David E. Sanger and Thom Shanker, "Gates Says U.S. Lacks Strategy to Curb Iran's Nuclear Drive," New York Times, April 17, 2010. Simon Tisdall, "Obama Feels the Heat on Iran's Threat," Guardian, April 20, 2010. Interview with former Iranian diplomat, June 30, 2010. Interview with Mohammad Khazaee, June 15, 2010. Interview with senior Obama administration official, October 27, 2010. Conversation with senior State Department official, November 9, 2010.

8. Interview with Ali Asghar Soltanieh, June 30, 2010. Interview with senior Obama administration official, October 27, 2010. Charlie Rose, November 6, 2009.

9. Interview with Ali Asghar Soltanieh, June 30, 2010.

10. Dana Moss, "Reforming the Rogue," Washington Institute for Near East Policy, Policy Focus #105, August 2010. Yahia Zoubir, "The United States and Libya: From Confrontation to Normalization," Middle East Policy 13/2 (summer 2006). Randall Newnham, "Carrots, Sticks, and Bombs: The End of Libya's WMD Program," Mediterranean Quarterly 20/3 (summer/fall 2009). Christopher M. Blanchard and Jim Zanotti, "Libya: Background and U.S. Relations," Congressional Research Service, February 18, 2011, http://fpc.state.gov/documents/organization/157348.pdf.

11. Mark E. Manyin, "The Vietnam-U.S. Normalization Process," Congressional Research Service, June 17, 2005, http://www.au.af.mil/au/awc/awcgate/crs/ib98033.pdf.

12. *Charlie Rose,* January 6, 2010.

13. Interview with senior Senate staffer, August 20, 2010. In the view of some of Obama's Senate allies, the president's pursuit of diplomacy was at times too timid. Interview with former Iranian diplomat, June 30, 2010. Interview with senior Obama administration official, October 27, 2010. Interview with former Iran Desk officer at the State Department, June 14, 2010.

14. Interview with Celso Amorim, July 15, 2010. Interview with senior Turkish diplomat, July 13, 2010. Interview with senior adviser to Lula, July 15, 2010.

15. Interview with Cengiz Candar, June 18, 2010. Interview with Celso Amorim, July 15, 2010.

16. On March 2–3, 2009, Acting Assistant Secretary of the Treasury Daniel Glaser gave a classified briefing to more than seventy EU nonproliferation and Iran experts on Washington's strategy-in-the-making toward Iran. According to classified U.S. State Department documents, Glaser made it clear that engagement alone was unlikely to succeed. Pressure and sanctions must be combined with diplomacy simultaneously, not sequentially, Glaser said. Classified U.S. State Department cable, "Iran Sanctions: AA/S Glaser Briefs EU on Priority Targets," April 8, 2009. Interview with senior State Department official, September 10, 2010.

17. Interview with senior Senate staffer, August 20, 2010. Interview with senior Senate staffer, October 5, 2010.

18. Interview with senior State Department official, July 2, 2010.

Chapter Twelve.
Epilogue

1. Trita Parsi and Reza Marashi, "The Geopolitical Battle for the Arab Street," *Cairo Review of Global Affairs,* May 16, 2011.

2. Matthew Duss, "Letter from Herzliya, Neocon Woodstock," *Nation,* February 14, 2011.

3. Helene Cooper and Mark Landler, "Interests of Saudi Arabia and Iran Collide, with the U.S. in the Middle," *New York Times,* March 17, 2011. "Saudi Soldiers Sent into Bahrain," Al Jazeera, March 15, 2011. Matthew Rosenberg, Jay Solomon, and Margaret Coker, "Saudi Bid to Curb Iran Worries U.S.," *Wall Street Journal,* May 27, 2011.

4. Interview with Danny Ayalon, October 4, 2010. In September 2010 Chairman Howard Berman (D-CA) of the House Foreign Relations Committee told an audience in Washington, D.C., that sanctions take "months, not years" to show results.

5. According to Moshe Vered of the Bar-Ilan University in Israel, war between Israel and Iran would last for "years and not weeks" (Tzvi Ben Gedalyahu, "War with Iran Could Last Years, Says Bar-Ilan U. Researcher," *Israel National News,* April 27, 2010). Jeffrey Goldberg, "The Point of No Return," *Atlantic,* September 2009. Classified U.S. State Department cable, "Assistant Secretary of Defense Vershbow Meets with Senior Israeli Defense Officials," November 16, 2009.

6. Jim Heintz, "Medvedev: Israel Not Planning to Strike Iran," Associated Press, September 20, 2009. Daniel Edelson, "Former MI Chief: Israel Can't Face Iran Alone,"

Ynetnews.com, March 11, 2009, http://www.ynetnews.com/articles/0,7340, L-3684 838,00.html. Gili Cohen, "Israel Won't Withstand War in Wake of Strike on Iran, Ex-Mossad Chief Says," *Haaretz*, June 1, 2011.

7. "Israeli Official Doubts Iran Would Nuke His Country," Associated Press, February 26, 2010. "Israel Defence Chief: Iran Not an Existential Threat," Reuters, September 17, 2009.

8. Interview with Danny Ayalon, October 4, 2010. Discussions with Israeli military and intelligence officials throughout spring and summer of 2010.

9. Interview with EU3 diplomat, July 6, 2010. Conversation with senior Obama administration official, October 10, 2010. Regarding the effect of sanctions on the prodemocracy movement, noted Iranian dissident Akbar Ganji has argued that the Green movement consists mostly of middle-class adherents and that "economic sanctions would destroy the middle class [and] . . . the Green Movement." Moreover, he said, "the more economic sanctions are applied against Iran, the more the government will control the economy" due to the prevailing structures (Jim Lobe, "Akbar Ganji Says Military Attack on Iran Would Destroy Opposition," Lobelog.com, May 12, 2010, http://www.lobelog.com/akbar-ganji-says-military-attack-on-iran-would-destroy-oppo sition/). Interview with Russian diplomat, August 26, 2010.

10. Interview with David Miliband, June 7, 2011.

11. John Limbert, "Engaging Iran: First, Break the Rules," International Relations and Security Network, May 30, 2011, http://www.isn.ethz.ch/isn/Current-Affairs/Secu rity-Watch-Archive/Detail/?ots736=4888caa0-b3db-1461-98b9-e20e7b9c13d4&lng=en&ots627=fce62fe0-528d-4884-9cdf-283c282cf0b2&id=129715.

12. "UN Sanctions Will Hurt Ordinary Iranians, Says Mousavi," *Telegraph*, May 23, 2010. Ladane Nasseri, "Iran Sanctions Won't Hurt Rulers, Top Dissident Says," Bloomberg, May 27, 2010. Conversation with Ardeshir Amirarjomand, June 10, 2011. Trita Parsi and Reza Marashi, "Want to Defuse the Iran Crisis?," *Foreign Policy*, November 12, 2010.

13. Ibid.

14. Interview with Russian diplomat, August 26, 2010. Interview with William D. Wunderle, September 2, 2010. Former U.S. officials involved in two-track diplomacy with Iran told investigative journalists that their message to Obama would be to "get off your no-enrichment policy, which is getting you nowhere" (Seymour Hersh, "Iran and the Bomb," *New Yorker*, June 6, 2011).

15. Matt Duss, "Ganji: Please Don't Talk About 'Regime Change' in Iran," Think Progress, May 13, 2010, http://thinkprogress.org/security/2010/05/13/176058/ganji-please-dont-talk-about-regime-change-in-iran/. Lobe, "Akbar Ganji Says Military Attack on Iran Would Destroy Opposition." Parsi and Marashi, "Want to Defuse the Iran Crisis?" Interview with Maziar Bahari, August 16, 2010. Interview with former Iranian lawmaker and prodemocracy activist, September 17, 2010. Conversation with Ardeshir Amirarjomand, June 10, 2011.

16. Parsi and Marashi, "Want to Defuse the Iran Crisis?"

17. Ibid. Ali Gharib, "Adm. Mike Mullen Supports Opening Up 'Any Channel' of Communication with Iran," ThinkProgress.org, September 20, 2011, http://thinkprog ress.org/security/2011/09/20/324318/mullen-iran-any-channel/.

Index